DAVID SUZUKI

THE AUTOBIOGRAPHY

DAVID

SUZUKI

THE AUTOBIOGRAPHY

To Emma & Mitch:
Thanks for your support

GREYSTONE BOOKS

Douglas & McIntyre Publishing Group

Vancouver/Toronto/Berkeley

Greystone Books
A division of Douglas & McIntyre Ltd.
2323 Quebec Street, Suite 201
Vancouver, British Columbia
Canada v5T 4S7
www.greystonebooks.com

Library and Archives Canada Cataloguing in Publication
Suzuki, David, 1936–
David Suzuki : the autobiography.

Includes index.
ISBN-13: 978-1-55365-156-7
ISBN-10: 1-55365-156-1

1. Suzuki, David, 1936–. 2. Environmentalists—Canada—Biography.
3. David Suzuki Foundation. 4. Authors, Canadian (English)—20th
century—Biography. 5. Broadcasters—Canada—Biography. I. Title.

GE56.S99A3 2006   333.72′092   C2006-900541-9

Editing by Nancy Flight
Copyediting by Wendy Fitzgibbons
Jacket design by Jessica Sullivan & Naomi MacDougall
Front jacket photographs: top left, top right, middle right, and
bottom left: courtesy of the CBC; bottom right: Chick Rice
Back jacket photograph courtesy of the CBC
Text design by Lisa Hemingway

Printed and bound in Canada by Friesens
Printed on acid-free paper that is forest friendly
(100% post-consumer recycled paper) and has been processed chlorine free
Distributed in the U.S. by Publishers Group West

We gratefully acknowledge the financial support of the Canada Council
for the Arts, the British Columbia Arts Council, and the Government of Canada
through the Book Publishing Industry Development Program (BPIDP)
for our publishing activities.

With deepest gratitude,
I thank and dedicate this book to the general public,
who made my life's work possible.

You watched and listened to my programs;
you read, thought about, and responded to
ideas I expressed in writing.

Your support added weight and
visibility to my efforts and carried me past
numerous roadblocks and detractors.

That support has been a great honor, privilege,
and responsibility, which I have tried in my fallible, human
way to live up to.

*My life and career in the university, research, and media
would not have been possible without the generous and enthusiastic
support of so many people in so many ways.*

With all my heart, I extend thanks to:

My elders—Mom, Dad, Freddy, Harry

My anchor and the love of my life—Tara

*The future—Tamiko, Troy, Laura, Severn, Sarika,
Tamo, Midori, Jonathan*

*The many students, postdocs, and associates who made my lab
such a vibrant, exciting, and productive community*

*The dozens of CBC radio and television staff, freelance researchers,
writers, and media professionals whose efforts have made me look good,
a job that Jim Murray reminded me is not easy*

*The hundreds of volunteers, staff, and associates who have made
the foundation such a supportive, joyful, and positive community*

*The tens of thousands of people who have contributed to
the foundation so generously*

Elois Yaxley, for bringing some order to my life

*Rob Sanders of Greystone Books and Patrick Gallagher
of Allen & Unwin Publishers for steadfast support and encouragement*

Nancy Flight and Wendy Fitzgibbons for making this prose readable

*And my kid sister Aiko, who taught me so much about life
and who died on the eve of 2006*

CONTENTS

PREFACE

IN 1986, THE year I turned fifty, I had the temerity to write *Metamorphosis: Stages in a Life*. It was not intended as an autobiography but as a series of essays. My publisher encouraged me to supplement the pieces with more and more personal material, until the essays were reduced to three at the end of the book. To my astonishment and delight, people were interested in my experiences, and the book sold more copies than any other I have written. At the time, at the relatively young age of half a century, I didn't feel I had matured enough to have a perspective on my life. Now, two decades later, I know I was still a child in maturity, and even now, looking in the mirror, I have difficulty reconciling the old man gazing back at me with the still-young person in the mind behind the face.

Although all people on Earth, as members of one species, share the same anatomy of the brain, the same chemistry of neurons, and similar sense organs, each of us "perceives" the world in a very personal way. We experience it through perceptual filters that are shaped by our individual genes and experiences, by our gender, ethnic group, religious background, socioeconomic status, and so on. Essentially, our brains "edit" the input from our sensory organs, "making sense" of it within the context of our personal history and the values and beliefs we have come to acquire.

Now, as my aging body imposes limits and tells me to slow down, I spend more time in reflection, trying to put my most memorable experiences into a kind of order. It's the way scientists write up a research report or paper: we follow different avenues of inquiry, going down blind alleys, hitting a fast lane or taking a shortcut, zigzagging along as we probe an interesting observation or phenomenon. Then, when it's time to "write it up," we shuffle through the experiments, tossing some out and organizing the remainder into an order that creates the illusion that a direct path was taken from the initial question to the final results.

So it is with my life story. I don't have a photographic memory (thank god), and certain events that might have passed unnoticed by someone else may have stuck in my mind, whereas other, seemingly more monumental moments have faded away. This, then, is a story I have created by selectively dredging up bits and pieces from the detritus of seventy years of life. The first five chapters skim over the first fifty years, giving a somewhat different emphasis from that of *Metamorphosis* and offering some different information about those years, and the rest of the book describes events since then.

Why would anyone else be interested in my life? I know people like to delve into the hidden parts of the lives of people who have acquired some notoriety, hoping to find juicy bits of gossip, signs of weakness, or faults that bring the subjects down off pedestals, or simply to expand on what one knows about a public figure. It's not my intention to satisfy that curiosity. Instead, as an "elder," I hope my reflections on one life may stir a reader to consider those thoughts in relation to his or her own life.

MY HAPPY CHILDHOOD
IN RACIST BRITISH COLUMBIA

JAPANESE IMMIGRANTS BEGAN arriving in Canada in great numbers at the end of the nine-teenth century, lured by the tremendous abundance of land, fish, and forests that promised money. Small, diligent, smelling of strange foods, speaking heavily accented English, these Asian newcomers seemed to be another kind of human being, willing to live in cramped quarters and squirreling away their hard-earned money. Laws were passed to bar them from voting, purchasing land, and enrolling in universities.

Like many other Japanese, my maternal and paternal grand-parents came to Canada less because they wanted to make a new life than because in Japan they were locked into extreme poverty. I can-not imagine the terrible conditions that made them take the chance to come to a country that regarded them and treated them as belonging to a kind of subhuman race. Japan was their home, and their intent was to return to it when they had made their fortune. But it was a journey to a distant land with no assurances they would ever return. After my birth, my father's parents never went back to Japan, and my mother's parents returned only after World War II, disillusioned by their treatment in Canada. They went back to Hiroshima, and both were dead in less than a year.

My grandparents started their lives in Canada with little more than hope and a willingness to work. They had no formal education, spoke no English, and were of a culture totally alien to Canadians of the day, who had different attitudes and perspectives about everything from family to customs. Like the waves of immigrants who have come to this place over the past two centuries, my grandparents saw Canada as a land of opportunity and plenty. There is a story that neatly encapsulates this belief. Two immigrants arrive in Canada on a Sunday and take a stroll together along the street. One of them looks down and spots a twenty-dollar bill, which he bends to pick up. He's stopped by his friend, who tells him, "Leave it there; we'll start work tomorrow."

Today I watch the Chinese family that operates the corner store, the Punjabi cab driver working long, hard hours, and the Mexican itinerants picking vegetables; all doing jobs that few Canadian-born folks are willing to endure, they are part of the stream of immigrants like my grandparents who have enriched what has become a highly multicultural society. They bring to it their vigor and their exotic practices, languages, and beliefs. But in the early part of the last century, there were no constitutional guarantees in this country.

My father and mother were born in Vancouver in 1909 and 1910, respectively, and survived the trauma of the Great Depression thanks to hard work and a strong extended family, which was held together by economic necessity and the forces of racism in British Columbia at that time. Asians, Canadian-born or not, differed from other Canadians in language, physical appearance, and behavior. My parents went to schools with other Canadians, and though Japanese was the first language each acquired at home, they soon were fluently bilingual and had many non-Japanese friends. Education was a very high priority for their parents, and Mom and Dad both completed high school, which was considered a good education in the 1920s. They stoically accepted encounters with bigots at school, in stores, and on the street, whereas only the most rebellious among Japanese Canadians of that time would ever have thought of dating, let alone marrying, a white person. Every one of the nine siblings of my parents' families married Japanese (today, among dozens of their children and grandchildren, only my twin sister, Marcia, is married to a Japanese). Even though their social lives revolved around family and other Japanese, however, my parents felt themselves fully Canadian.

Hard work was a constant part of their lives from childhood on. At about ten years of age, my father was sent to live with a wealthy white family as a "houseboy," performing small chores for the household and receiving room and board in return. Perhaps the most important effect of that period in his life was that in his time off he read the entire set of the encyclopedia *The Book of Knowledge,* and he retained much of that information. As a girl, Mom went out picking berries, something at which she became very adept. After the war, when we lived in southern Ontario, she, my sisters, and I worked on farms, picking strawberries and raspberries on piecework (that is, we were paid a set amount for each box we picked), but it was impossible to keep up with Mom.

Dad and Mom met while they were both working with Furuya's, a Vancouver company that until recently still existed in Toronto; it specialized in imported Japanese food and cooking paraphernalia. The company had a rigid rule of nonfraternization between the sexes, but Mom and Dad began to date on the sly. Eventually, Dad had to quit Furuya's to date Mom more openly. His Japanese had deteriorated when he went to school, and when he approached Mom's father to ask permission to take her out, he must have phrased it in such a way that it sounded as if he were proposing marriage. "You're both far too young," my grandfather replied in Japanese. "If you're serious, then wait, and come back in five years."

Well, they continued to see each other, and five years later, in the mid-1930s, Dad asked for permission to marry Mom and got it. Theirs was not a traditional arranged marriage; instead, they were imbued with the Western notion of romantic love. We kids took it for granted that they smooched, and on occasion we could overhear their active sex life.

After they were married, they received financial help from Dad's parents to start a small laundry and dry-cleaning shop in Marpole, a Vancouver neighborhood near the edge of the city and alongside the Fraser River. We lived in the back of the shop. Mom had a miscarriage early in their marriage, and then Marcia and I arrived in the world on March 24, 1936. Dad says Mom became enormous, and the delivery was long and harrowing. I was born first, weighing in at nine pounds, but Marcia took a lot longer—so long, in fact, that Mom had no strength left and finally the doctor reached in with forceps and dragged Marcia out. As the second-born of twins, she is considered in Japanese tradition to be the elder, who allows the younger one of the pair to exit first. But she was tiny, weighing less than three pounds, and the forceps delivery caused some damage that resulted in a weakened right side.

I was taken home when Mom left the hospital, but Marcia stayed behind. Visiting her daily, Dad was upset that she seemed to be left without any care, whereas I was at home and the center of attention. He told the doctor that if Marcia was going to be left to die, he would prefer to take her home where she could be loved and cared for. The doctor assented, and so this young couple took over responsibility for both babies, one requiring a lot of care and attention. And Marcia pulled through. As she grew up, I always felt Mom and Dad were too hard on her, treating her no differently from me and later our two sisters and demanding that she work alongside us. I learned later from my father that Mom was determined Marcia would grow up to be tough and able to take care of herself. She did; she became a terrific softball pitcher

Mom (Setsu Nakamura) and Dad (Carr Suzuki) on their wedding day, March 21, 1934

Dad and the twins, Marcia *(left)* and me, in 1936

and is competitive in anything she does. She had two children and is a wonderful grandma to her two grandsons.

Aiko arrived a year and a half later. Dad had hoped for another boy and had chosen the name Gerald, so when she was born, she was called Geraldine, or Gerry for short. We all had Japanese middle names, and in later life when she had assumed a more bohemian, artistic life, Gerry dropped her first name for Aiko, her second.

Sibling to twins, Aiko behaved like the stereotypical second child: a trickster, full of mischief, always wanting to explore. Dad had a classic Japanese attitude toward girls: they should finish high school, get a job, and find a husband. We later moved to London, Ontario, and both Marcia and Aiko took off for Toronto as soon as they finished high school so that they could become independent. Soon Aiko was immersed in an artistic crowd. I remember going home to London while I was in college in the United States and meeting her boyfriend, Alex, a big Hungarian with a beard and ponytail. This was the mid-

1950s, and a beard was shocking enough, but to us a ponytail on a man was unheard of. To top off the shame, Alex and Aiko were living together in an age when many men still hoped to marry a virgin. Aiko always pushed the edges, and I, Mister Square in a brush cut, was pulled into her exciting, scary world. I was with her when she died on December 31, 2005.

During the war, when we were living in internment camps in the interior of British Columbia, Dad had been separated from the family for a year as he lived in a road camp building the Trans-Canada Highway. He did manage to make his way to Slocan City, where we were imprisoned, for a couple of days before going back to the road camp. Nine months later, our youngest sibling, Dawn, was born. Dawn became Dad's surrogate second son and accompanied him on numerous fishing trips. She did not want to follow her older sisters by going straight to work after high school, and when she said she wanted to go to university, Aiko and I lobbied very hard to support her until Dad relented. She was also a wonderful ballet dancer and, after completing her degree at the University of Toronto, obtained a Canada Council grant to dance with Martha Graham in New York City, a position she held for years.

AS A BOY, I would stand for hours behind a steam-operated machine that Dad used to press shirts and pants, asking him a steady stream of questions as he worked. He was able to answer me with what he remembered from *The Book of Knowledge*. He would take me along when he delivered clothing to customers, and I would patiently wait for him in the car. He was a garrulous man, and toward the end of the deliveries his visits with customers got longer, probably because he was having a social drink or two while talking. Dad was a great friend, and I hope he found my companionship as much of a delight as his was for me.

He was also a dreamer. His parents were constantly nagging him to go out and make money and save for a home and security. As the eldest in a family of seven children, he was expected to be a role model for his brothers and sister, but he wasn't the kind his parents had in mind. He was not afraid of work and labored hard to earn enough to buy the necessities in life, but he didn't believe that we should run after money as an end in itself. He taught us it was bad manners to talk about money with others; we learned to pity the person who bragged about money, new cars, or fancy clothes. Dad loved fishing and gardening, and he was fascinated by plants. To my grandparents, he was a failure, and they constantly berated him to do better, but to me, he was my great hero and role model.

Dad loved to go on fishing, camping, and mushroom-hunting trips in the mountains, where he often encountered First Nations people. He would easily strike up conversations and often ended up being invited for dinner or to stay with them. In the mid-1960s, when he had returned to Vancouver, he became close friends with a Native family near Boston Bar along the Fraser River. On fishing trips he would often stop off to stay with them, and when they came to town, they and their children would drop in to visit and stay with him and Mom.

Once, I accompanied him on a trip to hunt for *matsutake*, aromatic pine mushrooms that are highly prized by Japanese. On that trip, I met this First Nations family. I was surprised at how uptight I was in contrast to my father, who felt right at home. I, a young professor in genetics, had never met Native people and only knew about them from snippets in the media. I knew nothing about Dad's friends or their background, and I didn't know how to relate to them in conversation. Dad was relaxed and simply accepted them as people who shared his interest in fish, trees, and nature, so he easily raised subjects of mutual interest about which they could converse for hours. But I felt alien and was especially afraid I might say something that would be insulting or patronizing. I was overwhelmed by the fact that they were Indians, and I never allowed our basic humanity to be the main point of interaction.

They probably wondered about this guy who had a great father but was too snooty to say much.

Dad's great characteristic was that when he met people, he was totally open, because he was genuinely interested in what they could tell him about their experiences and their world. Naturally, people loved him, because everyone loves to talk about him- or herself, and he was a terrific listener. I realize now that he automatically exhibited the quality that First Nations people tell us is so critical in order to communicate: respect. It would be a long time before I realized how much our shared genetic heritage—that is, our physical features—made First Nations people immediately more receptive to me.

Mom was a traditional Japanese wife, never arguing with or contradicting Dad in front of us or company. Her entire life was circumscribed by work. She was the first up in the morning and the last to go to bed at night, but I never heard her complain or nag my father. She took care of the family's finances, and as each of her kids began to babysit, waitress, or do farm work or construction, all of our earnings went to her. We didn't get an allowance; Mom and Dad bought our clothes, books, and other things we needed and from time to time doled out a little change for a treat, but I was never overwhelmed by a need for anything. I never acquired an interest in clothing fashions, perhaps because my parents bought my clothes for me. To this day, my wife tells me I don't know about color coordination when my socks clash with my shirt, something I still can't figure out. What on earth has the color of my socks got to do with the color of my shirt?

Mom's greatest gift to me was her unfailing interest in what I was doing. My sanctuary as a teenager when we lived in London was a swamp, and I would go home soaking wet, often covered in mud, but triumphantly brandishing jars of insects, salamander eggs, or baby turtles. She never scolded me but would ooh and aah over each little treasure as she helped me take off my clothes so that she could launder them.

Marcia and me on our first day of kindergarten, September 1941

In Vancouver, our next-door neighbors were the McGregors, steadfast friends to my parents. Their youngest son, Ian, was my playmate. The issue of race is not something I remember from those carefree days. On my first day of kindergarten, in 1941, I happily undressed to my undershorts in front of all the parents and without any sense of self-consciousness climbed onto a table to be examined by a doctor, although my parents told me later they were embarrassed that I undressed in front of the white parents.

The rest of my childhood memories are filled with fishing and camping excursions with Dad. We would make trips past Haney, then very rural but now on the eastern outskirts of Greater Vancouver, to fish in Loon Lake, a small lake so full of trout that most were stunted, growing to perhaps seven or eight inches at best. That's where I caught my first trout, for a limit of fifteen, while Dad practiced his fly-fishing. Today Loon Lake is part of the University of British Columbia's Demonstration Forest.

On other occasions, we would drive out to the Vedder Canal near Chilliwack in the Fraser Valley, where Dad arranged for horses so we could ride several miles upstream and camp. I was always fascinated that we could let the horses go at the end of our ride, and they would find their way home. Dad would catch steelhead and Dolly Varden trout as we fished down the river. The first time we went, I accidentally slipped off a rock and into the water. Looking up at Dad, I expected him to chastise me to be more careful. Instead, he told me to go ahead and jump into the creek and have fun—with my clothes on! It was wonderful.

Thinking back on my childhood, I understand that children live in a world of their own making, a fantasy life of real experiences, dreams, and imaginings that are jumbled together in the early state of coalescence into the filtering lenses through which we will see the world as adults. Even as an elder, I find those recollections changing as, more and more, I find my "memories" really are created by priceless photos, like the one of me dripping wet, rather than actual recall of the events.

Buffered from the world by my parents, I didn't know Japan had attacked Pearl Harbor in Hawaii on December 7, 1941, and I didn't sense any fear or consternation in Mom or Dad. Many years later, my father told me that when he heard the announcement of the attack, he immediately went to a barber and had his hair restyled into a crew cut, which he retained for the rest of his life. "I knew we were going to be treated like 'Japs,' so I figured I might as well look like one" was the way he put it. Cutting his hair was an act of both defiance and submission to what he knew was inevitable. The treachery implicit in Japan's "sneak attack" against the United States Navy and the terrible war that followed threw my family and some twenty thousand other Japanese Canadians and Japanese nationals into a turbulent sequence of events, beginning with Canada's invocation of the iniquitous War Measures Act, which deprived us of all rights of citizenship.

In 1941, Canada was still a racist society. In Prince Rupert in northern British Columbia, First Nations people existed under conditions akin to apartheid in South Africa: they were not allowed to stay in most hotels, they were refused service in restaurants, and they were forced to sit in certain designated sections of theaters. There were also prohibitions against any First Nations person in pubs. (My uncle Mar, who was quite swarthy, was once asked in a bar what tribe he was from. He replied, "The Jap tribe.")

Canada boasts of its high ideals of democracy and all the rights that are guaranteed by its Charter of Rights and Freedoms, but many have been hard won—for example, the right of visible minorities to vote, own property, attend university, or even to drink in a pub—and some have yet to become part of the accepted rights of all citizens. Even today, we are grappling with the recognition that gay people, transsexuals, and hermaphrodites as human beings deserve full legal rights, including the right to marry. Canadians have been prepared to fight and die for those principles. Yet by invoking the War Measures Act in 1942, the government declared that race alone was a sufficient threat to Canadian security to revoke all rights of citizenship for Canadians of Japanese descent.

One of the terrible dilemmas of democracy is that only under conditions of duress or crisis do those cherished rights even matter, but that's when they are often rescinded in the name of national security. What good are high ideals if we guarantee them only when times are good? We now know there was not a single recorded case of treachery among Japanese Canadians during the war, despite the conditions to which they were subjected.

But to the white community we looked different; we looked just like the enemy and thus deserved to be treated like the enemy. Most Japanese Canadians were totally loyal to Canada, and many young Japanese Canadian men signed up and willingly fought and died for Canada. Sadly, the evacuation of Japanese nationals and Canadians from the coast of British Columbia and their incarceration in internment camps generated enormous resentment within the community, and many Japanese Canadians gave up citizenship and abandoned Canada for Japan after the war. Under the War Measures Act, property was confiscated and sold at bargain-basement prices, possessions were looted, bank accounts were frozen, and people were warned they would be removed from coastal British Columbia, where they were thought to pose a threat. Within months we were sent to other provinces or relocated to hastily constructed camps deep in the interior of B.C.

As a child, I was not aware of any of these events apart from our relocation, and I can only marvel at how my parents shielded us from the turmoil they must have undergone. Much later, as a teenager, I realized that we—Japanese Canadians—had not been deemed worthy of full membership in the nation. It was an alienation not so much from my country, Canada, as it was from Canadian white society. In my teen years, my identity was based on the consciousness that in the eyes of white Canadians, I was Japanese first, Canadian second. All my life as an adult, my drive to do well has been motivated by the desire to demonstrate to my fellow Canadians that my family and I had not deserved to be treated as we were. And if that was the psychic burden I carried as a result of our experiences during the war, just think of the consequences for First Nations people from the terrible treatment they have been subjected to since first contact.

Of course, Japanese Canadians still held strong ties to Japan. Like those of English heritage who had lived in Argentina for generations yet felt enormous turmoil when Britain attacked the Falkland Islands, the Japanese who came to Canada (called Issei, or first generation) still had family and friends back in the "old country." Like all immigrant people, the first generation of Japanese-heritage kids born in Canada (called Nisei, or second generation) had to grow up without grandparents or an extended family here. This was a sharp break from traditional values surrounding family and elders, and Issei were especially concerned about the loss of those values. As a Sansei (third generation) born of Canadian-born parents, I did have grandparents living in Vancouver and saw them regularly, but, being unilingual, I was almost as cut off from them as I would have been had they lived on the other side of the Pacific. Most of those among the first wave of Issei were like my grandparents: desperately poor, lacking formal education, and in search not of freedom or democracy but of opportunity. They accepted the bigotry they encountered and the restrictions on their entry into society. The War Measures Act consolidated their belief that in Canada, equality and democracy didn't apply to everyone, only to certain privileged racial groups.

Ironically, it was in the internment camps that I became aware of the pain and irrationality of discrimination, and from the Japanese Canadian community at that. It was my first experience of alienation and isolation, and it gave me a lifelong sense of being an outsider. Soon after Pearl Harbor, my father had volunteered to go to that road camp where Japanese Canadians were helping to build the Trans-Canada Highway. He had hoped that by volunteering, he would demonstrate his good intentions, trustworthiness, and willingness to leave his family as hostages to ensure his continued good behavior, therefore ensuring we would be allowed to remain in Vancouver. But it wasn't to be. I am amazed that somehow my parents, still in their early thirties, were able to shield my sisters and me from the pain, anger, and fear that must have threatened to overwhelm them, as the only country they had ever known branded them enemy aliens who could not be trusted.

One day in early 1942, my father was gone. Yet I don't remember feeling any anguish leading up to his sudden departure, nor during the prolonged absence of the one male in my life, who also was my best buddy, hero, and role model. Left with three young children, my mother had to sort through our possessions, winnowing the necessities from everything else, which then had to be sold, given away, or discarded before we made the long train ride to our eventual destination in the Rocky Mountains. I didn't wonder why everyone on the train was Japanese. I just played games with Martha Sasaki, whose family was seated next to ours, and we had a delicious time.

Our destination was Slocan City, a ghost town. Built during the silver rush of the 1890s, when thousands of people mad with silver fever flooded into the beautiful, isolated Slocan Valley, the town was abandoned when mining declined. Now another wave of people poured into the mountains. I found myself surrounded by hundreds of other Japanese Canadians housed in rotting buildings with glassless windows. We lived in a decaying hotel that must have been quite impressive when Slocan City was booming but had become so derelict that I had to learn to avoid the hazardous floorboards on the porch that encircled the building. My mother, my two sisters, and I were placed in one of the tiny rooms, which were still reeking from past generations of occupants, and we would wake each morning covered in bedbug bites. Cleanliness for Japanese is like a religion, and I can imagine the revulsion my mother must have felt in those first weeks.

The massive upheaval, movement, and incarceration of twenty-two thousand Japanese Canadians who were supposed to be a threat to the country posed an immense logistical challenge. Camps made up of hastily thrown together tents and shacks were soon filled. Food had to be supplied by a nation already preoccupied with war across the oceans. There were shortages, especially of trained personnel like nurses, doctors, and teachers. There was no school for the first year, and for a kid suddenly plunked down in a valley where the rivers and lakes were filled with fish and the forests with wolves, bears, and deer, this was paradise.

I had lots of time to play. One of my playmates was a girl named Daisy, who was about my age and who had ended up in Slocan along with her Japanese Canadian mother. Her father was a Caucasian who was serving in the army, defending the democratic guarantees denied his family. Daisy was one of the few kids I felt comfortable playing with, but she was set upon cruelly by the other children, who would reduce her to tears by taunting her as an *ainoko,* which can be roughly translated as "half-breed." She was my friend, and I would never participate in harassing her, but I have felt shame that I didn't have the courage to stand up to the others and defend her. Years later, when we were teenagers, I met Daisy in southern Ontario. She was breathtakingly beautiful but filled with rage toward Japanese Canadians for the torment she had experienced in the camp. I understood the terrible psychic repercussions of discrimination, because I too was on the receiving end of that prejudice.

Although Dad had been taken to Japan for a month when he was about five, Mom had never visited that country. They were Canadians. Both my Nisei parents were bilingual, but they spoke English at home

Displaying my catch (with unidentified man) at Beatrice Lake
in what is now Valhalla Provincial Park

unless they didn't want us to know what they were saying. Almost
all the other children in the camps were Nisei, so they were fluently
bilingual and could switch into Japanese at will. I as a Sansei didn't
speak Japanese and often could not understand what they were saying.
Because of my linguistic deficiency, I was picked on by and isolated
from the other children.

About a year after we arrived in Slocan, a school was built in a
settlement called Bayfarm, perhaps a mile away. I had to knuckle down
and start in grade 1. I loved school and was a good student. Dad and
Mom would grill me on what I had learned each day, patiently listening
to me prattle on. I thought what I had to say was riveting, but now I
know their quizzing was a very effective way of going over lessons and
helping to correct or guide me along.

I was seven when I enrolled in grade 1, but I was soon skipped
through three grades and passed into grade 4 in a year. My father
said that at one point I seemed to lose interest in studies and began to

complain about having to go to school. He and Mom were very worried, because our education was one of their highest priorities, so one day Dad decided to go to the school to find out what was going on. As he walked along the railroad track that connected Slocan to Bayfarm, he saw a group of kids in the distance chasing a boy. It was winter, and there was a thick blanket of snow on the ground. The victim would slip and fall and the kids would catch up, kicking and hitting him as he struggled to his feet to flee again. The boy was me. Mercifully, I have no recollection of that particular mode of harassment, although I do remember much taunting in the school yard. It took a long time for me to overcome my mistrust and resentment of Japanese Canadians as a result of the way I was treated in those camp days.

White kids we saw rarely, and those we did encounter were Doukhobors accompanying their parents, who visited the camps to sell fresh fruit, meat, and vegetables. I am ashamed of one incident in which I took part as a result of ignorance and childhood stupidity. I have always felt grateful to the Doukhobor farmers, who perhaps were motivated in part by their own memories of repression and injustice in Russia, but to me at that time they seemed alien and mysterious as they rode into Slocan on their laden, horse-drawn carts. One day, a chum told me a "bad word" in Russian, giggling as he made me repeat it until I had it memorized. We didn't know what it meant, and I have no idea how he knew the word or even whether it was a curse or a sexual term. We leaned out of a second-floor window when a farmer's cart came trundling down the alley and stopped below us. My friend and I shouted out the word. When the farmer ignored us, we kept chanting until he picked up the knife he used to cut the tops off vegetables, shouted something at us, and climbed off the wagon.

I guess the shot of adrenaline from fear is why little boys do such things, but I did not enjoy being terrified for my life. We bolted out of that room and into my place and under the bed, trembling and trying to stifle our heavy panting. I doubt the farmer even came into the building, but I was absolutely convinced he was going to kill us. A long while later, we finally crept out of the room, and you can bet we never repeated that stunt. Years later, I apologized for the prank to an audience in the Doukhobor Centre in Castlegar and thanked the Doukhobor community for its support of Japanese Canadians during those trying years.

As the war was drawing to a close, those who renounced their Canadian citizenship and were to receive a one-way ticket to Japan were separated from those who chose to stay in Canada. There was strong coercion among camp members to demonstrate their anger at Canada by signing up to "repatriate" to Japan, and more than 95 percent did. Those who did not sign up were castigated as *inu,* or "dogs." My mother met regularly with a group of women to socialize and gossip, but after word got out that we had chosen to remain in Canada, someone in the group insulted her, nobody spoke up for her, and she never went back. To her death, she would not tell my father who had made the remark or what had been said. I have never forgotten that. My mother, one of the gentlest, kindest people I have known, a person who had had to work hard all her life, who would never have knowingly hurt another person, had been deeply wounded by people she considered friends. One of my worst characteristics is that I find it hard to forgive and forget insults and hurts, and this expulsion of my mother further estranged me from the Japanese "community."

Once the first boatloads of people (including my mother's parents and her older sister's family) arrived in Japan, word quickly came back to Canada that conditions were terrible. Japan had been flattened by bombing, and the people were further demoralized by the atomic bombs dropped on Hiroshima and Nagasaki in 1945 to finally prompt unconditional surrender. Food, clothing, and shelter were extremely hard to find, and people struggled to survive.

At that point, those who had renounced their citizenship began to change their minds and clamored to stay in Canada. They remained in the B.C. camps for so long as they fought deportation to Japan that the government finally allowed them to stay in Canada and resettle wherever they wanted. Many chose to return to the B.C. coast, and Dad was very bitter about that. He hadn't wanted to leave B.C., yet he had been evicted from the province, whereas those who had said they wanted to leave B.C. and Canada ended up staying. My father contemptuously referred to them as "repats" and said they were gutless. First they did not have the strength to decide to stay in Canada and fight for their rights, and then they chickened out of moving to Japan.

After we said we would remain in Canada, we were moved from Slocan to Kaslo, still in the Kootenay region but a much larger urban area on Kootenay Lake. For the first time, I attended a school with lots of white kids. But now they seemed alien, and I shied away from them, content to explore this new area of lakes and mountains by myself. The valley in the Kootenay region was rich in pine mushrooms, and that fall I learned where they were likely to be found and how to recognize the bulges on the ground, beneath trees, that indicated where the *matsutake* were. We filled potato sacks with them and my mother bottled the fragrant mushrooms. Today *matsutake* pickers do a thriving business exporting them to Japan. Kootenay Lake had a population of kokanee, which are landlocked miniature sockeye salmon. We took the *Moyie,* a passenger stern-wheeler steamboat, to Lardo, a landing at the head of the lake, where we witnessed a spectacular kokanee run. Like their oceangoing relatives, kokanee turn bright red at spawning time, and the river bottom was carpeted with undulating scarlet ribbons.

One summer day in Kaslo in 1945, I was in the communal bath with an old Japanese man when bells began to peal. "Damme! Maketa!" he exclaimed, meaning "That's bad! We've been beaten!" I didn't know what he meant by "we," because as far as I was concerned, my side must have won. I dressed and rushed out to the street, where people were celebrating and setting off firecrackers. I edged closer to the crowd, hoping someone might hand me a firecracker. Instead, a big boy kicked my behind and shouted, "Get lost, Jap. We beat you!" That's why the old man was rooting for the other side. The evacuation and the boy had shown me I was not a Canadian to the government or to him; I was still a "Jap."

WE FINALLY LEFT KASLO on a long train ride across the prairies, all the way to a suburb of Toronto where Japanese Canadians were kept in a hotel until we found places to go. Dad eventually located a job working as a laborer on a hundred-acre peach farm in Essex County, the southernmost part of Canada. We were supplied with a house, and my sisters and I attended a one-room schoolhouse in Olinda. There were probably thirty students, many of German background, but they were white and had not suffered the kind of discrimination we had felt during the war. My sisters and I were the only non-white kids in the area.

On the first day of school in Olinda, I was so shy that I couldn't look any other students in the eye. When recess came, I was stunned when the other children came up to us and dragged us into games and kept us at the center of all the fun. I later learned that our teacher, Miss Donovan, had told all the other students that my sisters and I were coming and that we were to be welcomed into their midst. What a wonderful gift she gave us.

I loved that year in Olinda, but we moved to the town of Leamington the next year when Dad found a job in a dry-cleaning plant. It was 1946, and when we arrived there, some Leamingtonians boasted to me that "no colored person has ever stayed here beyond sunset." We were the first "colored" family to move into the town, and we were nervous.

In postwar Ontario, Japanese Canadians were sprinkled across the province. In southern Ontario, a handful of families worked on farms, and they kept in touch and became the social circle for my parents. The adults would get together periodically to share stories, offer help, and feast on some of the treasured Japanese food prepared for the occasion. Dad became active in the Japanese Canadian Citizens Association, a group that sprang up to help people settle in their new province and to begin the long struggle for redress and apology. Meeting other Japanese Canadians filled me with mixed emotions because I still remembered the way I had been treated in the camps, but the hormones surging through my body spurred me to check out the only possible dating opportunities—Japanese Canadian girls.

Children are wonderful. They are blind to color or race until they learn from their parents or peers what to notice and how to respond. I was playing with one of my chums when my father came along on a bicycle. I called out to him, and he waved and cycled on past. My friend was dumbfounded and asked, "How do you know him?" When I replied, "Because he's my dad, stupid," he gasped, "But he's a Chink!"

In grade 6 at Mill Street School in Leamington, my teacher was a woman after whom the school is now named. I was an obedient, well-behaved student, so it was a shock one day when, as I was sitting quietly in class, she ordered me to get out. I stumbled into the corridor, stunned and humiliated, and trembled with apprehension as I sat on a seat. After an interminable wait, the teacher came out. "But what did I do?" I stammered. She retorted, "You were smirking at me. I know what you people are thinking. Now get back in there, and don't ever let me catch you looking at me like that again!" I was completely confused but seething with an anger I had to hide.

From that experience, I understood that my physical appearance must be threatening to people like her. Ignorance and the relentless propaganda during the war, portraying buck-toothed, slant-eyed

"Japs" in the cockpit of a plane on a kamikaze mission, must have caused mystery and fear just as today's image of a Muslim extremist strapped with explosives. Every time I looked in a mirror, I saw that stereotype. To this day, I don't like the way I look on television and don't like watching myself on my own TV programs.

One of our fellow students at Mill Street School was a Native boy named Wayne Hillman. I often wonder what happened to him, but back then I envied him because he seemed so carefree. He always had a smile on his face, and he was the personification of laid-back. I'm sure he suffered abuse from our bigoted teacher, too.

I graduated from Mill Street School to enter grade 9 in the only high school in Leamington. I think I was the only Asian enrolled; if anything, I was like a mascot or an oddity. I loved the school and begged my parents to allow me to finish my first year there when they decided to move to London, about one hundred miles away. They arranged for me to stay at a farm run by friends, the Shikaze family, some five miles from Leamington. In return for doing chores before and after school and on weekends, I was given room and board. I even learned some primitive Japanese, because Mr. and Mrs. Shikaze were Issei and spoke Japanese at home. At Leamington High, many students were farm kids who were bused to school, so I fitted in.

Just a few years ago, I happened on a Leamington High yearbook and was amazed to find one of my poems in it:

A WALK IN THE SPRING
David Suzuki
(Junior Poem, Phoebus, Leamington High School Yearbook 1950)

Let us take a walk through the wood,
While we are in this imaginative mood;
Let us observe Nature's guiding hand,
Throughout this scenic, colorful land.

Along a rocky ledge there dwells
A fairy with her sweet blue-bells;
Singing and dancing through the day,
Enchanting all things in her delicate way.

A brilliant bluejay scolds a rabbit,
Lecturing him on his playful habit.
A lovely butterfly flits through the air,
As though in this world it hasn't a care.

The many birds give their mating calls,
Lovelier than the Harp in Tara's Halls;
A wary doe and her speckled fawn,
Creep silently along on their moss-
covered lawn.

Water cress line the banks of a stream
That is the answer to a fisherman's dream;
Teeming with trout and large black bass
That scoot for cover as we noisily pass.

The V-line of the geese reappear,
Showing that spring is actually here;

The swampy marshes are full of duck,
In the water and on the muck.

The air is filled with a buzzing sound,
From above and from the ground;
The air is heavy with the scent of flowers,
Of new buds and evergreen bowers.

Thus precedes Nature's endless show,
Of all things, both friend and foe,
Living in her vast domain,
And under her wise rule and reign.

Thus within her kingdom lies,
Filling scenes for hungry eyes;
Also treasures of this natural world,
Which, if watched carefully, will be
unfurled.

DAD'S BROTHERS AND PARENTS had moved to London in southwestern Ontario during the war and missed the incarceration. After the war's end in 1945, they started a construction company that began to do very well in the postwar building boom. They had urged my father to join them in London, where the schools were better and he could work for them. In Leamington, Mom and Dad had managed to make a living, supplemented by what my sisters and I earned working on farms during the summer, but they were just getting by and had precious little to save. When we moved to London, we were still destitute.

Leamington was a town of perhaps ten thousand people, so when I arrived in London, which had close to one hundred thousand residents in 1950, it seemed a huge metropolis. I really felt like a hick. My cousins had attended elementary school there and were fully accepted into the community; Dad, though he himself hadn't wanted to leave his beloved B.C., had advised his kin to go east when the war started and thus had saved them from much of the distress of being Japanese in Canada. Out east, Japanese were rare, more of an oddity than a perceived threat. Dan and Art, my cousins, hung out exclusively with white kids and even went to parties where, they told me, they played spin the bottle! Wow, kissing a white girl was inconceivable to me, and I was so envious of them.

My uncles helped my family get on its feet. I don't know what the financial arrangements were, but Dad worked for his younger brothers as a trimmer, doing the fine carpentry of hanging doors, trimming along the floor and windows, and building kitchen cabinets. Years later, his outgoing personality made him perfect to sell insurance on the homes built by Suzuki Brothers Construction. In the first months after our family moved to London, my parents and sisters lived with my Uncle Minoru's family. I missed out on that by remaining with the Shikazes near Leamington, but I heard that it was cramped in that house in London and that the inevitable tensions arose between the families.

By the time I arrived in London, my parents had purchased a lot and the brothers had pitched in and helped to build a small house. When I moved in, the roof had been shingled, but the outside walls were sheathed only with raw plywood, the partitions inside were bare, and the floor was simply subfloor. The house was still being built, but the family had already moved in, covering the partitions with cardboard from boxes. Over the months that followed, as we all worked and contributed our earnings to the family coffer, we gradually bought the materials needed to complete the interior and then the outside. I had begun working as a framer for Suzuki Brothers Construction and loved it, working on weekends, holidays, and during the summers. I learned enough to frame, make sidewalks, build a fruit cellar, and pour a concrete slab at the entrance to our house. It took about two years to complete the dwelling. My sisters and I were embarrassed to be living in an unfinished house and would never invite anyone over.

Dad finally bought a car, the first in the family after the end of the war—a 1929 Model A Ford. It was in good shape, and today anyone would be thrilled to own one, but in the early 1950s, it was humiliating for a teenager. Whenever we drove anywhere, I would slump down, hoping no one I knew would see me. To make matters worse, in the autumn Dad went out to collect the leaves that had piled up on the streets and then been squashed into thick clumps as cars drove over them—perfect mulch for the garden. He made a box that could be hung on the rear bumper of the old car, and after dinner I would have to accompany him as he drove around to find an especially rich area of crushed leaves. We shoveled them into the box, drove home, and dumped the leaves in a pile in the front yard. The next day, after school, it was my task to wheel the leaves to the back of the house, where I would dig trenches in the garden and bury the soggy mess as compost. I lived in fear that I would be recognized as I toiled beside Dad under streetlights, piling leaves into the box at the back of the Model A. I admire Dad's gardening obsession now, but as a teenager, I found it excruciating. Like any boy going through puberty, I had sex on the brain, but I was too shy to talk with others about it. Encountering fellow students on buses or walking along a street, I would do my best to avoid having to make conversation by sitting alone or crossing the street.

At Leamington High School, I had felt comfortable in the student body and had even won the junior oratorical contest. But London Central Collegiate Institute was a different matter. Most students move to high school with friends from elementary school, and in the first year, old friendships are solidified, new ones are formed, and cliques coalesce. By the time I arrived for grade 10 at Central, social circles were pretty well established and I was a total stranger, a hick from a farm, an outsider. As adolescent hormones coursed through my body, I became consumed by thoughts of sex, but I was totally incapable of doing anything about it. It never occurred to me to ask a white girl out on a date, because the fear of refusal was too great. Of the ten Japanese Canadian teenage girls in London, three were my sisters.

In a civics class, we were asked what our parents did. To my surprise, I was the only person in the class whose mother worked; all the other students' mothers were full-time parents, and at that time, that was an indication of social status. To exacerbate my isolation, I was a good student, which in that era was like having leprosy. I was horrified when a teacher once asked each of us to tell what our grades had been the year before. I was ashamed to have to say all my marks had been first-class. "But I did get a second in one exam," I offered in a vain effort to soften the scorn. As well, for my sisters and me, weekends and summer holidays were not times to play and take vacations; they were opportunities to work and contribute income to the family. I was stunned to discover in another class that my fellow students spent the entire summer on holiday—that is, not working. Again, the situation set me apart from my classmates.

The only Japanese Canadians at London Central Collegiate Institute were my sisters and cousins. My cousins were well integrated, and my sisters had formed friendships in elementary school because they moved to London earlier than I, so for them the transition to high school was easy. Students at Central were pretty homogeneous, and there were even fewer Chinese Canadians than Japanese Canadians. I didn't realize the differences between gentiles and Jews were very important at London Central; to me, they were all whites who happened to go to different churches. When I was in grade 12, one of the candidates for president of the student council was Jerry Grafstein, now a federal Liberal party wheeler-dealer and senator. I voted for him since I admired his talkative disposition and tremendous popularity,

A carp caught in the Thames River in London, Ontario

and I assumed he was a shoo-in. I couldn't believe it when he lost, and I learned only later that Central just didn't elect Jews to student office.

My loneliness during high school was intense. I ached to have a best buddy to pal around with but was far too self-conscious to assert myself and make a friend. My main solace was a large swamp a ten-minute bike ride from our house. Any marsh or wetland is a magical place, filled with mystery and an incredible variety of plant and animal life. I was an animal guy, and insects were my fascination. Anyone who spotted me in that swamp would have had confirmation of my absolute nerdiness as I waded in fully clothed, my eyes at water level, peering beneath the surface, a net and jar in my hands behind my back. But I couldn't spend all my time in that swamp. I spent most of my waking hours daydreaming, creating a fantasy world in which I was endowed with superhuman athletic and intellectual powers that would enable me to bring peace to the world and win mobs of gorgeous women begging to be my girl.

I hung out with a few other marginal guys who were good students but not on any sporting team. In his fascinating 1976 book *Is There Life After High School?* Ralph Keyes makes the point that high school is the most intense formative period of our lives. Dividing high school students into two groups—Innies (football players, cheerleaders, basketball players) and Outies (everybody else, wishing they were Innies)—he suggests that our high school status remains with us psychically through adulthood. He's right in my case.

In my last year of high school, one of my fellow nerds suggested I run for school president. It was completely unexpected, and I said no. When I told my father, he was disappointed and asked why. "Because I'd lose" was my explanation. Dad was outraged. "How do you know if you don't even try? Besides, what's wrong with losing? Whatever you do, there will always be people better than you, but that doesn't mean you shouldn't try. There's no shame in not coming in first." I

Dad's Model A decked out for my campaign to be student president in 1953 (note the box on the back where we carried leaves to use for compost)

don't know how he acquired his wisdom, but his response stayed with me for life.

So I went back to my friend and said I'd give it a try. We campaigned as Outies and rallied all of those who weren't with the in crowd and wanted a say in student government. My sisters and our friends mounted the campaign with signs and posters saying You'll Rave About Dave. Dad let me take the Model A to school, and we tied a sign on the roof. My public-speaking experience at Leamington High served me well during the campaign at Central, and to my amazement, I won with more votes than all the other candidates combined. It was a powerful lesson—there are a lot more Outies than Innies, and together that means power.

All during high school and college, I worked for Suzuki Brothers Construction as a framer. I worked on houses, framing the footings, shoveling and pouring concrete, and then framing the house all the way to the roof. It was hard physical work, and it gave me a great deal of satisfaction to watch a house emerge from a hole in the ground. The structure we framers put up was later covered with shingles, siding, plaster, trim, and paint, until there was no outward sign of the work we had put into it.

In many ways, that house was like our childhood experiences. Over time, we acquire a veneer of personality that enables us to move among and interact with others, but beneath it remain all the unremembered experiences with family and the fears, hurt, and insecurities of childhood, which others cannot see. For me, the alienation that began with our evacuation from the coast of British Columbia and continued through high school has remained a fundamental part of who I am, all my life, despite the acquired veneer of adult maturity.

COLLEGE AND
A BURGEONING CAREER

I ATTENDED COLLEGE IN the United States as a result of a chance encounter with John Thompson, a former classmate in London. His father headed the business school at the University of Western Ontario, in London, and John, an American citizen, left London after completing grade 12 to enroll at Amherst College in Amherst, Massachusetts. I met him on the street while he was home visiting, and he raved about Amherst and suggested I apply. He had application forms sent to me, so I filled them out and sent them off. I hadn't taken the SATS or AP courses that many Canadian students now do, and I didn't have the extracurricular or athletic experiences that applicants to top universities usually have. All I had was my academic record. I learned later that John had made a strong pitch for me to the dean of admissions, Eugene Wilson, and I was accepted with a scholarship of $1,500, which at that time was more than my father earned in a year.

In the 1950s, the same grade 13 exams were written by all students in Ontario and acted as an academic filter. Most students left high school at the end of grade 12, and grade 13 was for those intending to go to university. But many of those who flunked grade 13 ended up going to American universities, so it was our common perception that U.S. universities had much lower academic standards than Canadian institutions. Not only that, Americans went only to grade 12 before entering university, and I had had an extra year of schooling. I thought Amherst would be a piece of cake.

Boy, did I learn in a hurry that there is a vast range among post-secondary institutions in the U.S. Yes, there are some universities and private colleges where academic standards can be pretty low, and state colleges and universities vary tremendously in academic stature and standards. Private schools also range in quality, but there are many top-rated liberal arts colleges throughout the U.S., including Amherst, Swarthmore, Reed, and Smith. The best and/or well-off students in the U.S. often attend private preparatory high schools, where the goal of the program is to gain admission into a leading academic institution. Over a quarter of my class at Amherst had been valedictorians in their high schools. Students with poor records wouldn't even bother applying, and of the students who did apply, fewer than one in ten was accepted. So these were pretty impressive students. As a scholarship recipient, I had to remain in the top 20 percent of my class to retain the support. No problem, I thought, since I'd had that extra year of a Canadian high school, which we knew was superior to begin with.

I sure had my comeuppance with the first midterm exams. I was not going to coast through Amherst as I had through high school. Suddenly I had to develop efficient study habits, learn to use the library, and write thoughtful essays. Amherst honed my academic skills, and I am grateful that I was able to attend a top-notch undergraduate school and receive an elite education that had no counterpart in Canada. I admire and support the enlightened policy that funded a foreign student like me in the belief that we added to the education of all at Amherst. I can't help contrasting that with Canadian universities that now accept foreign students merely to exploit them by charging exorbitant tuition fees.

I was the first person in my family to graduate from a university. Although my grandparents had not intended to remain in Canada, their Canadian-born children—my parents—had no interest in moving to Japan, because Canada was their country. They pounded home the importance of education as a means for us to escape the extreme poverty we found ourselves in after the war. The biggest fear I had during my youth was that my father might yank me out of school and put me to work.

Most of the students at Amherst came from families whose members had attended university for generations. They were well traveled, many having spent summers abroad. They went to concerts and listened to classical music. They read books for pleasure and attended the theater. These students were cultured, experienced, self-confident, and very bright, and I have never felt more of a yokel than when I first arrived on campus.

At Amherst I also found that most Americans knew almost nothing about Canada. If, on rare occasions, they thought about the country, they regarded it as an annex to the U.S. Nevertheless, I was classed as a foreign student and in my freshman year took advantage of the foreign-student program to stay with an American family for the Thanksgiving holiday. I was shocked when, during the traditional turkey dinner, the conversation became very serious and political and the mother began a loud and animated argument with her husband. In my family, women did not get into discussions in which there might be disagreements. My mother would leave the serious talking in public to my father (although I learned after her death that she was quite outspoken and influential with Dad when they were alone). And she would most certainly never confront him or disagree with him when there were others around. That Thanksgiving was my first intimation of what equality of the sexes might mean.

In London, puberty in a time of straitlaced attitudes toward sex, fear of pregnancy, and "shotgun marriages" was difficult enough, but as a Japanese Canadian scarred by the war and internment, I had a small potential field of girls to consider. Restricted by my father's edict that I must find a mate who was Japanese, I protested there were too few teenage Japanese girls in all of London, so Dad allowed me to consider dating a Chinese Canadian. "Dad," I pleaded, "there are only three Chinese families here and I don't know any of them." "Okay, okay," he relented, "a Native girl is all right." When I pointed out that there might be First Nations reserves on the outskirts of town, but I certainly did not know any Native girls, he added a black girl to the list of acceptables. The only black girl I knew was Annabel Johnson, and she certainly was not interested in me. "All right, I'll allow a Jewish girl," he said, grudgingly, having run out of visible minorities. Dad's descending order of potential mates was based on ethnicity and the extent to which he felt the women themselves would have experienced prejudice, but he failed to recognize that he implicitly accepted the stereotypes and limitations of the bigots.

In grade 12, I had asked the prettiest Japanese girl in London, Joane Sunahara, to go to a New Year's Eve dance. She turned out to be a terrific dancer and an even better kisser, and soon I had my first steady girlfriend. When I became student president at Central Collegiate, she became a vice president of students at Tech, and we were a couple at all the social events at the two schools. But once we had graduated, she went on to Ryerson in Toronto, and we understood that we would stay in touch but also date others.

Amherst College had been an all-male school since its inception in 1821. After a long, often rancorous debate, in 1974 the board of trustees voted to integrate the sexes, with female transfer students being admitted that fall and the first fully integrated freshman class admitted in 1976. Today, women and men are almost equal in number. When I was at Amherst, we dated women from the all-female schools Smith and Mount Holyoke colleges, seven and ten miles away, respectively. Each fall when I returned to Amherst, I would anxiously scan the freshman books from Smith and Mount Holyoke, looking for the three or four Asian students I would consider asking for a date. At social events, I was acutely conscious of being Japanese.

In my freshman year there was another Asian student, a Japanese American from Hawaii, on the same dorm floor, but he only exacerbated my sense of insecurity. Gordon was of very big physique for an Asian, and he had an outgoing personality. His father was a wealthy Honolulu dentist and businessman. Gordon was very conscious of clothes, and I learned from him that dirty white bucks were de rigueur and that wool challis ties, charcoal-gray suits, and pink button-down shirts were what the well-dressed person of that time wore. I couldn't afford them. But it didn't matter, because I had never been interested in clothing styles and was content to let my parents buy clothes for me. I hung around Gordon simply because he was another Asian who I felt shared with me a common background.

Nothing could have been further from the truth. Gordon had been reared in privilege. Japanese Americans in Hawaii had not been incarcerated during World War 11, and he had gone to Punahou, a private school in Honolulu. He was self-confident, and our shared Asianness was inconsequential to him. I think he tolerated me the way one tolerates a mutt, with a mixture of amusement and pity.

When his father visited in our freshman year, they invited me to go out to dinner with them. I was working on the breakfast shift in the Amherst dining hall, starting at 6:00 every morning and earning $1.50 an hour for spending money. They took me to a fancy restaurant, where I was floored by the cost of the offerings on the menu. When the bill arrived, I offered to pay my share with great trepidation. To my relief, Gordon's father picked up the tab, but I vowed never to go to dinner with them again. And I didn't. There was an enormous barrier created by our different experiences of the war. In Hawaii, the population of Japanese Americans was too great to consider their wholesale incarceration, even though the Japanese attack had been on Pearl

Harbor in Honolulu. Japanese Americans flourished in Hawaii, whereas my sense of self and personality had been sculpted by poverty, ignorance, and a sense of shame.

In the fall of 1957, my senior year at Amherst, an epidemic of Asian flu swept the world. Despite our rural setting, Amherst did not provide a sanctuary from it, and like many others, I finally succumbed to the virus. I staggered to the infirmary, only to find it filled with sick guys who booed me. There were only a handful of Asians on campus at that time, so it was easy to jokingly blame us for the Asian flu, but I was too sick to care anyway.

I collapsed into bed, feeling terrible, with only the radio as a diversion. I was jolted out of my illness when an announcer interrupted the programming to inform us that the Soviet Union had successfully launched a satellite called Sputnik into space. It was only the size of a basketball, but it was an electrifying achievement, the first man-made object to escape the atmosphere and orbit Earth. I had no inkling that there was even a space program, and the feat captured my imagination. But in the months that followed, I and the rest of America agonized as the United States initially failed in spectacular fashion to get a satellite into orbit while the USSR announced one first after another—Laika, the first animal (a dog) in space; Yuri Gagarin, the first man; the first team of cosmonauts; Valentina Tereshkova, the first woman.

In belatedly recognizing that the Soviets were very advanced in science, engineering, math, and medicine, the U.S. became determined to catch up by pouring money into students, universities, and government labs. In the post-Sputnik frenzy, every effort was made to attract students into science, and even though I was Canadian, I later received funding to carry on with my graduate studies at the University of Chicago.

There was an excitement that came from the infusion of money and government priority for science. We were taught in graduate school that science is the most powerful way of learning about the world. Through science we probed the deepest secrets of nature—the structure of matter itself, the edges of the universe, the genetic code. Implicit in our education was the notion that science rejected emotion and subjectivity and sought only truth.

The queen of all sciences was physics, especially theoretical physics. Biology was a fuzzy science; life is messy and does not readily lend itself to the kind of exquisite experiments done in physics. And within biology, there was a definite pecking order, with taxonomy and systematics (which geneticists contemptuously referred to as stamp collecting), ecology, and organismic biology on the bottom and molecular biology and genetics at the very apex (at least, that's the way geneticists saw it).

I had always wanted to be a biologist. In my early years, I dreamed of being an ichthyologist, someone who studies fish. As a child, I fantasized about being able to fly-fish for my experimental animals and then eat them when the experiment was finished. What could be more heavenly than that? Later, when I became an avid collector of insects, I considered entomology as a possible profession. But it was in my third year of college that, as a biology honors student, I was required to take a course in genetics and fell madly in love with the elegance and mathematical precision of the discipline. I loved reading arcane and difficult papers on exquisite experiments and discovered I had a knack for setting up complex experiments to solve very specific questions.

I had been assured of a place in medical school at the University of Western Ontario in London, but I decided to abandon medicine for genetics. My mother was disconsolate for weeks after I told her I was not going to become a doctor, and that I would study fruit flies instead.

By the time I had made this decision, it was too late to apply for scholarships or teaching assistantships. I had hoped to work with the famous geneticist Curt Stern at the University of California at Berkeley; although I had been accepted there, I was too late to receive any financial support. Joane and I were still an item and planned to get married, so I couldn't afford to go without such help. Bill Hexter, my

My professor Bill Baker, fellow PhD student Anita Hessler,
and me in the fly lab at the University of Chicago

thesis adviser at Amherst, called a friend, Bill Baker, a fruit fly geneticist at the University of Chicago, who offered me a position as his
research assistant supported by his grant.

When I graduated from Amherst in 1958 with an honors degree
(cum laude) in biology, I knew I could at least be a good teacher, but
upon entering graduate school at the University of Chicago I found I
had a burning desire to do experimental science. I enrolled as a student
in the Zoology Department, and Joane, whom I had married in August
1958, worked as a technician preparing specimens for the electron
microscope, a highly demanding task at which she excelled. I had taken
a course on marriage and sex in my last year of college, so I figured I
knew all I needed to plan ahead. Unfortunately, passion and sloppiness
intruded, and all of our plans for the future went out the window when
Joane became pregnant. So much for the significance of an A grade in
the course I had taken. Tamiko was born in January 1960, a wonderful
surprise who took over my life.

Joane and Tamiko

Tamiko's arrival put a lot of pressure on me to complete my degree. Joane would work in the day while I took care of Tamiko, most often taking her to the lab, where she could sleep in the buggy while I counted fruit flies. I would take her home for dinner and then leave to spend long nights continuing the experiments. The work paid off, as I completed my doctorate in zoology in less than three years after graduating from Amherst.

The Zoology Department at the University of Chicago had had a long and distinguished record in the classical fields, whereas cell biology and genetics were relatively recent arrivals. Aaron Moscona was a top developmental biologist there, and Hewson Swift was a cell biologist with expertise with the electron microscope. Bill Baker was the geneticist. As well, there were terrific people in other departments such as botany, microbiology, and biochemistry, and there was an atmosphere of intellectual excitement. I took courses with two of the "grand old men of ecology," Alfred Emerson and Tom Park, both of whom gave me a grounding in ecology and introduced me to students in the area.

But exhilaration about the recognition that deoxyribonucleic acid (DNA), was the genetic material, the James Watson–Francis Crick model that explained it, and other advances in molecular biology seemed to extend into every area of the life sciences. I remember Tom Humphreys, one of the bright grad students in Moscona's lab, protesting, "You geneticists seem to want to take over all of biology." He was right—we did. As far as we were concerned, the entire field of developmental biology was the consequence of differential activation and inactivation of genes. We grad students in genetics were pretty puffed up with ourselves as a result of the recent discoveries and tended to be condescending toward the more traditional, descriptive sciences. Now that I realize how important it is to bring an ecological perspective to environmental issues, I feel a need to serve penance for my youthful arrogance.

In June 1961, I received my PhD and had the added thrill of receiving the sheepskin directly from the university's new president, George Beadle. He was a Nobel Prize winner who had begun his career working with corn, then switched to fruit flies, and finally settled on the bread mold, *Neurospora crassa*. Through this research, he and Edward Tatum had discovered the one-gene/one-enzyme relationship that suggested each gene specified the production of a specific protein or enzyme. I became a fully licensed scientist upon receiving my degree from an eminent fellow geneticist.

My thesis adviser, Bill Baker, had worked for years at the Biology Division of the Oak Ridge National Laboratory (ORNL) in Tennessee and strongly recommended that I apply for a position there. I did, and I was delighted to receive my first full-time job as a research associate in the lab of Dan Lindsley, one of the world's experts in manipulating chromosomes.

ORNL had been created in the mountains of Tennessee as a top-secret project to purify uranium for the Manhattan Project, set up in

Yataro Tazima *(right)*, a silkworm geneticist from Japan, visiting Dan Lindsley
and me at the Oak Ridge National Laboratory in Tennessee

1942 to develop the atomic bomb. After the war, research on radiation
continued in the Biology Division, but by the time I applied, the division had shifted its research emphasis to basic biology. Once there, I
was free to follow any avenue of research I wanted in the company of
some of the best scientists in the world. There was a wonderful spirit of
collegiality and helpfulness that encouraged cooperation and exchange
of ideas as the best way to develop one's skills. I came away much more
confident in my abilities as a scientist.

World War II had created Oak Ridge, and, ironically, the institution that had been the source of material for the bombs that had
demolished Hiroshima and Nagasaki was now a hotbed of world-class
research and international cooperation, and I was part of it. There was
another legacy, from the Great Depression of the 1930s. Tennessee
had been one of the poorest regions of the U.S.; the forests had been
cut down long before, and farmers had overworked the soil, leading
to loss of the land's fertility and to erosion. During the Depression,

U.S. president Franklin D. Roosevelt had galvanized people with his vision of a New Deal to create wealth and get people working. At his urging, Congress established the Tennessee Valley Authority (TVA) in 1933 to oversee a massive make-work project. The TVA was a radically new approach that took a more holistic view of problems like malaria control, flooding, deforestation, navigation, and erosion. A network of lakes created by dams provided flood control and, most important, power for industries and home use.

Around Oak Ridge, there were TVA dams that supported populations of fish. Below the dams, I would fish for trout and shad, and above in the lakes, silver bass were plentiful. I would take the family camping in the Smoky Mountains. Dad came to visit and was soon driving along back hills, meeting hillbillies and sharing their moonshine.

But Tennessee had been a slave-owning state and a part of the southern Confederacy in the Civil War. There were still overt signs of racism. Because of my own experience during World War II, I identified strongly with the black community. Most of the scientists at ORNL came from the North, so the facilities were an oasis of liberalism. In Dan Lindsley's lab, the chief technician was Ruby Wilkerson, an African American who lived with her husband, Floyd, in the nearby village of Philadelphia. Ruby and I would sit at our microscopes across from each other, and she would regale me with stories about the many geneticists who had gone through Lindsley's lab.

When Joane and I visited Ruby and her family, guests sat at the table with the men while the hosting women stood behind and filled our plates and glasses as needed. The TV was always blaring. Once I was holding forth when I suddenly realized that no one was listening to me—they were all riveted by the appearance of a black actor on the TV screen. It was a stunning illustration of their desperate need for someone with whom they could identify.

There were lots of black employees at ORNL, including Ruby's husband and his brother, but almost all worked in support positions—as

My Oak Ridge lab companion, Ruby Wilkerson; her husband, Floyd; and her daughter, Patricia with trout at Dad's pond near London

janitors, kitchen help, and animal caretakers. I became involved in the local chapter of the National Association for the Advancement of Colored People (NAACP) and, in empathizing with the problems of discrimination in the South, began to resent all white people. Joane and I traveled into the Deep South, where I was distressed by the blatant racism in signs restricting the use of drinking fountains and washrooms.

Although I could have stayed on at Oak Ridge and had been offered several faculty positions in the U.S., I felt deeply estranged from the culture because of the overt racism. Even though Canada had invoked the War Measures Act against Japanese Canadians, the country was smaller, and I believed there was more of a chance to work for a better society. The opportunities for a scientist in the U.S. were much greater at that time, but I have never regretted my decision to return home.

A position as assistant professor arose in the Genetics Department at the University of Alberta, which I eagerly applied for, and I was gratified to be offered the job. I accepted it. Edmonton was an excellent place to begin my career, although I took a cut in pay compared with what I would have received had I stayed at ORNL. The province was booming and provided far more support for research and staff than most universities received. When I arrived in the summer of 1962, I would leave the lab at 2:00 or 3:00 in the morning and was thrilled that it was still light out because of Edmonton's northerly latitude. I was not so happy when I was assigned to teach an Introductory Genetics course to a group of agriculture students, but they turned out to be the hardest-working and hardest-playing group I've ever had.

However, that winter, the thermometer plunged to minus forty degrees Fahrenheit, a temperature I had never experienced and did not wish to experience again. So when a position came up at the University of British Columbia (UBC), I applied and was invited out for an interview. When I left Edmonton to try for the job, the temperature was minus thirty degrees. I arrived in Vancouver, where it was thirty above, and everyone was moaning about the cold! I took the job but also another pay cut. It was a good thing I stayed at UBC, because at the rate I was going, I might have ended up having to pay for a job.

When I had taken up the position in Edmonton in 1962, I applied for a research grant from the National Research Council (NRC) in Ottawa and was shocked to be awarded only $4,200. I was told later that a first-time grant for a new professor was $3,500, but since I'd had a year of postdoctoral studies, mine had been bigger. It was a shock because, at that time, the people with whom I had graduated in the U.S. were receiving first-time grants of $30,000 to $40,000. Canada had simply not moved into the post-Sputnik era, as the U.S. had, with a huge commitment to science as part of the Cold War competition.

Canada's granting policies had grown up when there was far less research money to support a small community of poorly paid scientists who did research simply because they loved it. In Canada, one aged into respectability—the longer one hung in doing research, the bigger the grants became. When I returned to Canada in 1962, heads of departments often held the really big grants, even though they were usually fully occupied with administrative duties. They were powerful because of the money they controlled and the people they could support and hire.

That has slowly changed. In those early days in Canada, University of Toronto microbial geneticist Lou Siminovitch worked hard to get better support for junior scientists. He attracted a top-notch group of young people to the University of Toronto, and I believe his advocacy of better support for such researchers was part of the reason my own grants began to rise as the lab became productive. Lou recognized that Drosophila (fruit fly) genetics would be an important area of molecular interest and offered me a position at the University of Toronto that would have led to increased grants and support. But I really loved British Columbia and couldn't see living in a large city.

Canada did have Nobel laureates in science, the most famous being Frederick Banting and John Macleod in 1923 for their discovery of insulin. It was the Nobel Prizes awarded to University of Toronto chemist John Polanyi in 1986 and UBC DNA chemist Michael Smith in 1993 that galvanized greater support for research. In 1972, the Senate Special Committee on Science Policy headed by Senator Maurice Lamontagne had released its recommendations, and among them was greater emphasis on "mission-oriented research"—that is, research dedicated to a specific goal.

The problem with that approach is that science does not proceed from experiment A to experiment B to C to D to a cure for cancer. If it did, we would have solved most of the problems of the world by now. Science cannot proceed in this linear manner. From the moment we begin experiment A, we have no idea what the results will be or where we will end up. The way we maximize "return on our investment" is by supporting top people, not top research proposals. Increasingly, universities are encouraging arrangements in which academics are supported by money from the private sector—in forestry, agriculture, pharmacy, biotechnology, and so on. This policy has had a negative effect on the open, free flow of discussion, criticism, and information that is the essence of a university community.

At the very beginning of my career, I was ambitious and determined to make a mark, not to make money or acquire power but mainly to receive the approbation of the scientists I most admired in *Drosophila* genetics. But I simply would not have been able to carve out a career on such a piddling grant as $4,200 from the National Research Council, and I reluctantly began to make inquiries about positions back in the U.S.

Then the picture changed. As I was leaving Oak Ridge in 1962, George Stapleton, an administrator I had come to know, had advised me to apply to the U.S. Atomic Energy Commission (USAEC) for research money. Once I got to the University of Alberta, I applied to USAEC, but I did not expect to receive any money, because I was doing basic genetics that did not involve radiation in any way. To my surprise and delight, I received a substantial grant, about ten times my NRC grant and certainly enough to get my lab off the ground. It is such an irony that the U.S. gave me, a foreigner, the support that enabled me to remain in my own country.

I had worked day and night at ORNL, and there were always other people around working just as hard. When I took my academic position in Canada, I was confident in my abilities as a teacher and scientist and anxious to make a name in research, so I continued to work in the lab into the evenings and on weekends. Students responded to this example and worked right along with me, so the lab was lit up well after my colleagues and other students in the department had gone home.

I was still in my late twenties when I arrived at UBC in 1963. Faculty members in the Zoology Department wore jackets and ties, and their students addressed them as "Doctor." I certainly did not wear a jacket and tie, and my students called me by my first name. This more "American" style was frowned upon. I was never caught up in the social sphere with other staff either, because I was so enthralled with setting up my own lab and getting our research off the ground. The Canadian faculty still acted like a small, exclusive club. I felt disgusted at a meeting when another professor boasted that we were one of the best zoology departments in Canada. I was only interested in being among the best in the world.

Evenings were the best time to be in the lab. No one, including me, had classes then, so we could count fruit flies, drink coffee, and talk— my, how we talked, mostly about genetics but also about sex, politics, and the world. With the revolution in molecular biology, we were all agog at what was being found and kept hatching crazy ideas for experiments. The students I attracted were enthusiastic, and the lab became a kind of family. We worked hard, but we also played hard, going to the pub, skateboarding in the basement, camping together on weekends and in the summers.

Harvesting salmon pituitary glands for future Nobel Prize winner
Michael Smith's biochemical studies (yup, I used to smoke)

DAVID SUZUKI

But the self-sufficiency of my lab, our enthusiasm, and no doubt our arrogance, set us apart from the rest of the department. We looked down our noses at the folks in fisheries and wildlife biology, snorting that they were just descriptive biologists, not real experimental scientists like us. I cringe when I think back on that cockiness and sense of superiority. Yes, that feeling of excitement about our work created a strong sense of community, but it also alienated me from most of my fellow faculty members. Confident in my teaching and research and absorbed in my own community of students, I had little interest in the local politics of academia and lived in a kind of self-imposed isolation from the rest of the university. If they didn't bother me, I was happy to be left alone.

Not surprisingly, as I spent more and more time in the lab, Joane and I had less and less time together. Besides Tamiko we now had Troy, born in 1962; dinner, bathing the children, reading to them in bed—that was a steady part of my routine before going back to the lab. But even on our family camping trips, the lab often went along. Joane had every justification for demanding more of my company. She had worked hard so that I could go to graduate school even with a child, and once I was settled as a faculty member, we should have had more opportunities to be together. But I was too ambitious to give up the time; I was much more focused on doing a really elegant, important experiment. Our marriage was ending. Soon after the birth of Laura, our third child, in 1964, Joane and the children moved into a home we had just bought. I did not.

On April 4, 1968, American civil-rights leader Martin Luther King was assassinated, and students at UBC organized a rally on the steps of the library to express our sorrow. I was an associate professor and spoke out, telling British Columbians that this was a time for us not to smugly reaffirm our sense of superiority over Americans but to reexamine our own society. I reminded them of the incarceration of Japanese Canadians during World War II, the treatment of Native people, and the fact that Asians and blacks were not allowed to vote in B.C. until the 1960s. The *Vancouver Sun* wrote a scathing editorial that chastised me for opening old wounds, for raising issues that were not relevant on the occasion of a King memorial. It was then that I realized how important tenure was as I was subtly informed that university administrators were nervous about faculty members who might attract negative publicity.

When Joane and I had separated in 1964, my department head warned me that a broken marriage could jeopardize my career. A faculty member from Microbiology drove me home from campus one evening, and as I was about to get out of the car, he said, "I would be remiss if I didn't say that by breaking up your marriage, you will pay a price within the university."

On many fronts, the university was still adjusting to rapidly changing values in society.

WHEN I HAD RETURNED to Canada from the U.S., I had been consumed by a passion to study cell division in *Drosophila* and thought I had some clever tricks up my sleeve. But I also enjoyed teaching and put a lot of time and energy into it. My early years of public-speaking contests and courses paid off in my abilities as a "performer." I encouraged students to interrupt me at any time if they were confused or had a query.

Students were interested in far more than how many points an exam was worth or what would or would not be on the final test paper; they wanted to explore the implications of the work I was discussing—societal issues related to genetic engineering, cloning, and eugenics—so I was forced to read up on the history of genetics, which I hadn't been taught in college. It was devastating to me to discover that geneticists early in the twentieth century had extrapolated from their studies of the heredity of physical characteristics in mice, fruit flies, and plants to make pronouncements about the heredity of intelligence and behavior in humans. Back then, genetics was an exciting new science making huge inroads in our understanding of the mechanisms of heredity, and no doubt seemed to them as if we were on the threshold of acquiring incredible powers to manipulate human heredity. But these grand claims ended up in discriminatory legislation prohibiting inter-racial marriage in some U.S. states, restricting immigration of certain ethnic groups, and permitting sterilization of inmates in mental institutions for genetic reasons. It was a shock to discover that the grandiose declarations of geneticists had been used in Canada to justify the fears of treachery from Japanese Canadians that led to our evacuation and incarceration, and in Nazi Germany to support the Race Purification Laws that culminated in the Holocaust.

I decided I had to speak out about the potential abuse of genetics. For my colleagues in that field, this did not sit well, especially as revolutionary insights and techniques for manipulating DNA seemed to presage a cornucopia of wonderful applications. I kept trying to remind geneticists of the disastrous consequences that had resulted from claims made by equally eminent geneticists only two generations before. It has been a lonely role for a geneticist to raise issues of concern when there was and is so much enthusiasm and so much apparent potential for revolutionary applications.

In 1991, I was invited to host an eight-part series of one-hour television shows on the genetic revolution, in a coproduction between the American PBS and the British BBC networks. In Britain, the series was called *Cracking the Code,* in the U.S., it was *The Secret of Life,* and it was broadcast in 1993. It was a huge success for nonprofit PBS, earning a review in *Newsweek* magazine that said the series was the "first sign of intelligent life in the television season." Because of the success of the series, I was asked to be the moderator of an all-day symposium in Oklahoma City in April 1995, only two weeks before the tragic bombing of the Alfred P. Murrah Federal Building by an antigovernment extremist that killed 168 people.

The symposium participants were eminent geneticists discussing the exciting implications of their work, and the star of the meeting was Nobel laureate James Watson, co-discoverer with Francis Crick of the double helix. I was effusive in my introduction of Watson, talking about how few scientists were as successful as he was, living to see their work become the stuff of textbooks, blah, blah. When I called for questions after his talk, people were shy at first, so I took the initiative and asked Watson what I thought was an innocuous question about the social and ethical implications of the revolutionary techniques in molecular biology. To my astonishment, in response, Watson lashed out and attacked me personally: "I know what people like you think," he snarled. "You want everyone to be the same." Then he proceeded to mock those who raise moral and ethical issues around modern genetics.

I was truly offended, disappointed, and embarrassed, all at once. He had put words into my mouth that made me into a straw man he could easily knock down. As moderator of the session, I felt it would be wrong for me to start debating him, so I let him finish and called for the next question, my cheeks burning with rage. I knew that later that evening, when I was no longer moderator, I could rebut Watson, but he left immediately after our session was over. My rebuttal felt pretty hollow, but I gave it, saying Watson was totally wrongheaded. "Yes," I said, "I believe in the concept of equality before the law, which is a magnificent concept. But as a geneticist, I know diversity and difference are a part of our makeup, and no one should want to diminish that."

Over the years, Watson has made many statements about his outlandish faith in the benefits of genetic manipulation on virtually every aspect of human development and behavior. But even today, merely thinking about Watson's outburst raises my blood pressure, though I know he was just being Jim.

During the 1960s, as science departments everywhere were growing, there was tremendous competition for faculty members. Canadian research grants were so small that there was no way a hotshot scientist could be lured away from the U.S. As the elite American universities skimmed off the best candidates from Canada and the rest of the world, we were left competing with other Canadian universities and third-level American institutions for the rest. At a faculty meeting, I suggested that one way to build a top-grade research faculty at UBC would be to focus on recruiting women.

At that time, most women still had difficulty finding tenure-track positions and were usually recruited as research associates or teachers in non-tenure-track jobs. It would have been far easier for a Canadian institution like UBC to recruit excellent female prospects and become a world-class school. At the time, the Zoology Department had one woman with tenure out of perhaps twenty-five faculty. The response to my proposal was dead silence; then discussion abruptly shifted to other matters. Once again I felt I had marginalized myself in the department with what was thought to be another kooky Suzuki idea.

When I had been recruited by UBC, about 60 percent of the faculty in the Zoology Department were Canadians, and the rest were Britons and Americans. Canadian universities exploded in size as more and more students enrolled, so by the 1970s, Canadian institutions were graduating substantial numbers of students with PhDs. Yet we were hiring more and more Americans and Brits, and the proportion of Canadians in my department fell below 50 percent. At a departmental meeting, I suggested that when we received applications for a position, we should separate them into two piles, one for Canadians, the other for all the rest. We should then examine only the file of Canadians to see whether any applicants met our academic standards and needs. If there was someone who did, I recommended we try to recruit that person without even looking at the applicants in the other group. Only if we couldn't find someone of high enough caliber in the Canadian applications would we then look at the second group.

I couldn't believe the response. One young professor from Britain called me a "fascist" and raised the specter of jackbooted Nazi-like brownshirts if my advice were followed. It was astonishing to see the equally angry reaction from others to my attempt to make it possible for Canadians to compete in a more equitable way without compromising academic standards. After all, by grading all applications together, Canadians would immediately be at a disadvantage just in numbers of competitors for the job.

I don't want to imply that I suffered by being an outsider. In large measure, I chose to remain in that position by not playing the game. The politics of rising through the academic ranks never interested me, and so long as I had research support and great students, I was happy. I also remembered my father's admonition that if I wanted to be liked by everybody, I wouldn't stand for anything. If I was going to say what I believed, I had to be prepared for the reality that some people would always be pissed off at me. Many times in meetings, when I knew I would be a minority of one on an issue and would anger a lot of people, I would agonize over whether to let it pass and make my own life simpler. But I couldn't help responding if it was a matter of principle, even though everything in me just wanted to fit in and not make waves. My fellow faculty members would roll their eyes, suggesting they were thinking, "There goes Suzuki, grandstanding again."

An outsider sees things from a different angle and thus, I believe, often recognizes what others may not see. A scientist working in biotechnology with the prospect of making a lot of money from a product can be resistant, if not blind, to questions of hazards or risks that someone without a vested interest might see with greater clarity. For me, status as an outsider has been a mixed blessing. When I was younger, I so wanted to fit in and not stand apart, to be accepted and liked. However, on the outside, not only do I see things from a different perspective, but also I don't have a vested interest in the status quo or in companies, groups, or organizations of which I might be critical.

chapter THREE

A NEW CAREER

IN 1954, WHEN I graduated from high school and went away to college, my family had never owned a television set. At that time in London, Ontario, television was still a novelty, and a pioneer who purchased a TV set required a giant antenna to pick up signals from Cleveland or Detroit. I remember the thrill of sitting in my uncle's living room watching shadowy on-screen images flitting through a curtain of heavy electronic snow—it was the technology more than the programs that fascinated us. But watching television had never been part of my early family life, and when I went away to college and then graduate school, I was too busy to watch TV.

On another front that would turn out to be a thread in the fabric of my life, my father had encouraged me to take up public speaking. In Japanese culture, extreme deference is paid to authority and social position, and self-deprecation and politeness often mean people are reluctant to speak out or stand up for themselves or their ideas. In Canada, a culture in which outspokenness or aggressive self-promotion is often admired, the inability of many Japanese Canadians to stand up and speak with enthusiasm or authority is a disability.

My father was a very rare Japanese Canadian, outgoing, gregarious, and articulate, and he wanted me to be the same way. "You've got to be able to get up and speak in public," he told me over and over when I was a teenager. He worked hard to train me to give speeches, and at his urging, I entered oratorical contests and won a number of them.

Amherst College in the 1950s aimed to graduate students who were well rounded in the humanities and the sciences. Every Amherst undergraduate of the time, regardless of area of specialty, had to take such courses as English and American Studies and a foreign language; one of the more idiosyncratic requirements was that all students had to be able to swim two lengths of the pool. Amherst men also had to take public speaking in sophomore year. The course was a joke among the students, because no one ever failed, but I took it seriously and won top marks in the six speeches we had to give over two semesters. As well, as an honors biology student, I was required to make a scientific presentation to students and professors in each semester of my senior year, and I discovered I had an ability to present complex scientific topics in a way that not only was understandable but also excited the listeners. I realized teaching was something I enjoyed and could do well, and in graduate school this awareness was reinforced in the seminars and discussions I led.

After I arrived at the University of Alberta in 1962 to take up my first academic position, I soon earned a reputation as a good lecturer and was invited to give a talk on a program called *Your University Speaks*, broadcast on a local television channel. It featured university professors lecturing on subjects in their areas of expertise, aided by slides. As the title of the show suggests, it was a pretty stodgy series. But I was curious and accepted the invitation (I think we were even paid twenty-five bucks), and apparently I did all right, because I was asked to go back the next week and the next and the next until I ended up doing eight programs. The series was broadcast early Sunday mornings, so

I was shocked when people stopped me and told me how much they had enjoyed one of the shows I had done. Initially I couldn't understand why anyone would watch TV on a Sunday morning, but I began to realize television had become a powerful vehicle to inform people.

I moved to the University of British Columbia a year after returning to Canada, and in Vancouver I was asked to appear on television to do the occasional book review or commentary on a scientific story. I became more interested in the medium as a way to communicate and ended up proposing a television series to look at cutting-edge science. Knowlton Nash was head of programming at the Canadian Broadcasting Corporation (CBC) and approved the series to come out of Vancouver. At one point, he called Keith Christie, who had been assigned to produce the series, and asked how "it" was going. Keith asked what he was talking about, and Knowlton replied, "You know, that Suzuki-on-science series." Keith tells me he said, "That's it," and the show was called *Suzuki on Science*. It was broadcast across the country in 1969 and was my first involvement in a television series with a national audience. It ran for two seasons and was renewed for a third, but I quit: we had a lousy time slot and low budget and I saw no future for the show, exciting though making the series had been.

In 1974, Jim Murray, longtime executive producer of *The Nature of Things* on CBC Television, began a new show called *Science Magazine*, a weekly half-hour collection of reports on science, technology, and medicine. He had known about my Vancouver-based series, and after we met and talked, he hired me to be the host of the new one. It was an immediate hit, drawing an audience that was 50 percent larger than the long-running popular series *The Nature of Things*, which had begun in 1960. I took a leave from UBC to host the program.

Halfway through that first season, Knowlton Nash informed us the series would be dropped. We were shocked, but we carried on. At the end of the last show, I told the audience this was the final segment,

Being interviewed by students in the late 1960s

thanked them for watching, and said goodbye. I didn't lament our passing or plead for support, but viewers responded with letters and phone calls objecting to our cancellation. The series was restored and ran for four more years.

During the first season of *Science Magazine*, Diana Filer, executive producer of the CBC Radio series *Concern*, attended a speech I gave at the University of Toronto. She had proposed a new science series for radio called *Quirks and Quarks* and hired me to host it when it went to air in 1975. I was host of both *Science Magazine* on television and *Quirks and Quarks* on radio, which was a full-time job, until 1979.

Diana also introduced me to Bruno Gerussi, whose CBC Radio show had been a forerunner of Peter Gzowski's *This Country in the Morning*. Bruno became a good friend, and I would often drop in on him in Gibsons on the Sunshine Coast just north of Vancouver, where he lived while filming his long-running CBC Television series *The Beachcombers*. On one of those visits, he met my father and grew very fond of him, eventually inviting him to play a guest role on an episode.

Bruno also had a script written in which I played a scientist in search of a rare coastal tree. In one segment of that episode, I appeared with the First Nations actor Chief Dan George, who had starred so powerfully in the film *Little Big Man* with Dustin Hoffman. I was awed and thrilled to be in his presence, but by then he was quite old and frail. In the story, I seek his advice on where the rare tree might be. When I arrived for the shoot, Chief George was seated in a rocking chair on a house porch and covered with a blanket. As the crew went about setting up the lighting and camera, I tried to chat with him. He replied in a barely audible voice, so I realized I was draining his energy and left him alone; I worried about whether he could perform.

Once the camera was rolling and the producer called out "Action!", Chief George threw off the blanket, straightened up, and delivered his lines forcefully with that unique voice. As soon as the director shouted "Cut!", the chief immediately drew the blanket up around his shoulders and slumped back into the chair. He delivered like a trouper by conserving his strength between every take. Now that's being a professional.

In 1979, I left both *Science Magazine* and *Quirks and Quarks* to become host of *The Nature of Things*, which had been reformatted and was to become an hour-long program called *The Nature of Things with David Suzuki*. I left radio with great reluctance. It was the medium I enjoyed most, because interviews were relaxed, and there was an opportunity to be spontaneous, humorous, and even risqué, since tapes could be edited and still retain warmth and intimacy.

In contrast, television is very controlled, because airtime is so valuable. After I've given a speech, I often encounter people who tell me I'm so different from my persona on TV. But it shouldn't be a surprise; that person on-screen is a creation of the medium. My on-camera appearances are carefully planned and controlled, then prepackaged, and the narration is laid down in a studio, where my reading is carefully delivered to fit the pictures. Because radio burns through material and, as host of *Quirks and Quarks*, I had to do all of the interviews, it demanded far more of my time than television. There was also no denying the much greater audience size of television and therefore, potentially, its greater impact. So I reluctantly gave up *Quirks and Quarks*, but I continue to take vicarious pride that it has endured and flourished under a number of excellent hosts.

When I began to work in television in 1962, I never dreamed that it would ultimately occupy most of my life and make me a celebrity in Canada. I thought I might have a knack for translating the arcane jargon of science into the vernacular of the lay public, and I felt that speaking on television was a responsibility I had assumed by accepting government research grants and public support in a university. When I appeared on a television show for the first time, I enjoyed the novelty, but I did not anticipate the notoriety that would come from being on-screen regularly. Looking back, I realize how incredibly naive I was.

Nim Chimpsky, who was taught to use sign language by Herb Terrace of Columbia University

I just didn't understand the relationship between a viewer, television, and information.

Television is an ephemeral medium; a program we might work for months to create flashes onto the screen to an audience often distracted by other activities—feeding the kids, answering the phone, going to the toilet, walking the dog, getting a drink. Viewers aren't fully engaged through the entire program, and what is ultimately remembered may be a snippet. And if a show is part of a series such as *The Nature of Things with David Suzuki*, in which diverse topics are covered, the subject matter of any given show may be forgotten, but the one constant feature from week to week—the host—is remembered.

Over time, a relationship is established wherein the audience comes to trust the host and to believe in what he or she is conveying. Think of the enormous following of people like American journalist Walter Cronkite and Canadian counterpart Peter Mansbridge.

In the same vein, I too am transformed from being the carrier of information to an "expert." People assume I am an authority on each subject we cover on the series and that I must know everything in the area of science, the environment, technology, medicine, and so on. Strangers often approach me to ask a very specific question about treatment for a disease, a new technology for cleaning up the environment, or an obscure species discovered in the Amazon. When I answer that I have no idea, they stare in disbelief and demand, "What do you mean, you don't know? I thought you knew everything!"

Even back in the 1960s, when I was dabbling in television, it was referred to as "the boob tube," and I knew program offerings were mainly idiotic or dull or both. When I entered television as a new career, I was conceited enough to think my shows would be different, glistening like jewels in the muck. Because I was not in the habit of watching television, I thought people would carefully read the program listings to find out what important, interesting, or entertaining show was coming up, look forward to it with great anticipation, turn on the set just before the show was to appear, and sit riveted through the entire program. When it was over, I thought, people would turn off the television and then discuss the show with someone else.

Well, of course, now I know that's not how we watch television at all, especially today, with so many choices available. More likely, we come home from work and turn on the set as we go about doing other things. Often the TV is on during dinner and remains on until we go to bed. Even when we are watching a program, our attention may be distracted. By the time we go to bed, we won't remember whether something was on *That's Incredible!* or *The Nature of Things with David Suzuki*.

In the 1970s, Bob McLean was host of a noon talk show on CBC and invited me to be a guest. At one point, he asked me out of the blue, "What do you think the world will be like in one hundred years?" My answer went something like this: "If there are still humans around by then, I think they will curse us for two things—nuclear weapons and television." Surprised by my answer, he ignored both my suggestion that humans might not survive another hundred years and the nuclear issue to blurt out, "Why television?" My response was, "You've just asked a pretty profound question. Suppose I had replied, 'Bob, that's a tough one. I'll have to think about it' and then proceeded to think, not say anything, for ten seconds. You'd cut away to a commercial within three seconds, because TV can't tolerate dead air. That's the problem; it demands instant response, which means there's no profundity." Thinking back on that reply, I'm rather impressed with it, because I still believe that today.

I worry about the impact of computers and television, because the cyberworld is seductive—not because it is so real, but because in many ways it's *better* than reality. You can have the kinkiest sex yet not worry about getting caught by a partner or contracting AIDS, and you can hit the wall in a car race or get shot down in a dogfight in the air and walk away undamaged. Why bother with the real world when you can get all the heart-thumping thrills of the real thing and none of the risks or harm? I always thought our programs on nature would be different; they would show people the natural world through wonderful images that would teach them to love and treasure it. But now I realize that I, too, am creating a virtual world, a fabricated version of the real thing.

If we want to do a program on diverse life forms in the Arctic or the Amazon, we send a cameraperson to those places to spend months trying to get as many sensational shots as possible. Then, back in an editing room, from hours of film we pull together the best pictures and create a sequence of images—polar bears, seals, and whales in the Arctic or parrots, Indians, piranhas, and jaguars in the Amazon. In the end we have created an illusion of activity that belies the truth. If anyone actually visits the Amazon or the Arctic expecting to see what they saw in a film, they will be very disappointed, because the one thing nature needs is the one thing television cannot tolerate: time. Nature needs time to reveal her secrets, but television demands the juxtaposition of one hard-earned shot after the other, a kind of nature hopped up on steroids to keep the viewers' attention so they don't run out of patience and switch channels. Without understanding the need for time, what is perceived is a Disney-fied world providing so many jolts of excitement per minute.

Today, in almost any city in the developed world, cable television provides instant access to sixty to one hundred channels, and a satellite dish can deliver hundreds of channels. Merely grazing through such a vast offering with a remote control is liable to consume half a program. Whizzing through the channels, one is struck with the sense that Bruce Springsteen is right when he sings, "Fifty-seven channels and nothin' on." As the viewer clicks past, every program tries to reach out of the set, grab the person by the throat, and insist, "Don't you dare change channels!" How does a show do that? By becoming louder, shorter, faster, sexier, more sensational, more violent. It's no accident that *The Nature of Things with David Suzuki* has offered programs on psychopaths, female castration, and the penis. But there is a price to be paid to acquire that audience: when you jump into a cesspool, like everyone else you look like a turd.

In 1992, before the Earth Summit in Rio, I screened a program on the first United Nations–sponsored conference on the environment in Stockholm in 1972 as reported by *The Nature of Things*. In 1972 there might have been two or three channels competing with CBC, and *The Nature of Things* was only a half hour long. To my surprise, there were three- to four-minute on-camera interviews with the anthropologist Margaret Mead and the biologist Paul Ehrlich. Today, *The Nature of Things with David Suzuki* is an hour long (although up to fourteen minutes may be taken up by commercials), but we would never run an on-camera interview longer than twenty to thirty seconds. Images, far more than words or ideas, determine what is on television programs today, and depth and content are sacrificed. What I find creepy is that I too felt the 1972 interviews dragged and were boring; in spite of my desire for more meat in my information, I wanted it sped up.

When I began a career in television, I realized how important the applications of scientific ideas and techniques were to people's lives, and I thought my role was to make those applications accessible to the general public. By watching my programs, I thought, the audience would acquire the information they needed to make informed decisions about how science and technology would be managed. I wanted to empower the public, but the opposite happened because of the nature of the medium. Regular viewers of *The Nature of Things with David Suzuki* watch the program on faith that what we present is important and true, and they come to expect me to tell them what to do or to act on their behalf. If I phone a politician's office, even the prime minister's, chances are very good that my call will be returned within half an hour—not because I'm an important person, but because an informed politician knows that a million and a half people watch my shows regularly. Those viewers have empowered me, putting an enormous weight of responsibility on me and on the producers of our programs to ensure that the shows are impeccably researched.

AS THE HEAD OF a large research lab, I was constantly at the center of activity. If not actually carrying out an experiment myself, I would be having discussions with various members of the team, reading new publications, arguing about what we should be doing next, talking about student projects, and so on. What a contrast with making a television program; although a shoot involves moments of intense activity and concentration, those are punctuated by long periods of sitting around waiting, and the host is the least important factor.

Each member of the filming team has a very specific role, though we all chip in when there's gear to be packed, lugged, or unpacked. Depending on the amount of funding we have, the size of the ensemble varies. On a well-funded shoot, there may be a producer, writer/researcher, cameraperson, camera assistant, soundperson, lighting person, and me, the host. I contribute the least in creating the film, yet I receive most of the credit for the final product. A producer, having conceived of a program and been intimately involved in the research, shooting, and editing, is often understandably ticked off when the program airs and that producer then meets someone who says, "Hey, Suzuki's show last night was great."

My main preoccupation in a shoot is what I am going to say on-camera or what questions I need to ask in an interview to elicit the responses we want. When we are doing an interview, we generally know where the subject is going to fit in the show and what we want or expect that person to say. When the interviewee is, say, a spokesperson for a chemical company that is polluting a river, everyone knows *The Nature of Things with David Suzuki* is not going to be interested in all the good things the PR representatives tell us it is doing. The company spokesperson will try to stick to a message worked out beforehand whereas I will probe and spar, hoping the subject will let down his or her guard, reveal some emotion, or stray from the set refrain. At the same time, the company line will often be so patently false that, when backed up against the evidence, it will clearly be revealed as just a PR stance. An interview in those circumstances is an elaborate dance by both sides.

One of our two-hour specials was a program on logging practices, produced by Jim Murray. It was called "Voices in the Forest," and one segment included an interview with loggers who were working on a MacMillan Bloedel cutblock near Ucluelet on Vancouver Island. The loggers had been warned we were coming and had permission from the

Publicity shot for *The Nature of Things with David Suzuki*

company to talk to us. After we had parked the car and were getting the camera ready, four burly men spotted us and stopped their chain saws to come over. They started badgering me, blaming "environmentalists" for taking jobs away from them, while I tried to argue that it was technology, big machines, and computers that were putting them out of work. It was great theater and never got out of hand.

As we ended the interview and the crew began packing their gear, I continued to talk to the loggers. I told them, "I worked in construction for eight years. To this day, carpentry is my great joy. I love to work with wood. I'm not against logging, and I don't know any environmentalist who wants to shut down the forest industry. We just want to be sure your children and grandchildren will be able to log forests as rich as the ones you're working in now."

Immediately one of the loggers retorted, "There's no way I want my kids to be loggers. There won't be any trees left for them." I was stunned, and I regretted that we didn't have the camera still rolling to record his comment, which made it so clear that we weren't arguing about the same things. The loggers were focused on the immediate paycheck to put food on their plates and pay the mortgage, and I was discussing the long-term sustainability of the forests. Those loggers clearly understood that the way forestry was practiced, the trees were going and wouldn't be replaced, but they were trapped by the need to keep their jobs and the money coming in. And that's the way it is in so many areas, whether in fishing, petrochemicals, industrial agriculture, or forestry—the problems are viewed either from the short-term perspectives of employees and investors or from the long-term perspective of environmentalists.

One of my more interesting interviews was with Jack Munro, then head of the International Woodworkers of America-Canada (IWA), who once suggested that people who encountered a spotted owl should shoot it to preserve jobs for his union. He is a big, blustery man, and he went after environmentalists with a vengeance. For the show on logging, our researcher did a preinterview with Munro and won his agreement to be interviewed by me. I knew the session would be heated and argumentative, but I wasn't all that nervous, because I knew he was blunt and forceful and that the interview would be great television.

We arrived early at the union offices to set up our lights and camera and were all ready when Munro arrived. He acted as if he were surprised, and when he was told that David Suzuki was there to interview him, he boomed in a loud, gruff voice, "Suzuki! I don't want to talk to that asshole!" He knew damned well I was there to interview him, and I assumed it was all an act to impress his own staff or to intimidate me. Finally I growled back at him, "Listen, if you don't agree with me, well, here's your chance. Sit down and talk about it." And he did.

I knew Jack was a lot of bluster, and that was okay with me. What I didn't respect was his caving in to his employers, who convinced him that environmentalists were his enemy. From the 1970s to the '90s, the number of jobs in the forestry sector had fallen by more than a third, and the volume of wood being cut in B.C. had doubled. Yet he was blaming environmentalists and the creation of parks as his enemy for taking away jobs. He accepted the industry line that to be globally competitive, the forest sector had to bring in big machines that displaced men and to apply computers that also increased productivity while reducing jobs. I never understood why the IWA wasn't an ally of environmentalists. We should have been working together to maintain forests, and therefore jobs for loggers, forever.

MY MAIN ROLE IN *The Nature of Things with David Suzuki* is to perform "stand-ups," the segments I do on-camera to introduce or end a program or act as a link from one section to another. I write the pieces according to my viewpoint and then work with both the producer and the writer to shape my script to fit the show as they picture it. Sometimes, when the film is finally edited, a stand-up turns out to be irrelevant or totally off the mark and is discarded, but often it is useful and helps the flow of the program.

Once the stand-ups are honed and accepted (by the producer and me), I have to commit them to memory, which I do by repetition, just the way my father taught me to prepare for oratorical contests. I either rehearse the script in my head or say it out loud, memorizing a line or sentence until I can deliver it without a stumble or mistake. Then I go to the next line or sentence, repeating the entire sequence up to that point each time. If I flub or forget, I start over. I do this until I can repeat the whole thing over and over without a mistake.

If the piece lasts a minute or less, I can usually memorize it in just a few minutes, but when the stand-up is a minute and a half or two minutes, it might take ten or fifteen minutes to get it down pat. Once I know I have to do a stand-up, I withdraw from banter with the crew and become totally uncommunicative, because all I'm concentrating on is the stand-up. Unfortunately, to outsiders it can I look as if I'm not doing anything, so they approach and try to talk to me.

Memorizing lines is the most stressful part of television for me. I always thought Roy Bonisteel, the craggy, deep-voiced host of the CBC television series *Man Alive,* was perfect for his job. In person, he was down-to-earth, salty, and humorous, but on-camera, he had a gravity that was just right for the religious show. He told me he would tape his on-camera pieces exactly as he wanted them to be said and then play the tape through an earpiece hidden by his hair. That way, he could hear himself and simply repeat what he had said, perhaps lagging behind the tape by four or five words. It worked for him.

I always felt my life as host would have been so much easier if we had had a teleprompter from which I could read the script. But Jim Murray was adamant that I had to memorize my lines because, he said, he would be able to tell if I was reading a teleprompter. As I watched newsreaders and other hosts of television programs render their lines naturally and effortlessly from prompters, I felt sure I too could do it while conveying the impression of naturalness and spontaneity—that's what it is to be a professional.

One day, when I was supposed to be filming a stand-up at Allan Gardens in Toronto, I urged Vishnu Mathur, the producer, to get a teleprompter for me to use. He did, and I recorded several pieces. It was bliss, because now I could relax, joke with the crew, and generally feel human for a change, delivering my lines flawlessly for each take. When the stand-ups were done, Vishnu was satisfied that they were fine, and we turned them over to Jim, who insisted on screening all my stand-ups so he could select the ones he felt worked best.

Jim was an outstanding executive producer and paid close attention to every aspect of *The Nature of Things with David Suzuki*. As money for the series began to be cut back during the '80s and '90s, he kept the budget for each show high and reduced the number we put out, rather than lower the quality to maintain the count. He was a stickler for detail, screening rough cuts, deciding on every stand-up, poring over scripts, even checking on color correction of final prints. Producers approached him for his approval at each stage of production with great trepidation, as he was known to tear shows apart and demand that they be completely reedited or even that new footage be shot. But I've always believed it was Jim's attention to detail and demand for quality that made our series so enduring and powerful.

Although Vishnu had gone along with my request to use a tele-prompter, he was worried that Jim would see what we had done when he looked at the footage. To our enormous relief, Jim screened the stand-ups and approved them without a murmur—he couldn't tell I was reading off a screen! Now, I thought, the days ahead would be so much easier.

But Jim's temper was notorious. Vishnu was too intimidated to tell him we had fooled him, and I didn't want to get Vishnu into trouble by squealing on him. If we continued to use the prompter, Jim would eventually notice the cost of its rental on our expense sheets. So I kept memorizing my pieces and suffering through the shooting because we didn't have the courage to confront our boss. When Jim reached mandatory retirement age and his replacement, Michael Allder, was appointed, I timorously asked whether we could start using a prompter. To my great relief, Michael's response was, "Of course."

I know that, to the viewer, working in television might seem exciting and glamorous. But it isn't. Oh, there are moments when one witnesses something spectacular, such as a group of elephant seals on land or whales emitting a curtain of bubbles to surround and drive fish. Those occasions are special, and what adds to that is the knowledge that very few people in the world will ever have that firsthand experience. Through television, it has also been my great privilege to meet some amazing people—lots of Nobel Prize winners and other remarkable people; for example, the English scientist James Lovelock, who coined the term "Gaia hypothesis" to express his idea that Earth is a single living entity; the English primatologist Jane Goodall; the Kenyan paleontologist Richard Leakey, and many others. But most of the time on location, we are filming wide shots, close-ups, and the same scenes over and over from different angles so they can be edited to form a sequence the viewer seldom realizes is a collage.

We usually have one camera on a shoot. When we do an interview, we keep the camera trained on the person being interviewed. When that's over, the camera is repositioned for a "reversal" and I "re-ask" the questions, this time with the camera on me. It's a challenge to remember the way a query was originally asked from off-camera. I also do "noddies," in which the camera films me nodding or shaking my head, smiling, or looking puzzled, all to provide material an editor can blend to give an illusion that there were two cameras shooting the whole thing. These "reaction shots" also allow an "edit point" in an interview. If a long reply has to be cut at a certain point and then connected to a later part, we cover the edit by putting in a reaction shot. If we shoot a scene without recording sound, it is said to be shot "MOS," reputedly a take on the Austrian-born American film producer Otto Preminger, who would shout, "This shot is mit out sound," which became MOS.

WORKING IN TELEVISION HAS been very rewarding and has given me a great deal of pleasure. I have also enjoyed the traveling it has entailed, but there has been a downside as well.

In 1993, Nancy Archibald began to work on a two-hour special on dams. Nancy was Jim Murray's partner and had become the executive producer of *The Nature of Things* when Jim was recruited to take over *The National Dream*, the blockbuster series based on Pierre Berton's book and hosted by the prolific Canadian author. Nancy proposed to look at megadams around the world and ascertain whether they had lived up to their promise.

Protests had been launched against a dam proposed on the sacred Narmada River in India, and the charismatic firebrand Medha Patkar had spent years rallying indigenous people who would be flooded out by it. In 1985, the World Bank had committed a $450-million loan to build the dam at Sardar Sarovar, but, led by Patkar, public protest forced the bank to set up an investigative committee in 1991. It was chaired by former United Nations Development Program administrator Bradford Morse of the U.S., and he took on Canadian lawyer Tom Berger as deputy chair.

Having represented the Nisga'a First Nation in a landmark case and consulted other First Nations as commissioner of the ground-breaking Mackenzie Valley Pipeline Inquiry, Berger had a long track record of working with aboriginal people in Canada. The Morse Commission traveled extensively in western India, listening to the people who would be affected most by the project. In the end, the report came down heavily against funding the dam, and the World Bank withdrew its promised support. By then, it had become a matter of national pride, and the Indian government went ahead and built the dam on its own.

When Nancy started filming, the Narmada dam was not yet complete. We applied to the Indian government for permission to film but were turned down when officials discovered that we would be focusing on dams. We decided to film without a permit. As we expected, the country is so vast and complex that there was no way our activity could register in the upper echelons of government before we were already in and out.

We went in December, and although the weather was still warm by Canadian standards, it was winter, when a tremendous amount of coal is burned even by the poorest street people. The air was unbelievably polluted. As we rode in a three-wheeled taxi through the streets of Bombay in early morning, coal dust hung in the air and swirled about in great clouds as we passed by. I found it hard to take a breath and couldn't imagine what the pollution was doing to our lungs. When I returned home, I became very ill with lung congestion. I couldn't shake it, and after ruling out a viral, bacterial, or parasitic infection, my doctors decided I had asthma. Subsequent tests revealed I do not have asthma, but I have been left with chronically weak lungs and allergies that flare up whenever I visit a new city or there is heavy smog.

Another difficult shoot was in 1999, when Geoff Bowie produced a program on the tragedy of the Aral Sea in central Asia. Bounded by Uzbekistan, Tajikistan, Kazakhstan, and Turkmenistan, only a few decades ago this great inland sea was a rich source of fish, including sturgeon, salmon, and plaice, and villages dotting its shores were magnets for summer tourists. The Aral Sea was the fourth-largest inland sea on Earth when the Soviet Union decided to make the surrounding region the cotton center of the world. Soon, vast areas of land were growing cotton, one of the most chemically demanding crops we have.

Heavy use of pesticides and fertilizers polluted the sea, and so much water was drawn from the two main rivers, the Amu Darya and Syr Darya, that they were reduced to a trickle.

After 1960, the level of the sea began to drop. Biodiversity was heavily affected. Before 1960, more than 70 mammalian species and 319 bird species were known, but by the end of the twentieth century, those figures had dropped to 32 and 160, respectively. What were once beaches became wide swaths of toxic sand that spreads on the winds.

Today the Aral is the tenth-largest inland sea, most of its fish species are extinct, and the shoreline has retreated more than sixty miles from the once-seaside villages. Child and maternal mortality levels around the Aral Sea are the highest in the former Soviet Union. People in the region suffer high levels of respiratory diseases such as tuberculosis and asthma, as well as diseases of the liver, kidney, blood, thyroid, and heart. And poverty ensures they have no way out. It is a stark story that informs us we must pay attention to the ecological ramifications of our projects.

To film the Aral, we flew to Tashkent and then drove to a number of communities, ending at the former edge of the sea, where the beach sand was a witches' brew of toxins. We flew to the retreating seashore, where I was reluctant to breathe deeply because I knew how polluted the air was. The food and water were contaminated. It was heartrending to visit hospitals, where medical staff were unable to help the patients. I found the entire trip unpleasant, because I knew I was taking in all those toxins, and I couldn't wait to finish. But unlike the fifty million people around the sea, I had the option of leaving. The story of the Aral Sea is a fable for our time, the result of ignoring the effect of our megaprojects on the surrounding ecosystems.

STAND-UPS AND FALL-DOWNS

IT'S ONE THING TO memorize lines and deliver them before a camera; it's quite another to move or even gesture while also speaking. Add factors beyond those and the task becomes even more challenging.

I am filled with admiration for David Attenborough, the British host of countless natural history television programs. His stand-ups set a very high standard. Actually it was a often sit-down rather than stand-up. In one instance, somehow he and the film crew had been able to move close enough to a group of wild gorillas to get them into the shot without spooking them. Attenborough was almost whispering his lines, when a female gorilla sidled up to him and began to check him out in a rather friendly manner. No amount of preparation could have anticipated the animal would move in like that, but Attenborough incorporated this unexpected intrusion into his words and kept going without blowing his lines.

In the same way, Australia's Steve Irwin is very impressive in the way he delivers his lines in his TV series *The Crocodile Hunter*. He works at close quarters with wild snakes and crocs in a very physical way while conveying tremendous enthusiasm, yet he is able to evade a snake strike or a croc's mouth or tail without losing his cool or a limb.

I had an unscripted close encounter with a creature when we shot a stand-up for *A Planet for the Taking* that pondered the mystery of our relationship with the apes. I was seated on a stool as I posed the question of our evolutionary history; a trained chimpanzee sat on a stool next to me. In the opening shot, the camera was focused on me—the idea was that when I mentioned our nearest relatives, the shot would widen and reveal the animal.

As we began to shoot and I started talking, the chimp reached into the frame and tickled me under the chin! It was a probe of curiosity that we could never have rehearsed or trained the animal to perform, and it worked as a perfect surprise for the piece—but I blew it. I was so shocked at the chimp's initiative that I stuttered and then broke out laughing. Too bad, but I'm just not the calm and cool type.

We've tried to create fun in stand-ups, though. When we were filming a story on location at Cambridge University in England for *Science Magazine*, I did a stand-up while poling a punt on the Cam River that runs through the campus. As I finished my piece, I pretended the pole had stuck in the mud, and I flipped off the punt and into the water. It had to work on the first take, because I didn't have dry clothes to change into. It worked.

Another time, I was hired by an energetic dynamo, Margie Rawlinson, to narrate a film she had commissioned to raise money for a science museum in Regina. She would show the film at a fund-raising dinner to be attended by special guest Gerald Ford, former president of the United States. During his presidency, Ford had been filmed stumbling, and it was widely joked that he couldn't walk and talk at the same time. I was filmed on a skateboard, and my opening line was something like: "Well, I can ride a skateboard and talk at the same time." Then, following the script, I slid right into a lake and finished my piece while soaking wet. I thought it was hilarious and so did Margie. Apparently Ford didn't.

We once did a two-hour special on drugs for *The Nature of Things*, at a time when George Bush Sr. was U.S. president and waging war on drugs and drug users. Vishnu Mathur was the producer of the program and Amanda McConnell was our researcher and writer. We traveled to Liverpool, where there was a very successful program of prescribing heroin to addicts so they could remain healthy and avoid the AIDS-causing HIV. We then went to the Netherlands, where, with approval of the police, "coffee shops" were selling marijuana and hashish.

I did a stand-up seated at the bar in a coffeehouse. On one side of me was the owner of the shop, and on the other side was a regular customer. The plan was for me to start talking on a tight close-up so that no one else appeared in the frame. As I expounded on the Dutch experiment, the camera would widen out to reveal the two men, one puffing on a joint and then passing it in front of me to the other, while I finished the piece.

Well, it was a huge joint, more like a cigar than a cigarette. We were just starting to use videotape rather than film, and the crew was still getting used to it. We had filmed several takes with these two guys sucking on this huge stogie before John Crawford, the soundman, discovered he had not flicked the right switch on the camera; my mike had not recorded my piece. I was annoyed, because we had already put these guys through a lot. But they seemed quite cooperative and we began to shoot again.

It took a lot of coordination to get the joint being passed across at the right moment in the script, so Rudi Kovanic kept shooting and reshooting as the smoldering dope was passed under my nose. Finally, everyone pronounced the take to be perfect; we then shot a "safety" that was also great, and we were done. The crew had to reset lights to film a scene in the coffeehouse, but my work was over. I told them I would walk to the van and wait there for them to finish.

I set off walking. And I walked. And I walked. It seemed I had been walking for miles, yet still the vehicle was way down the street. I started to freak out. I had taken ages to get here, but if I turned around, would I be able to make my way back? I turned around, only to discover that I had walked maybe half a block. All that joint passing had affected the host as well.

People ask whether it's dangerous filming for *The Nature of Things*. They're usually thinking about encounters we might have with wild animals. The cameraperson who does the filming is the one who may be at risk; doing a stand-up is pretty controlled, and I can remember only a couple of times when I even worried about danger from animals.

One of those occasions came when we were filming elephant seals. They get their name from the incredible proboscis of the males, who can blow up those snouts into trunklike structures that are quite intimidating, exactly as intended. A male can weigh up to a ton. Elephant seals were pushed to the very edge of extinction early in the last century and have made a remarkable comeback, now numbering in the tens of thousands.

We set up a stand-up on an island just offshore from Los Angeles, where the animals go to breed. Several huge males were lying on the beach, looking most benign. Rudi lined up a shot so that I could give my lines with the seals visible behind me. I delivered my lines, and Rudi said, "That was good, David. Now, would you mind backing up to get closer to the animals?"

The thing about camerapersons is that they are totally focused on what they see through their eyepiece. Often they seem completely unaware of the danger or discomfort others may feel. But I was up to the task. We had a usable stand-up "in the can," so now we could try for a more impressive shot. We filmed another piece, which Rudi also pronounced fine, and then he had me move closer. My back was to the animals, but they didn't seem to mind, so I kept backing up. We did four or five takes.

I began my spiel once more, then realized that Rudi's free eye wasn't squinting as usual but was opening ever wider, staring at me. The nearest elephant seal was practically under my bottom, and I thought he or another must have woken up. In fact, a huge male had lifted his head and body to tower above me. I'm no Attenborough; I fluffed my lines and scrambled out of the way.

When we were filming for *The Sacred Balance,* a series of four one-hour shows, one of our first trips was to Pond Inlet on Baffin Island in the eastern Arctic. It was a wonderful time: the sun remained above the horizon twenty-four hours a day, and we often found ourselves filming at 10:00 PM with light streaming down on us. The ice was melting, and we were able to film hunters shooting a narwhal at the edge of the ice sheet.

One spectacular shot from a helicopter was to show me walking alone across an immense expanse of ice. All our gear and the crew had to be taken far away so they wouldn't be in the shot. Neville Ottey, the cameraman, was perched in a chopper that hovered above me for a while as I walked along, and then it pulled straight up until I became just a dot on the ice.

Before we took the shot, at the insistence of our Inuit guides I had carried a rifle, because polar bears are virtually invisible on the ice. They can jump up and attack so quickly and powerfully that I wouldn't have been able to get help before I was killed. That shoot is the only time I have felt the hair on my neck stand up; all of my senses were wide open as I walked along. I can't tell you how happy I was when Neville announced that he had the shot and we could leave.

More common hazards have arisen in urban areas. Once, for a film about magic and illusion, producer Daniel Zuckerbrot had a cute idea: we would start a stand-up with a "medium" shot from below of me on the strut of an airplane, wind blowing through my hair, propeller roaring, sky in the background. Next we would cut to a wide shot of the plane in the air with me outside it, then to a close-up of my face as I continued talking "to camera." Finally, I would let go and drop out of the frame. In the following shot, we would reveal that I was standing on the strut of a plane that was still on the ground, with the propeller spinning; I had merely stepped onto the ground.

The sequence was edited together perfectly, and until the last shot it did indeed seem I had jumped out of a flying plane. But in order to get the sequence, I actually had to fly while being filmed from another plane. Yes, I had to get out onto the strut, talk to the camera on the other plane and hang on until the cameraman signaled he had the scene.

Even more hair-raising, I couldn't be tied or attached to the plane. I had to wear a parachute and be prepared to use it in case I fell. I was quickly instructed on how to pull the cord and release the chute. I had never jumped from a plane; somehow, a one-minute instruction that ended with "if you slip off, just pull this cord and you should be fine" was not that reassuring. Nevertheless, I did it, and for some reason I felt no fear when I got out onto that strut. Actually, I was half tempted to jump. I instructed the cameraman to keep shooting if I did fall. No point wasting the opportunity.

I think the most dangerous urban shoot was a stand-up for that same show on drugs. Vishnu said we had to do a stand-up in New York City to convey the flavor of a "drug neighborhood," so I flew down to New York on a Saturday to meet the crew that night. We drove to the middle of Harlem and parked the van at the corner of Martin Luther King and Malcolm X streets. It's the only time I have ever felt white, as if my skin were shining like a beacon.

When we hauled out the camera and gear, a cluster of young black men formed around us. "What are you guys filming?" they asked. Perhaps Vishnu felt oblivious to the attention we were attracting, but I was scared. When he told them we were doing a film on drugs, the response was exasperated. "You mean you are going to do another film showing us bad-ass niggers doing drugs!" a young man exploded. A big fellow put his hand over the camera lens and told us: "You are not going to film a f---ing thing here."

"Let's get the hell out of here, Vishnu," I hissed, as he seemed about to argue with the group. Filming in that location seemed to me the most horrendously stupid idea I've ever been involved in, and I believed we were lucky to get out of there intact. So where do you think we ended up shooting the stand-up? On a street where all the buildings were boarded up because they were occupied by gangs of crack and heroin dealers. I did my piece under a streetlight with the dark, shuttered buildings behind me, expecting to feel a bullet in my back at any moment. And the CBC doesn't even give danger pay for a shoot like that.

A lot of the time, the danger seems real only in retrospect. When we are shooting, we are so intent on getting the piece in the can that any danger seems minor. For *A Planet for the Taking*, we filmed a sequence on a kibbutz in Israel near the Jordanian border at a time when Arab–Israeli hostilities had broken out. As we filmed, we could hear gunfire and the drone of planes along the border, but it was only after I had left Israel that I wondered how dangerous it might have been.

Another shoot was very plainly hazardous. It was a story about off-shore oil drilling before the Hibernia oil field off Newfoundland had been fully developed. We dressed in survival suits and flew in a large helicopter far out over the ocean to an immense drilling platform where dozens of men lived. From there, a smaller helicopter lifted our gear in a sling and transferred two of us at a time, clinging to the outside of the net, to a barge where we would film the stand-up with the platform in the background.

As we soared into the air and over the water, I was confident in my ability to hold onto the netting, but I learned later that camera-man Neville Ottey was terrified on that ride. I am impressed with his courage, because in spite of his fear, he did the job. I realized how

Preparing to dive for an underwater shoot near Halifax with unidentified scientist from Dalhousie University

dangerous the whole operation was when we were being dropped onto the barge. It was rising and falling many feet at a time; at one moment we would be way above the deck and then suddenly, splat, right on it. It turned out to be a spectacular stand-up, with the barge surging up and down with glimpses of the oil rig behind me.

I have had many uncomfortable stand-ups, usually involving squeezing into spaces such as an astronaut's suit at the National Aeronautics and Space Administration center in Houston, Texas, or a hard-hat diving outfit for deepwater exploits. But two are particularly memorable for their unpleasantness.

For *Science Magazine*, producer John Bassett was doing a report on hypothermia and decided the best way for me to do a stand-up was in the ocean. But it was December, and although we shot it in Vancouver, which has a relatively mild climate, it was snowing that day. I was wearing street clothing, but underneath that I had a wet suit of vest and short pants. Since the mid 1960s I had been an avid scuba diver, and in British Columbia the best time is in winter, when the cold water is clear and visibility is excellent. So I knew what it felt like when a wet suit first filled with water.

But on this shoot, I had minimal protection for my torso and no hood, gloves, or booties. I was not prepared for the shock when I jumped in. The water sloshed onto my skin and literally took my breath away. I could barely gasp out the lines as I had memorized them, my teeth chattering and my breaths coming in spasms. I can't remember how many times I had to do the stand-up, but when I crawled out of the water, it took me hours to warm up.

By far the most disagreeable shoot was for *The Sacred Balance*, filmed in a gold mine just outside Johannesburg in South Africa. It was bad enough going two miles underground: I had worried for days about developing claustrophobia, because in a huge, packed crowd, I get panicky at being swept along. What would happen when I was so far below ground in dark, narrow tunnels? I think the fear of being regarded as a wimp was the major factor that got me through those two days of shooting. But the biggest discomfort was not the noise, confinement, or darkness, it was the heat. The rock was 120 degrees Fahrenheit, and the air was almost as warm. We were advised to drink at least a quart of water an hour, which I did without having to pee—the water simply poured out of our skin.

We were there for a fascinating story. Until very recently, it had been believed there was no life below a few hundred feet underground. Oil drills had kept clogging up with microbial contaminants, but over the years those were dismissed as having originated above ground. However, the persistence of such findings finally induced scientists to determine whether there was life at a deeper level than was then known.

We followed the scientist Tullis Onstott of Princeton University in Princeton, New Jersey, who had discovered life embedded in rocks deep underground. Now bacteria are found up to five miles deep and probably farther. (Writer/researcher and my sometime coauthor Holly

Dressel's response when I told her about this was, "I always knew rocks are alive.") What Tullis has discovered are bacteria that belong to entirely new groups of organisms, which may have been isolated hundreds of millions of years ago. They metabolize so slowly they may divide once every thousand years.

We were going to film a sequence in which I would assist Tullis as he took samples of water flowing out of the rocks. He would explain to me what he was doing and what he had found. As we hunkered in front of the camera, the heat was overwhelming; it was so hot that the camera had been taken down the day before to allow the fogged lenses to clear as the camera heated up. We shot for a few minutes, then all of us retreated about one hundred feet down the tunnel to where one of the ventilation ducts blew cooler air into the shaft. We cooled down, then rushed back to film for another couple of minutes, then fled back to the vent.

After we had done this for about an hour, I was beat and was relieved to be told my part was finished, so I could stay by that vent. But Tullis was the star of the piece and had to be there to the end. He was beginning to stumble over his lines, and I warned the producer to watch him because I was worried. Sure enough, Tullis passed out from overheating and had to be dragged to the vent of cool air. The collapse of a worker is a nightmare, because at least two others are required to pull him to cooler air, and the rescuers are at risk of overheating and collapsing themselves. Pretty dicey, but our dogged scientist survived to talk another day.

Sometimes I have to juggle several stand-ups in a shoot. I had remarried in 1972; my wife, Tara, was pregnant with our second child when, in 1983, filming started for *A Planet for the Taking*, the biggest television series I had ever been involved with. We had slotted in a three-week interval around the time the baby was due when I could be in Vancouver. The anticipated date for the baby's arrival came and

A publicity shot with illusionist David Bens for a film on Martin Gardner called "Mathemagician" for *The Nature of Things with David Suzuki*

went, and day after day the amount of time I would have available to stay home shrank.

We had three camera crews out filming at the same time, one in India, the other two in Europe, and I was absolutely needed to do the stand-ups because they would hold the entire series together. If I couldn't be there when filming was going on, I would have to be sent out with a crew later just to shoot stand-ups, and that would be terribly expensive. I kept getting messages from India asking when and where I was arriving there so I could be picked up. Finally, the day I was supposed to leave for India came and still no baby. Sarika arrived three days after that, so I stayed around for another two days and then flew to India, five days late.

I did my stand-ups in India over several days, then moved on to Europe, Egypt, and Israel before flying to Kenya, where producer Nancy Archibald was filming a sequence on baboons. At this point, I had not seen Tara or Sarika for over three weeks. Tara had received clearance from doctors to fly with Sarika (and three-year-old Severn) to meet me in England, where I would be shooting a segment on the mathematician Isaac Newton, so I had to leave Nairobi on a certain date. As you might imagine, I was very antsy to leave for England.

Three days before the day I was to meet my family in England, I met up with the crew in Kenya. We filmed a number of stand-ups, and the day before my departure, we were scheduled to film a series of stand-ups with the baboons in the background. Shirley Strumm, the baboon expert who was advising us for the filming, had assured us that once the baboons were awake, they would move and forage for food for two or three hours, then settle down in midmorning for a couple of hours, and that's when we could film our stand-ups. If all went well, I could be out of there by noon.

We had followed the troop of baboons until they bedded down for the night, so we knew where they were. The next morning, we woke very early when it was still pitch-dark and set out so we could follow the animals once they started to move; they would tolerate us in close proximity as long as we were unobtrusive and didn't look them in the eye. I had four long stand-ups to deliver, which meant a lot of material to memorize. As soon as we were on the trail, I began to go over and over my lines, feeling the pressure both because there were wild, unpredictable animals involved and because I just wanted to get the hell out of there and onto the plane.

As Shirley had predicted, the animals woke up in the dawn light and began to move in a leisurely way. Lugging all our gear, we followed them for a couple of hours, until they finally seemed to be settling down to rest and digest their food. Nancy whispered, "Okay, David, stand-up number 1."

Rudi pushed me around so that the baboons were nicely arranged behind me as I concentrated on stand-up number 1 over and over again. Just as Rudi was ready to shoot, the animals would get up and shift around. We'd scramble to find another spot where they had settled. "Okay, number 4 this time," Nancy instructed, and Rudi and I repeated the process.

We followed the monkeys for the entire day and didn't complete a single stand-up. "I'm so amazed," Shirley insisted. "They always settle down for a rest." My brain had slowly turned to mush as the day dragged on and I was cranked up to shoot stand-up 1, then 4, then 3, then 2. All I knew was that I was going to miss my plane, and I did. The next day, the animals performed perfectly, and I was out of there.

One shoot I did had an absolutely amazing effect. Actually, it was a shoot for a still photo, not for a program. In the 1970s, when a program of *The Nature of Things* failed to get more than a million and a half viewers, we would worry. But with cable and dozens of competing channels, our numbers fell steadily until our average, while still robust for a CBC program, sank below a million. I kept saying, half jokingly, that we could get dynamite numbers if we did a program on the penis, a perfectly good subject for a science show. When Michael Allder became the executive producer, I mentioned the idea and he immediately expressed interest. So he commissioned the program to be done and it focussed on the male obsession with size and some of the techniques used to enlarge the organ. The show was called "Phallacies."

Michael had wanted a series of new style photos of me for publicity and arranged for a shoot at his cottage in Georgian Bay. As we were leaving the CBC for the shoot, Helicia Glucksman, our publicist handed me a couple of fig leafs and said "If you have time, please have a photo wearing this for 'Phallacies'." It was all said lightheartedly and I didn't know whether she was serious or not.

To get the best light, we shot very early the next morning with the rising sun. The photographer was very efficient and we soon had all the pictures Michael wanted, so as a lark, I taped the fig leaf to my crotch and we set up a bench to stand on and pose. Now it was quite cold out so I had to drape a blanket over my shoulders between shots so I wasn't covered in goosebumps. It was a very large fig leaf, so I felt it was pretty modest, but I can tell you, if it had fallen off, it wouldn't have made much difference. As I told you, it was cold. Of course, my Haida friends who saw the picture teased me for needing such a "small leaf."

Helicia arranged for the photo to be on the cover of the *Toronto Star TV Guide* and I was astonished to see the reaction when it came out. It was picked up by dozens of newspapers across the country and written up as if it was incredible for me to pose that way. I did receive a couple of letters and one nasty phone call (all from women) expressing disgust at my "obscene photo." Overwhelmingly, the response seemed to be surprise that even a 64 year old man could still be in reasonable shape. There was even a suggestion that my head had been superimposed on someone else's body. Well, I'll tell you, if we were going to do that, I would have selected a much better body.

I am not a bodybuilder and at my age, testosterone levels are too low to allow me to build up muscle mass, but I had been exercising regularly for decades, ever since I had married a much younger person. Once when my daughter admired a photo of someone's "abs" by saying "Wow, look at this six-pack," I had interjected, "What about mine?" Sarika retorted, "Dad, you've got a ONE-pack!" I have been gratified that even in my sixties, my body has responded to exercise and after Sarika's jibe, I had developed a series of exercises for my belly and it worked.

We got the best rating for "Phallacies" than we had had for many years but it was bittersweet for me. Staff at my foundation worked hard for years for every story we got into the media on environmental issues. Then I take off my clothes for one shot and we get gangbuster exposure. It wasn't fair.

FAMILY MATTERS

I WAS BECOMING MORE involved in television when Joane and I separated in 1964. By that time, we had two children and a third was on the way; we didn't divorce until two years later.

Troy had been born in January 1962, and his name came from the father of my roommate in college. In 1956, at the end of my second year at Amherst, my roommate, Howie Bonnett, from Evanston, Illinois, invited me to spend the summer with him with the promise that I could get a job that would pay much more than I made working for Suzuki Brothers Construction back in London. So I went and stayed with his family. Howie's father's name was Troy. I had never known anyone by that name, and I loved the antiquity and masculinity of it. I vowed that if I ever had a son, I'd call him Troy. The high-paying job in Evanston never came through, but I didn't forget that name.

As with so many second-borns, Troy may have suffered from seeming to repeat what his father had already experienced with a first-born. Tami continued to enthrall me with every new behavior and activity. Troy was of a different gender, which was fascinating, but my attention kept turning to Tamiko and the new things she did every year. As he grew older, Troy certainly suffered from the expectations teachers inadvertently laid on him. "Oh, are you going to be a scientist like your father?" they would ask innocently. Or, because Tamiko was a good student, they might say, "Oh, you're Tami's brother," implying they expected him to do as well. Troy reacted by not trying at all to compete academically.

Troy grew up in a household of a mother and two sisters but, I believe, suffered from the absence of a male figure. My father had played a huge part in his life and tried to be a role model for him, but Troy needed me to be there to help pick him up when he hurt himself, to revel in his successes, to lay down the line when he needed the discipline, and I simply wasn't around enough to fully fill that role. I'm so grateful Troy and I have become closer as the years have gone by, but I have no doubt he bore a heavy burden through my absence.

Laura was conceived before Joane and I had agreed to separate. She was born prematurely, on July 4, 1964, at the very same time I went into the hospital for a month in isolation after contracting hepatitis B from eating contaminated oysters. She developed jaundice, which apparently is quite common among preemies, and the treatment was incubation with light of a certain wavelength. I don't know whether that was the cause, but she developed problems with a "wandering" or "lazy" eye; that may have been a result of her prematurity, but it was never fully corrected by surgery. She was a beautiful child, always quite self-sufficient and happy playing by herself.

When I left hospital, I moved into an apartment near the family so I could still see the kids every day. But when Michael Lerner, an eminent population geneticist at the University of California at Berkeley, invited me to teach a course there, I eagerly accepted. It was an exciting time, and I was thrilled to be living in Berkeley when "flower power" and Haight-Ashbury were blossoming. During my stay, the battle over

Television host of *Suzuki on Science* (late '60s)

People's Park broke out, and I took part in the demonstrations that ended in tear gassing, buckshot, and death at the hands of the California National Guard, called in by Governor Ronald Reagan. I was appalled at the violent attempt to put down American youth and realized then that my decision to return to Canada in 1962 was still the right one.

I had gone to Berkeley looking like a square, and I came back decked out in granny glasses, a moth-eaten mustache and beard, and bell-bottoms. I had been transformed, much to the discomfort of my fellow faculty at UBC, especially because of what became my trademark—long, nearly shoulder-length hair held in place with a headband.

But the University of British Columbia, like Berkeley, was swept up in revolutionary fervor and the sexual revolution. Physical appearance didn't seem to matter anymore, and I no longer felt such intense self-loathing because of my small eyes and my Asian appearance. In the pre-AIDS period before the 1980s, there was rampant experimentation with drugs and sex, and although I was too unhip and insecure to ever try the drug LSD, it was widely believed I was "into" psychedelics and I heard rumors (totally false) that "acid" was being synthesized in my lab.

I was a child of the 1950s, still imbued with the notion of stable relationships and marriage. After Joane and I split up, I had two very serious relationships, one lasting three years and the other close to four years. Both broke up as much as anything because of my own insecurities about whether I was good enough and expectations I had as a spoiled male. I was not ready to commit again to a long-term relationship, and I was still driven by desire to make a name as a scientist.

On December 10, 1971, I was scheduled to give a talk at Carleton University in Ottawa. I entered the lecture room at the top of Carleton Towers to find it packed with several hundred students filling every seat, the aisles, and the floor in front of the podium. As I began to speak, I noticed a sensationally beautiful woman sitting near the front.

With long, blonde hair, a full mouth, and high cheekbones, she looked like the American film star Rita Hayworth.

After I gave my speech and answered questions and people began filing out of the room, a handful came down to the front to carry on with a dialogue. The beautiful woman was one of them. I had never acquired the self-confidence to "pick up" someone or even start a conversation in that direction. Instead, as I was leaving, I announced in a loud voice, "I hope you're all coming to the party tonight," and I left.

I had to sit on a panel early that evening and did not see the beautiful woman in the audience there, so I figured I had failed. Afterward I was driven to the party, which was packed with students, a number of whom immediately surrounded me to engage in serious conversation. About half an hour later, the woman arrived, and I spotted her. I ducked out of the ring of people, popped up in front of her and asked her if she wanted to dance. As I moved away toward the dancing, she looked inquisitively at the woman next to her, who said, "I think he meant you." So she followed me to the dance floor, and the rest, as they say, is history.

The sensational woman was Tara Cullis, who was working on a master's degree in comparative literature at Carleton. She was twenty-two; I was thirty-five. I learned later she used to watch *Suzuki on Science* with her boyfriend and had attended my talk out of homesickness for British Columbia. After hearing my lecture, she felt for the first time in her life that she could imagine marrying someone—me.

Later that evening, my good friend Gordin Kaplan, in the Biology Department at the University of Ottawa, invited me to Nate's Restaurant for a snack, and I took Tara along with me. Afterward Gordin drove us to Tara's apartment, where I left her, and she promised to see me in B.C. when she went home for Christmas. I kissed her, and we knew this was pretty special. As I got back into the car, Gordin commented, "She didn't have much to say." Well, neither had I—Tara and

I were both so overwhelmed that we were almost speechless to each other during the meal, but we remember Nate's with great fondness.

How helpful that she was from B.C. Her father, Harry, was superintendent of schools and lived in Squamish, and as soon as I got back to Vancouver, I left a message with her parents that I had called. Soon Tara and I had a date in Vancouver, and we both knew this was serious.

On New Year's Eve, we hiked up Mount Hollyburn in North Vancouver with one of my students, his girlfriend, and another couple, to stay in a cabin there. It was buried under snow, but we dug our way in, got the woodstove going, and soon the room was warm and the table set with food and drink. That night, when we were in our sleeping bags, I asked Tara to marry me. And she did, on December 10, 1972, exactly a year to the day after we had met.

My children have been my pride and joy, but getting Tara to marry me was the greatest achievement of my life, and our marriage continues to be an adventure. Even now, when I come home from a long trip, my heart flutters at the thought of being with her. I had never believed in love at first sight—it was actually lust at first sight—but whatever it was, it was powerful, undeniable, and ongoing.

Tara was always years ahead of her age group in school. She graduated from high school when she was fifteen, but her father kept her there through grade 13 so that she would be a year older when she went to university. She was a top scholar, having been part of the accelerated program in West Vancouver, as well as a champion hurdler and an all-round athlete. And aside from her beauty, she made me feel like a slow learner when it came to discussing literature and history.

When we met, I had told Tara I anticipated her parents would have objections to me because of my race and my age. To my amazement and everlasting respect, neither of those were issues—only my divorce was. They were concerned that I had been divorced and that I had children. But they welcomed me into their home and have been bulwarks

Wedding photo of Tara and me, December 10, 1972, with
(left) Dad and Mom and *(right)* Freddy and Harry

in supporting Tara and me in all we have done and in being terrific
grandparents. I love and respect them enormously.

When we were buying the house that is our home today, I had to
ask them for help to make a down payment on the mortgage and suggested that when Harry retired, I could add another story to the house
and they could come and live with us. We bought the house, added a
story to it later, and they moved into their separate apartment with us
in 1980, an arrangement that has worked wonderfully for all of us.

Harry loves a good discussion and often provokes arguments by
taking a position he may not even believe in, yet I fall for it over and
over. As a result, there have been times when I was so mad at him that
we were yelling at each other while the women hovered, trying to calm
us down. Every human relationship has its ups and downs—there are
times when I know Tara is furious at me and times when I'm ticked at
my children, but that's the nature of human relations. On the whole,
living with Harry and Freddy has been wonderful. They have Tara

and their grandchildren right there to visit and fuss over them, and Tara can go upstairs to seek their advice while looking after them now that they are getting older. I am away a lot but can relax because Harry, especially, takes on the care of the house and garden as he has since he moved in.

BEFORE WE MARRIED, TARA said she would keep her maiden name, and I agreed wholeheartedly. She had been called "Cullis" all her life; it was part of her history and persona, and she didn't want to give it up. Today, no one would give it a second thought, but in the early 1970s, many looked on such a decision with disdain. (One annoying consequence of the antiquated, patriarchal practice of adopting another's surname is encountered when searching for a high school friend and discovering she has disappeared, having taken on the identity of Mrs. Harry Smith.) We found out that in Canada, it was illegal for a married woman to keep her maiden name.

We did not go on a proper honeymoon. Because I had been invited to spend a month in the Soviet Union on an exchange program in the summer of 1973, we decided we would wait a few months after marriage and take a long trip. Tara had emigrated from England when she was five and most of her extended family were still there. We planned to stay in England for a month to visit relatives, then travel through continental Europe for another month before flying to the Soviet Union, where an itinerary had been arranged. Next we would fly from Moscow through India, Thailand, and South Korea before spending a month in Japan. We would fly home to Vancouver via Honolulu, completing a four-month round-the-world trip.

Tara had never taken out Canadian citizenship, but before we set off, she needed a passport, and she wanted to travel as a Canadian. She and brother, Pieter, went to the passport office to each apply for a passport, expecting no problem, because they had lived here since they were children. Sure enough, Piet's application was readily accepted.

Tara then stepped up, and the clerk saw she had the same last name as Piet. "Oh, you're his wife?" he asked. "No," Tara replied, "he's my brother." The clerk was confused: "But you say on the forms that you are married." "Yes, I'm keeping my maiden name," Tara told him. The clerk told her that was illegal, and her application for a passport was rejected.

That was a shocker, and she returned home furious. She needed a passport if she were to travel with me, and she intended to travel on a Canadian passport. She found that so long as a woman never used a married name, she could continue to go legally by her maiden name. We were outraged at the rejection of her passport application, so I called *The Vancouver Sun* and told someone in the newsroom about the situation. I thought it would make a good story, and I was stunned after the journalist listened to my spiel and responded, "So what's the news? Besides, I happen to have a wife who loves to use my name." Click; that was it. Ironically, only a few weeks later, *The Vancouver Sun* ran a front-page story about an American woman who was denied an American passport because she refused to use her husband's name. If it's in the United States, that's a good Canadian story.

Eventually, Tara found someone in the federal External Affairs Department in Ottawa who didn't reject her application out of hand. This was a precedent-setting request, he informed her, and she could go to Ottawa to make her application in person. "You will get your passport," he promised her, "but I can't guarantee it will be made out in your maiden name." She was given a date to make her case and flew to Ottawa, full of trepidation because we didn't know what the outcome would be.

In the end, she was granted a passport in her maiden name, a precedent that few are aware of and most today simply take for granted. Our daughters have assumed both of our names, as Cullis-Suzuki, but what happens when more and more children take on double-barreled names and begin to meet and marry? In any case, I'm proud that Tara stood up to the authorities.

OUR FIRST YEAR OF marriage was a truly happy time in my life. We traveled, got to know each other's foibles, and found our relationship deepening beyond anything I could have imagined when we became engaged. So I was shocked when Tara told me that although she had loved being with me and traveling to new places and meeting new people, she wanted to pursue studies beyond a master's degree. She could have taken the easy path and applied for a doctoral program at UBC (where, as a faculty member's wife, she could enroll free), but her area was comparative literature and there was no such department at UBC. I encouraged her to apply to schools with extensive programs in her field of interest, and she ended up being accepted at the University of Wisconsin in Madison.

We were happy newlyweds, and the thought of being separated while Tara studied elsewhere was daunting. I moaned to Shirley Macaulay, my secretary, "How can I be apart from her for two or three years?" To which Shirley replied, "Right now, two years seems like a long time. But believe me, in a few years, it will seem to have been nothing." And she was right. Tara went away, and that separation was very hard. But I had a busy life, and she threw herself into her course work.

We had decided we would call each other every day, regardless of the cost. That call became our lifeline, something we continue to this day when we are apart. My contract with the CBC stipulates that when I am away on a shoot, I am allowed one call each day to Tara. I was amazed at how many times I could schedule my trips so that I could take in Madison on my way. I don't think we ever went longer than a month without seeing each other, and while the intervals apart seemed horrendously long, she had soon completed all her course work, selected a professor to work with, and thought of a thesis topic.

I thought her thesis was brilliant. Tara's father and brother were trained in science, and she had done well in math and science in school. Focusing on French, German, and English literature, she showed that during the nineteenth century, serious thinkers were writing about science and the implications for society (Mary Shelley's *Frankenstein* was a classic in the genre), but in the twentieth century, when science and technology had become the dominant element in our lives, writers seem to ignore it altogether.

Tara's thesis, "Literature of Rupture," used the metaphor of the two hemispheres of the brain to suggest that in the nineteenth century, writers integrated science and literature just as the corpus callosum in the brain connects the two parts. But in the twentieth century, it was as if the corpus callosum had been severed, as is done for severe epileptics, so that a situation analogous to what C.P. Snow called the "two cultures" was created. It was a brilliant analysis, and we were delighted when Tara graduated with a PhD in 1983, a remarkable achievement when you realize she had given birth to two children in the interim.

MY THREE CHILDREN WITH Joane were a very high priority to me, but Tara and I agreed it would be great to have children together. However, my children were still young, and Tara and I, in the flush of new love in 1972, didn't want to risk a pregnancy. To avoid relying on the birth-control pill, Tara had an IUD, and it worked fine.

In the meantime, we had many good times with my children. In the summer of 1976, after René Lévesque and the separatist Parti Québécois he founded were elected to form the government of Quebec, Tara and I decided to take Tamiko and Troy, who were teenagers, to Chicoutimi in Quebec for six weeks of total immersion in French. We were appalled by the notion that the province might try to secede from Canada, and becoming bilingual seemed to be one small way to show Québécois how much we cared about them.

Tara and I were two of only three adults among the students in the course in Chicoutimi that summer. The rest were like Tami and Troy, teenagers there to learn some French and have fun. We were all billeted with different families, Tara and me together and Tami and Troy with the other kids. We had chosen a good area, because this was the heart of separatist country and most people we met did not speak English, so we had to speak French. We moved to three different villages, Baie-des-Ha!-Ha!, Saint-Félicien, and Chicoutimi, where we stayed with different families.

It was an intense program, six weeks with teachers who not only drilled us in classes during the day but also accompanied us on various outings and on evenings at the pub. Tara and I were serious about learning to speak French as well as we could; for Tara, it had the added interest of being one of the languages she used in her field of comparative literature. We decided we would try to speak French all the time, not just in school and on field trips but when we were alone at night. Although we were still almost newlyweds, we quickly found that concentrating on speaking an unfamiliar language definitely cooled our ardor. We decided the French-only edict was lifted when our feet were no longer on the floor.

In a group of teenagers, it didn't take long until we were "Dave" and "Tara" and a part of the group, playing volleyball, going to the pub, and just hanging out together. I reverted to high school days, taking great delight in following the crushes, dating, and breaking up among the group. In our gang, there were a couple of boys who had driven to Chicoutimi in their cars, and just as it was in high school, they were the popular ones because they had wheels.

One night we all played volleyball, and when we finished, we hung around outside, trying to delay going home so early. One of the young fellows drove up in his car and three or four giggling girls—including Tamiko—jumped onto his fenders and hood. The driver revved his engine a few times, then took off very quickly and jammed on the brakes after a hundred feet or so, causing the girls to slide off. They jumped back on the car, squealing, and he took off again. Everybody else seemed amused, but I was horrified. Suddenly I wasn't Dave, one of the gang. Now I became "David"—DAD.

I had been running for years and was in pretty good shape, so I took off after the car and finally caught up to it when the driver stopped at a light. I yanked the door open, dragged him out of the car, and slammed him up against the side of the vehicle. "What the hell do you think you're doing?" I screamed, so pumped from fear I was almost hoarse.

I looked over and saw Tamiko staring in horror—I must have looked half crazed, and I knew she probably was humiliated to have her father behaving this way. "Get to your room!" I yelled, not caring any longer to be one of the gang. She looked away and disappeared down the street. Fortunately, I calmed down enough to restrain myself from slugging the boy. I was gratified the next morning when he came to me, apologized for his stupidity, and ended with, "You should have hit me. I deserved it." Tamiko wouldn't look at me for days.

Six weeks is a long time. Not only did we pick up a good deal of French, we became a little community, despite the spread in ages. Although we were often referred to by our teachers as *maudits anglais* ("damned English") or *vous américaines* ("you Americans"), we took it in good humor and grew quite fond of our young separatist teachers.

When it was announced that we would have a *spectacle,* or performance, at the end, we took it seriously. Tara and I wrote a drama around two individuals, one speaking only English, the other only French. All the rest of the characters spoke only in French. I played a Dr. Frankenstein character who decides he's going to try an experiment and sew these two, an anglophone and a francophone, together to see what will happen. We had lots of fun with the scene in which we got the two "volunteer" main characters operated on surgically behind a curtain and then revealed them joined together as Siamese twins.

At first as a unit they fought, pulling in different directions; then they yelled at each other. The yelling turned to blows. Finally they told the doctor it was intolerable and demanded to be cut apart. "But together you have more than the strength of two," I said in French. "Apart, you may not even survive." I know, I know, it was pretty ham-fisted, but we wanted our hosts and teachers to know that we valued the concept of a Canada that included Quebec and that Anglos also had a culture, spirit, and élan. At the end, we all sang "My Country Is a Cathedral" in English. Many people in the audience remarked later that they hadn't known English Canadians had that kind of spirit.

We had formed a close friendship with André and Louis-Edmond Gagné and their children, our hosts in Chicoutimi. They were rare for the Lac Saint-Jean/Chicoutimi area—outspoken opponents of separation and highly critical of the Parti Québécois. In 1979, the Gagnés came to Vancouver to visit us. We took them fishing, had them stay in our cottage at Sechelt, and showed them around English Canada. They spoke almost no English, and I was very proud to watch Vancouverites go out of their way to help and accommodate them. Twenty years later, when *The Nature of Things* did a program on bilingualism called "You Must Have Been a Bilingual Baby," I arranged to interview the Gagnés in Chicoutimi. It was a happy meeting after so many years, but I was stunned and disappointed to learn the entire family had become staunch separatists.

DURING THEIR VISIT TO Vancouver, I had taken the Gagnés to the UBC Faculty Club. We were having a drink in the bar when Tara arrived, obviously upset about something. I took her aside as soon as I could and asked her what was wrong. She poleaxed me with her answer: "David, I'm pregnant."

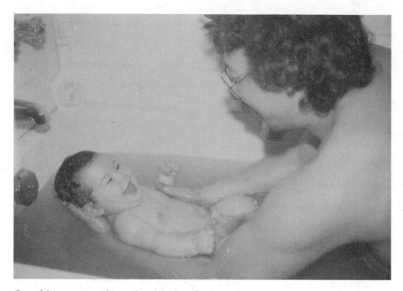

One of the great joys of parenthood, bathing Severn

It seemed as though we had made up our minds we wanted children and it simply happened, but I always think of an embryonic Severn struggling around that IUD, embedding herself in the lining of the uterus and hanging on for dear life. The IUD had to be removed, but the risk of miscarriage at this early stage was very high, and we worried about the amount of bleeding after it had been removed. But Sev was well embedded, and eight months later a wonderful gift arrived.

I had tried to devote as much time as I could to my first offspring, but the lab and research had dominated my life and the children had paid a price for this obsession with the end of my marriage to Joane and even beyond that. I was determined not to let that happen again. Research was not taking as much of my time as it did when I was younger and more ambitious, but now I was caught up in both television programming and activism on the environmental front.

Severn arrived to the great joy of my parents, who were retired. All of my sisters and their children lived out east, but now my folks could devote their full attention to this new baby. During Tara's pregnancy, we had begun renovations on our house so that Tara's mother and father could move in with us, and Severn was their first grandchild, so they were thrilled too.

As with my other children, we took Sev on camping trips from the time she was an infant, and she was soon catching fish in the ocean or freshwater lakes with my father, who was a fishing nut. From infancy, she accompanied us on Vancouver's annual Peace March as well as to protests against clear-cut logging.

We moved to Toronto the September after Severn was born, so that Tara could commute to Boston to teach expository writing at Harvard while a nanny and I cared for Sev and, later, Sarika. For five years after that, we relocated to Toronto each autumn so Tara could teach the fall semester; I would work on the new season of *The Nature of Things*. We'd move home to Vancouver at Christmas and stay there until the next fall.

We thought it was cute when Severn, at age five, gathered a group of children on the block in Toronto and decorated a wagon with signs saying things like Save Nature, and Protect the Animals. That summer, back in Vancouver, we found Sev had removed a number of hardcover books from the house and had set up a table outside, where she was selling them for twenty-five cents apiece to raise money to help protect the Stein Valley. It was a noble cause, so we couldn't chastise her just because she didn't understand economics. I hope I managed to hide my annoyance.

When Severn was born, it had been sixteen years since the 1964 birth of my youngest child in my first family, Laura, so having Sev seemed like starting anew. When Sarika arrived three and a half years later, Sev was running and talking and entertaining us with her cleverness. Sarika was a placid baby—we even thought of calling her Serena—so we could put her down and she would gurgle away happily as Severn cavorted at the center of attention. As Sarika grew and

Sarika in an Inuit outfit I brought back from the Arctic

started to talk, we would often call her "Little Me Too" because of her insistence that she not be ignored. It was hard when her sister was constantly attracting the limelight. Sarika was very shy, but she was fearless and always up for any family adventure.

IN THE MEANTIME, AS our young family was growing, Mom was beginning to show signs of forgetfulness. She was constantly misplacing things—checks, clothing, letters—that might turn up weeks or months later or not at all. Dad and my sisters insisted she had Alzheimer's disease, but I denied it, because Mom exhibited no change in temperament. She did lose some of her inhibitions, however, and I took great delight in teasing her and telling off-color jokes, which would cause her to giggle.

By the early '80s, though, it was clear she was losing her short-term memory. She never became incontinent or failed to recognize her family, although Dad said she sometimes confused him with her brother.

As Mom lost interest in taking care of their finances, sewing, and cooking, Dad took on these responsibilities. He never complained, but I could see it was a heavy load, so I urged him to let me hire someone to help him. He resisted. "She devoted her life to me," he said. "Now it's my turn to pay her back." As Mom's needs increased, I saw a patient side of Dad—he was compassionate, considerate, and loving, and I admired him for it. But it was not easy. I once dropped in to my folks' place in the evening to find Mom in bed and Dad weeping with sadness and frustration about the condition she was in.

The day Sarika was born, I was in the hospital with Tara and Sarika when Dad arrived and asked anxiously, "Is Mom here?" She wasn't. My parents had come to the hospital to see the new baby, but as they were walking down the hall, Dad spotted an acquaintance and ducked in to see him, instructing Mom to "wait right here." When he came out a few minutes later, she was gone. We began a frantic search for her, first running along all of the corridors of the hospital, then driving along streets in the neighborhood. Poor Tara had just given birth but was now worried sick about her mother-in-law. Tara's brother, Pieter, joined Dad and me as we drove along a series of grids looking for Mom, with no success.

Night fell, and we decided to wait at home and hope the police would find her. A call came at about 3:00 in the morning, and Dad and I raced down to the police station. A cab driver had picked her up and realized she was confused and needed help. Dad leaped out of the car when we got to the police station and raced up the stairs, where Mom was waiting at the top. He was crying as he hugged her. "What are you crying about? Let's go," she said, as if nothing had happened. Her stockings had been worn right through, and she had been spotted in the Marpole neighborhood of Vancouver, miles away from the hospital, and trying to get into a blue Volkswagen van like the one Dad owned. Much later, the taxi had picked her up in a completely different part of the city.

On April 25, 1984, a month after they celebrated their fiftieth anniversary, Dad and Mom walked a few blocks to a local restaurant, had a meal together, and then went to a movie. As they were walking home, arm in arm, Mom had a massive heart attack and dropped to the sidewalk. Someone called a paramedic crew, who arrived within ten minutes and resuscitated her. They were doing their job, but the ten minutes of anoxia would have caused further damage to the brain already ravaged by dementia.

I was in Toronto at the time and was able to rush home and be with her for the week before she finally "died" on May 2. As Dad said, "She had a good death," she didn't suffer, she was not incapacitated physically, and she had been with him right up to the heart attack. An autopsy revealed that she did indeed have the brain-tissue plaques characteristic of Alzheimer's.

HAIDA GWAII AND
THE STEIN VALLEY

A LONG THE WEST COAST of Canada, extending south from the tip of the Alaska panhandle, is a chain of islands that some call Canada's Galápagos Islands. During the last glaciation, some ten thousand years ago, most of Canada was entombed in an ice sheet more than one mile thick. It is thought the ice might have encircled but not completely enveloped the islands, which became refuges for species that could move away from the ice. As ice formed, plants and animals moved up the mountainsides, which eventually became islands in a sea of ice and the repository of the survivors. Today many of their descendants are found nowhere else on the planet. This is Haida Gwaii, the land of the Haida people, which was named the Queen Charlotte Islands by more recent arrivals.

In the early 1970s, a combination of citizens, First Nations, and environmentalists on Haida Gwaii had become appalled at the logging practices on the islands and called for the British Columbia government to intervene and protect the land from the depradations. A symbol of the contentious areas was Windy Bay, a pristine watershed covering 12,350 acres of Lyell Island near South Moresby Island in the southern third of the archipelago.

In 1974, a group of citizens on Haida Gwaii demanded protection of critical parts of the islands from clear-cut logging. In response, the provincial government set up the Environment and Land Use Committee, made up of representatives of the various interest groups. In 1979, one of the committee's recommendations was not to log in Windy Bay. That was not an acceptable option to the forest company, which continued to press the B.C. government to allow logging. But Premier Bill Bennett could not ignore the environmentalists' increasing outspokenness or the public's greater awareness of environmental concerns. So in 1979 yet another group comprising a broad spectrum of environmentalists, forest company representatives, and other interest groups was set up as the South Moresby Resource Planning Team, chaired by Nick Gessler, an American expat who was running the Queen Charlotte Islands Museum.

I first heard about this controversy in 1982, when I received a handwritten note from the New Democratic Party member of Parliament representing the Skeena riding, which includes Haida Gwaii. In his note, Jim Fulton, the young social worker who had defeated the beautiful, charismatic incumbent and cabinet minister, Iona Campagnolo, wrote: "Soozook, you and *The Nature of Things* should do a program on Windy Bay." At that point, I had no idea what the battles were about or even where Windy Bay was. But as I learned the issues, I could see it would be an important story and I suggested to Jim Murray, executive producer of *The Nature of Things with David Suzuki*, that we do a program on the fight over its fate. In fact, Dr. Bristol Foster, a wildlife biologist who had worked for the B.C. government for years before quitting in frustration, had already contacted Murray about the Windy Bay story.

Jim assigned the program to producer Nancy Archibald, and after the show's writer, Allan Bailey, had researched the background of the issue, Nancy and a crew flew to the islands to film. I followed days later to do some critical interviews and stand-ups on location in different parts of the archipelago. It was expensive to hire a helicopter and fly to the significant sites, so there wasn't a lot of time. Working frantically with Allan, I wrote, rewrote, and memorized the on-camera pieces as we flew by helicopter to different locations. Looking over those stand-ups today, I am gratified that they still resonate with relevance. I began the report this way:

> The vast forests of Canada are more than just a potential source of revenue: they're part of the spiritual mystique of the country. I'm on Windy Bay in the Queen Charlotte Islands off the coast of British Columbia, and this virgin forest began its existence over eight thousand years ago. Many of these trees were already mature adults long before Christopher Columbus discovered America. It was here that the Haida Indians hunted and fished. They used these trees to build their dugout canoes and their longhouses. It was these trees that inspired Emily Carr to paint some of her most haunting pictures. Having existed for thousands of years, this forest could disappear in a matter of months through logging. Tonight we face a special issue that could affect all Canadians and asks us to redefine our notion of progress.

I continued with a piece on location in a clear-cut on Talunkwan Island, not far from Lyell Island, where logging was speeding along:

> There's nothing subtle about logging. It's the application of brute strength to efficiently clear large tracts of land. This is Talunk-wan Island across from Windy Bay. Ten years ago, it was covered in forest just like Lyell Island. Then it was logged. It'll be a long time before the land recovers. We often hear of "harvesting" trees, but in areas like this, you can't farm a forest the way you do corn or tomatoes. The topsoil takes thousands of years to build

up and the population of trees changes slowly over long periods of time. Now the thin layer of soil is exposed to easy runoff—and it rains a lot here. No one can say what these hills will look like in a hundred years, but you can be sure the forests will look nothing like the ones that once were here.

At the end of the program, this was my conclusion:

> The Queen Charlotte Islands are at the outer edge of the west coast, a unique setting where we can be transported back to pre-historic times when only natural laws prevailed. It took thousands of years and countless seeds and seedlings before giant trees like those at Windy Bay took root and survived. Many of them are more than six hundred years old. Once it took two men weeks to cut one of them down—today one man can do it in minutes. Is this progress? Wilderness preserves are more than just museums for relics of the past, they're a hedge against our ignorance, a tiny reserve from which we might learn how to use our powerful technologies more wisely. But in the end, our sense of awe and wonder in places like this changes us and our perspective of time and our place in the nature of things.

I have often been accused by vested-interest groups like loggers and forest company executives of being biased in my reporting. Viewed through their perspectives of immediate jobs and profit, my statements may seem slanted, but nature and so many other values are ignored by the lenses of such priorities. I believe a huge problem we face today is the overwhelming bias of the popular media that equates economic growth with progress.

For the program I interviewed Tom McMillan, then federal minister of the environment; environmentalist Thom Henley; Bill Dumont, with Western Forest Products Limited; forester Keith Moore; Nick

The Big Four on Haida Gwaii—me, Miles Richardson, Jim Fulton, and Alfie Collinson

Gessler; Bristol Foster; traditional Haida Diane Brown; Miles Richardson, then president of the Haida Nation; and Guujaaw, a young Haida artist and carver. Ruggedly handsome, long hair loosely braided, a twinkle in his eye so you never knew whether he was serious or kidding, Guujaaw changed the way I viewed the world and set me on a radically different course of environmentalism.

I knew that unemployment in Skidegate and Masset, the two Haida communities, was very high, that some of the loggers were Haida, and that the non-Haida forest workers often spent money in the two communities. If economic opportunities were desperately needed, one would think the Haida would welcome forest companies; yet Guujaaw had been a leader in opposing logging. When I asked him why, he answered, "Our people have determined that Windy Bay and other areas must be left in their natural condition so that we can keep our identity and pass it on to following generations. The forests, those oceans, are what keep us as Haida people today."

Windy Bay, forests, and oceans were critical to Haida identity? This was a statement of a fundamentally different relationship with the "environment" than most of us have, a sense that we are where we live, a relationship that is essential to future generations for whom present Haida people feel a responsibility. I wondered how many executives of forest companies—or of any company for that matter—would consider future generations a fundamental part of their planning and actions.

I continued my interview: "So if the trees are logged off—" Before I could finish my question, he responded, "If they're logged off, we'll probably end up the same as everyone else, I guess."

"The same as everyone else"—such a simple statement, yet so deeply significant. It was only days later, while I was watching the rushes, that I recognized the enormity of this insight. Since then, Guujaaw has confirmed that my interpretation of his remarks is correct: Haida people do not think they end at their skin or fingertips. Guujaaw opened for me a window into a radically different way of seeing the world. As I reflected on his words, it became obvious that these words are true for me and for all of us.

If we looked at another person with a machine that registers temperatures in different colors, we would see a gradient of heat exuding from her body into her surroundings. Water vapor and tiny electromagnetic emissions also fan out from any body while we exchange oxygen and carbon dioxide with plants on land and in water. Each of us is connected to our surroundings, just as the Haida see that the air, water, trees, fish, and birds of their land make them who they are. Talk to most Haida and within a few minutes it becomes clear that Haida Gwaii, "Island of the People," the islands they consider home, not only embody their history and culture but also are the very definition of who they are and why they are special and different.

Miles Richardson once told me about a meeting of the Fourth World Wilderness Congress, held in Colorado and attended by delegates from fifty-five countries and indigenous representatives from

around the world. Miles was there for his expertise in aboriginal politics. One evening, he found himself in a circle with other First Nations
representatives, including some elders. He was lamenting that the
Haida had lost so many of their ceremonies and cultural traditions, as
well as their language. An elder sitting next to him, who Miles had
thought was snoozing, lifted his head and remarked: "You know those
ceremonies, those songs, those traditions you're talking about—they
haven't gone anywhere. They're in the same place your forefathers
found them. They're in the forests, they're in the ocean, they're in the
birds, they're in the four-leggeds. You've just forgotten how to listen.
I have a suggestion—before you take another step forward [meaning,
do more politicking], take a step back and remember how to listen."
Miles was tremendously moved by this and says he hardly said a word
for the next three days.

My grandparents, like most newcomers to North America over the
past five centuries, arrived with a very different attitude to the land. To
them, Canada was a totally alien country. Many earlier immigrants survived only because of the knowledge and generosity of the aboriginal
people. The attraction of North America may have been freedom from
the tyranny of church or despots, opportunity in a resource-rich region,
land for farming, ranching, mining, or other development. But most of
those immigrants were incapable of learning from the aboriginal people or the indigenous flora and fauna because they lacked the respect to
watch, listen, and learn from them. Instead, they attempted to "make
over" the land to what was familiar, bringing their domesticated plants
and animals, clearing the land of its native forests and prairies, draining wetlands, straightening or damming rivers, and dumping wastes
without a thought. And once they were established, they attempted to
remove the indigenous people by killing them or forcing them to abandon their languages, culture, and values to become Canadians.

The Nature of Things with David Suzuki program on Windy Bay
was broadcast in 1982 to a large audience and elicited more letters in

response than any other show in the series since its inception in 1960. After the program had run, the South Moresby Resource Planning Team reached the same conclusion as the committee before it—Windy Bay, a jewel set in the misty isles, had to be protected from logging.

Premier Bennett still resisted the team's recommendation because of immense pressure from logging interests. He did what politicians often do in such circumstances—he punted, setting up yet another group, the Wilderness Advisory Committee, headed by the respected lawyer Bryan Williams. But so many battles over logging had broken out all over the province that the committee was charged with examining sixteen contentious areas and coming up with decisions on all of them in three months! After years of deliberation and no decisions about Haida Gwaii, Bennett set a ludicrously short time to decide on all these areas. Environmentalists immediately pointed out there wasn't enough time to perform the job responsibly, adding that the committee's membership was too heavily weighted toward the logging industry.

By then I was fully engaged in the battle over Windy Bay, and I made a submission to the Wilderness Advisory Committee. The body included Les Reed, a forest economist who occupied a chair at the University of British Columbia funded by the forest industry. He once boasted that in contrast to people like me, he did not have tenure; I don't know what he was trying to imply, because tenure is a privilege conferred on academics to free them to speak out on issues about which they are knowledgeable, without fear of reprisal. In contrast, Reed was completely dependent on the forest industry for his continued support—like someone who works for the tobacco or nuclear industry, he was too dependent on vested interests to be credible.

At one point during my submission to the committee, I mentioned that I had just driven through forests in France while filming and had noticed the roadkill—animals killed by motor vehicles. Before I could finish my sentence, Reed interrupted me to blurt out, "We have lots of roadkill in B.C. too." I responded that the point I was making was that in France I hadn't seen any roadkill. Instead, I saw a lot of tree plantations of the kind the forest industry wanted to substitute for old-growth forests, but judging by the lack of roadkill in France, there was little wildlife in them compared with our forests—as Reed had pointed out. The audience hooted its delight as Reed scowled at me.

The really hot area examined by Williams's committee was Windy Bay. In the end, the committee came through, recommending that 363,000 acres, including Windy Bay, be set aside as parkland. Response from the forest industry was furious, as well-known radio talk show host Jack Webster took on the issue and attacked environmentalists (it was revealed later that he was a shareholder in one of the companies logging the area). In the heat of the controversy, I was invited to debate the issue on Webster's show. I was very nervous, because I was a latecomer to the controversy and didn't know all the details, as others who had been involved for years did.

To my surprise, when I arrived at the studio, I could see immediately that Jack was equally scared of me. No doubt he too felt insecure about his facts. Once he opened his show, he was very polite and respectful as we sparred over the issue. Finally I said, "Jack, it's disgraceful how little land we set aside to protect. Do you know how much we protect on the coast?" Now, in a way I was bluffing—I had heard Thom Henley quote a number that was very small but had not seen the evidence for myself. If Jack had answered, "No, I don't. How much do we protect?" I would have had to sound foolish by replying, "I don't know either, but it isn't very much." To my relief, he began to stutter, then paused and finally said, "Well, I have to admit I don't know," and he lobbed me an easy question on a different subject. He was as shaky on the land issue as I was at that moment.

Bennett was still under too much pressure from the forest industry and loggers to be able to accept the Williams recommendation. Even though a mere sixty to seventy logging jobs were at risk if the area were set aside as a park, the industry held the rest of the province to ransom, railing against the "greedy" environmentalists who cared more about trees than people. I heard of a public meeting that was held in Sandspit, the community where most of the men logging South Moresby lived. Debate was heated as loggers demanded their right to make a living on Haida Gwaii like anyone else. At that point, a Haida elder stood up and asked how many loggers were buried in Haida Gwaii. After a long pause, the answer came back: "None." The elder responded that her people had lived there for thousands of years and their bones could be found throughout the islands.

At last, in 1987, new premier Bill Vander Zalm decided to include the disputed land in a park to be jointly administered by Parks Canada and the Haida people and known as Gwaii Haanas National Park Reserve and Haida Heritage Site. It was a massive area of almost six hundred square miles, representing 15 percent of the islands of Haida Gwaii.

Vander Zalm had been vacillating back and forth, leaving environmentalists whipsawed between the excitement of potential victory and despair at the possibility of losing. He was in direct phone contact with Prime Minister Brian Mulroney as they debated the amount of money the feds would kick in. I was in Russia filming, and it seemed that each time I called Tara, a different outcome was imminent. I was writing a weekly column for the *Globe and Mail* newspaper in Toronto at the time and had to go through all kinds of machinations to send the columns from different parts of the Soviet Union. I was filming along Lake Baikal in Siberia when the decision was finally made, but I had written two columns—one congratulating politicians for the wisdom of their decision, the other decrying their cowardice in making the wrong choice.

Frank Beban, the owner of the company that was doing the logging, ordered his men to cut on Lyell Island around the clock, dropping the trees as fast as possible and just leaving them on the ground until the deadline in July when all logging had to stop. Then they could haul them out more leisurely. I flew over Lyell Island with Tara, and her eyes filled with tears at the sight of the trees lying crisscrossed on the ground, the wanton destruction a last-gasp thumbing of the nose at all the "preservationists."

I was invited to the provincial government buildings in Victoria for the July 1987 signing of the agreement between B.C. and Canada that would help to create Gwaii Haanas National Park Reserve. It was a rare moment when environmentalists could celebrate a victory and rub shoulders with politicians. Tara had already flown to Haida Gwaii, where a great feast was being prepared in Skidegate to welcome home *Lootaas* ("Wave Eater"), the fifty-foot dugout canoe carved there for Expo 86 under the supervision of the Haida carver Bill Reid. In Victoria, Premier Vander Zalm signed along with Prime Minister Mulroney. Afterward, Elizabeth May, who was a special assistant to federal environment minister Tom McMillan, was given permission to take a government jet to Haida Gwaii, and we flew off in a state of euphoria.

Our elation ended abruptly as we stepped out of the plane onto the tarmac at Sandspit, the logging community in Haida Gwaii. We were met by a mob of women pushing against the fence and screaming at us. It was an intimidating situation that none of us wanted to exacerbate by entering the airport building. Undaunted, Elizabeth noticed that there was a military Sikorsky helicopter parked on the tarmac; flashing her government credentials, she commandeered the machine. Without even entering the airport building, we climbed onto the chopper and in a few minutes had left the bitter crowd behind. We were whisked across the water and landed in Skidegate, where the people were in a high state of excitement.

We were ushered into the village's great hall, where tables were set for a feast. A row of hereditary chiefs in full regalia presided over the long head table. Many people, including Minister McMillan, were feted and honored in speeches and with gifts. The tables sagged under the weight of the food from the ocean—salmon, halibut, herring roe, crab, and eulachon, as well as bannock, pies, cakes, jelly, and so much more. Speeches, drumming, and dancing followed dinner, including the demanding eagle dance; the most admired performances of this require the dancer to squat as low as possible while hopping and swirling, a feat that leaves me breathless in just seconds. (The next day I encountered children who told me they had seen me dance. Then they giggled.)

Alan Wilson, a Haida hereditary chief, was one of the Royal Canadian Mounted Police officers at the protest line at Windy Bay. He had been caught in an agonizing position—he understood that the confrontation was about the land that made the Haida who they are, yet as an RCMP officer, he had to enforce the laws of the dominant society. The three elders who had insisted they be the ones to block the road and be arrested included his own aunt, Ethel Jones. Alan had approached the elders with tears streaming down his face in a scene that would appear on national television. "It's all right, dear," his aunty assured him as she took his arm and walked to the helicopter that would whisk her away to jail.

Alan leaped up at the Skidegate feast and publicly announced that he was giving me his dance apron, part of the formal regalia. Decorated with strips of copper, buttons, and figures of whales and birds, it was the first piece of regalia I ever received and is a much-treasured gift. Each time I wear it, great memories flood back.

The Gwaii Haanas National Park Reserve and Haida Heritage Site agreement was signed in January 1993, after almost six years of negotiation between Canada and the Haida Nation. The official title recognizes that the Haida designated Gwaii Haanas a Haida Heritage Site in 1985.

ANOTHER BATTLE THAT TOOK place during this period was the fight to protect the Stein Valley, at 425 square miles the last large unlogged watershed in southwestern B.C., relatively close to Vancouver.

In 1984, I received a request from organizer John McCandless on behalf of Chief Ruby Dunstan of the Lytton First Nations band and Chief Leonard Andrew of the Lil'wat band to speak at the first of what it was hoped would become an annual festival to celebrate and protect the Stein Valley. The First Nations who had roamed the valley for thousands of years claimed it as a spiritual place. Unfortunately, I had a previous commitment at the time of the inaugural festival in 1985 and was unable to make it, but John invited me early so that I could attend the next year.

John was an American who had left his country during the Vietnam War; he ended up moving his family to the Fraser Valley in B.C. and working for the Lytton band. As was common practice in British Columbia at that time, a forest company had been granted a license to log the Stein Valley, without any consultation or approval from the people who had been using it for their sacred burial sites and as a source of berries and salmon long before Europeans arrived. Environmentalism was growing in British Columbia, aided by the high-profile fight against clear-cut logging by the Haida.

John had conceived of the idea of raising the profile of the Stein Valley by holding a First Nations–run festival that would feature speakers and musicians. That first gathering attracted up to five hundred people, who hiked high into the alpine at the valley headwaters in a terrific kickoff to what would become an incredible success.

What impressed me over the years was John's ability to manage all the details required to hold the Stein Valley Festival. He eventually inspired the support of hundreds of skilled volunteers from the two host communities, but try to imagine the logistics involved in pulling off a celebration that hundreds (eventually tens of thousands) of people would attend in a very remote and wild part of B.C. Posters and advertising had to be arranged; parking sites had to be found for hundreds of vehicles; trails had to be cut for hikers. As the success of the festival grew, loggers went in and felled several huge trees across the

Sev, Guujaaw, and Tara at a Stein Festival in the alpine meadows

path of hikers, creating a lot of tension over possible violence. Camp-sites and cooking facilities were needed; food was arranged for special guests, elders, and staff; portable toilets had to be installed before the festival and removed after; first aid was necessary for everything from sunburn to broken bones; a stage and a sound system were needed for performers; garbage had to be dealt with; elders and VIPs who couldn't hike had to be helicoptered to campsites; tepees were set up for special guests; guards were recruited in case of confrontations with loggers or rednecks, and cleanup crews were needed during and after the event. And, of course, the money had to be raised. It was like mounting a major battle, but somehow, with the help and direction of chiefs Dunstan and Andrew, year after year John pulled it off.

For the second festival, Tara and I were delighted to have the chance to camp in a part of the province we hadn't seen before. The festival site was alongside the lower Stein River, in a meadow, and there might have been a couple of hundred people there. In preparing for my talk, I had to integrate my ideas about the environment with what little I knew about the traditional values of First Nations.

The first night, Tara and I and our two very young daughters were put up in a large tepee with several other people. We had settled comfortably into our sleeping bags and were about to drop off when a group right outside the tepee began to drum and chant. For hours! Tara was beside herself with frustration at first, but in the end our daughters slept through it all. The night grew bitterly cold, the drumming and singing droned on, the wind blew the dry soil under the edges of our tepee, and we felt so far from our world that we were finally transported to a different state: we knew this was a watershed experience in our lives.

In the next tepee were Miles Richardson, the young, charismatic president of the Haida Nation, involved in his own battle over the land; Patricia Kelly, his Coast Salish girlfriend; and Guujaaw, the Haida artist who played such an important role in my education and who would himself become president after leading the fight against logging in Haida Gwaii. They would become our dearest friends and companions over the years.

Time changed for us. The drumming continued through the night as we drifted between our dreams and the people outside. The lead drummer was a young man who called himself "Seeker," and in the following days, Tara and I found he had much to teach us. He told us the reason this valley was important to him and his people. "White people go to church, but I come here. When I bring my kids here," he told us, "all my problems fall away and I feel at peace. This is my sanctuary." I began to understand what the word "sacred" means.

Because of its relative proximity to Vancouver, the Stein Valley became a favorite place for my family to hike and fish. When Sarika was six, we backpacked along the river one Thanksgiving. We reached the Devil's Staircase, a steep climb over a rocky scree that was a formidable challenge for the children. As we began to climb, Sarika lay

Severn and Sarika admiring a spawned-out chum salmon in the Stein Valley

down on the trail and refused to go any farther. I took the pack off her back and urged her on for a few hundred yards, at which point she stopped and refused to go on. I ended up carrying not just her pack but Sarika herself until we got over that hump. But she has never refused a hiking challenge since.

Thanks to the increasing attendance at the festival, interest in the Stein Valley grew. The environmental community rallied to the cause. Colleen McCrory of the Valhalla Wilderness Society in New Denver, B.C., had successfully led a fight to have the area where Dad and I fished while at the wartime camps in the Slocan Valley set aside as Valhalla Provincial Park, and she took part in the later Stein festivals. The Western Canada Wilderness Committee, one of the oldest and most effective grassroots activist organizations in B.C., had pioneered the issue and continued to pitch in with posters and papers publicizing the Stein.

Celebrities began to lend their names to the cause. I called and recruited the Canadian singer Gordon Lightfoot, who flew his entire band to the Stein to perform free. Later, Gordon became a very good friend and donated a large sum of money that pulled the festival out of debt. He had asked me to tell John McCandless how much he would give, and when I did, John's face sagged with relief and his eyes welled with tears.

Somehow, in 1987, I was able to find a phone number and call the American singer John Denver, who answered the phone himself and said he knew who I was. He accepted my invitation to perform at the Stein, and, like Lightfoot, he traveled in at his own expense, flying his plane to the Kamloops airport. His performance in the alpine meadow high up in the valley was the highlight for the two thousand people who had hiked up the mountain.

John became a friend and invited me to give talks as his guest at Windstar, his retreat/think tank near Aspen, Colorado. He was a huge talent, and he supported environmental groups around the world; yet he was surprisingly insecure about his failure to have a big hit record for years. He told us proudly how, when visiting China, he had come upon a peasant who did a double take and shouted, "John Denba! Countly Load!"

In 1997, Tara and I were driving back to Vancouver from Williams Lake and stopped at the same Lytton motel that had always been our Stein headquarters, overlooking the ferry that crossed the Fraser River to the trailhead of the Stein. Out of the blue, the radio announced that a plane being flown by John Denver had plummeted into the Pacific off Monterey, California, killing him. We were stunned. I'm glad John knew before he died that the Stein Valley had been set aside as a provincial park.

Tara worked full-time on the Stein campaign as the unpaid Vancouver coordinator. She was able to get the Hawaiian phone number of the Canadian First Nations singer Buffy Sainte-Marie and called to ask her to sing at the Stein Valley Festival. Buffy had to go to an audition for a job in Washington, D.C., and agreed to perform on condition that we pay for an executive-class round-trip plane ticket from her home in Honolulu to Vancouver and then to Washington. That would be a very expensive item, but she was a huge star and we agreed.

That summer, she flew in to Vancouver, where she was put up in a hotel. She didn't want to drive all the way to the Stein, so we had to charter a helicopter, at great expense, paid in advance, for her flight the following morning. Tara and I were already at the festival site when we learned that Buffy had slept through the morning flight-departure time and now insisted she be flown up in the afternoon. We had no choice but to pay for the helicopter a second time.

But when she arrived at the festival, her impact on the First Nations people there was electric. I immediately saw the value of having a headliner with whom the First Nations could identify. The audience was ecstatic, and it was clear to me that however much of a pain she had been, she was worth it. Buffy was a real pro, her unique voice projecting

John Denver and his wife, Cassandra, at the 1987 Stein Festival

warmth and charisma onstage while telling the rapt audience how happy she was to be there. Afterward she climbed into a car to go back to the airfield and disappeared in the chopper back to Vancouver and on to Washington.

In October 1987, B.C. forests minister Dave Parker, who had been chief forester overseeing the clear-cutting of the Nass, the sacred valley of the Nisga'a, gave the go-ahead to log the Stein. The rationale was that it was "only" to be 22,000 of the 260,000 acres in the watershed, but it would have cut out the heart of the valley bottom. However, the buildup of support for protecting the valley paid off: because of the festivals, the Stein had become too well known and support for its protection too great to send the loggers in.

By 1988, 3,500 people were attending the Stein Valley Festival. The following year, 16,000 people drove to the event, held at the rodeo grounds near Mount Currie. They were entertained by Canadian stars Bruce Cockburn, Gordon Lightfoot, Colin James, Valdy, Blue Rodeo, and Spirit of the West, among many others. The festival had become so huge that it now made money, and I was sure the size of the crowd ensured the valley would never be logged. In one of many dramatic moments, Woody Morrison, a Haida, rose and told us he had served in the U.S. military in Vietnam, but even the most heavily bombed land he had seen there had not been as devastated as the clear-cut area visible behind him. In another, Hollywood director and Canadian Norman Jewison got up on the stage to announce that he and American singer Cher were contributing $5,000 to the cause.

That was the last Stein festival I attended, because, as with Windy Bay, I was sure public support had reached a level that meant no politician would ever dare allow the valley to be logged. That goal had been the rationale for the festival in the first place. In 1995, B.C. Premier Mike Harcourt held a ceremony with Chief Ruby Dunstan and Chief Leonard Andrew to set aside the entire watershed as Stein Valley

Nlaka'pamux Heritage Park, administered by the Lytton First Nations and B.C. Parks. Now, each time I return to hike up the valley, it is gratifying to think the ecosystem will continue to flourish long after we are gone.

IN BOTH HAIDA GWAII and the Stein Valley, the battle was led by First Nations. Theirs was a struggle over land, not for the superficial needs of money, jobs, or control, but for the most powerful need of all—to remain who they are. In the past, and even in the present, environmentalists often recruited First Nations communities to support their agenda of protecting forests, rivers, and wildlife without regard to the people's even broader cultural and spiritual needs. In sharing their land as park reserves, the Haida and Lytton people gained tacit recognition that these areas are part of their territory but are to be protected for all people for all time. It is a generous gift.

chapter SEVEN

ADVENTURES
IN THE AMAZON

W HEN I WAS A BOY, I would sneak a peek at
Dad's adventure magazines, which carried
tales of true-life adventures in exotic places. The ones that would make
my heart beat wildly described the Amazon, a place I yearned to visit.

I loved reading about the Indians who wore feather headdresses,
their bodies painted in patterns blending with the dappled light beneath
the tree canopy as they hunted for game with blowpipes and arrows
tipped with deadly poisons. In the 1940s there were still many parts
of the globe that had not been explored by people from the industrialized world; the Amazon rain forest remained a vast and mysterious
ecosystem, rife, according to the magazines, with terrifying diseases
and parasites. Piranhas and giant anacondas filled the rivers; jaguars
and armies of deadly ants lurked in the forest. These terrors were bal-
anced by the spectacles of colorful parrots and dazzling butterflies and,
most of all, beetles. I had fallen madly in love with insects, but beetles
especially held me in thrall.

In 1988, at the age of fifty-two, I had my chance to realize my boy-
hood dreams. In August, *The Nature of Things with David Suzuki* crew
traveled to Brazil to begin filming for a special program on the rain

forest's ecosystem. A month later, filled with anticipation, I flew to the outpost of Pôrto Velho, capital of the state of Rondônia, to hook up with the crew. But my first glimpse of the legendary forests was bittersweet: we were there to bear witness to its destruction.

For years, Brazil's urban poor had been promised opportunities in the Amazon under the slogan "Land without people, for people without land." They had flooded into remote villages in the rain forest, cutting trees to make into charcoal as fuel for factories and to clear land to cultivate crops, which grew for only a year or two in the meager soil. Then the peasants were forced to leave their plots and move on, taking their poverty and malaria with them, as they continued the cycle of burn and cut to plant crops for another year or two.

When I caught up with the crew in Rondônia, they had not been able to take aerial shots because smoke from the burning forest was so thick it was too hazardous for airplanes to take off. I was excited to be there, depressing as the scene was, but the team was demoralized by what they had filmed—poverty, malnutrition, malaria, and children so painfully thin the crew ended up giving them money for medicine and food.

The red soil that had so recently been cloaked with an ancient forest was now exposed in fields that barely supported a pitiful crop of vegetables inadequate for the needs of the large families. Immense trees were cut down without a thought for their ecological role or the organisms they supported (Harvard's E.O. Wilson records that he found more genera of ants on a single tree in the Amazon than are found in the entire United Kingdom).

One of the most destructive activities in the Amazon is the cutting of huge trees to be burned anoxically in sealed ovens to produce charcoal. We filmed dozens of domes in which the wood smoldered to be rendered into lightweight, high-energy fuel, which was then piled in sacks. Magnificent trees were reduced to skeletal pieces of charcoal in pile after pile. I found this devastating. I knew I was witnessing an ecological holocaust, a crime against future generations who would never know the full wonder of this magnificent ecosystem.

We filmed endless scenes of burning—trees, fields, whole forests going up in smoke. At one point we were searching a burn and drove down a narrow road, which suddenly ended in a pond. Rudi Kovanic and the crew lugged their gear around the pond to film the fire on the other side. Since I had plenty of time before I had to appear on-camera, I pulled out my fishing rod and cast toward some logs in the water. On shoots like this, where we were filming scenics rather than interviews with scientists, I might do only one or two stand-ups in a day, so I had a lot of time to stand around and watch. That's why, when we encountered water, I often would pull out my rod and reel and see what might be caught. This time, surrounded by the desolation of burning, I did not expect to catch anything, but at least I had something to do.

I felt a strike on my first cast and watched a beautiful tucunare, a peacock bass that is green and has a characteristic spot on its tail, hit the lure and leap into the air. Tucunare are aggressive predators and attack a lure violently, then fight like mad. They are also one of the most exquisite-tasting freshwater fish I've eaten. When the crew got back to the car, I could promise them a wonderful meal of fresh fish. But I was sure there would be no tucunare left a year or two later, even if there was still water, because the forest cover and the water cycle were being so disrupted by the destruction going on. It was with mixed feelings that I fed the crew—I love fishing and eating fresh fish, but here I was part of a "terminal fishery."

A crew member who liked to fish was Terry Zazulak, the camera assistant. One night, when we were ensconced in a shack for the night near the Amazon River, we decided to hike to the river and try fishing. It gets dark suddenly and early—6:00 PM—near the equator, and we soon found ourselves squinting in the fading light. The river was flowing very fast, and our gear was too light to sink far enough below the surface to attract a fish. I couldn't see where my lure landed and

the river was too noisy to hear it plunk into the water. I began retriev-
ing my lure, then realized the line wasn't coming up out of the water
toward me but seemed to be floating in the air. I reeled in faster, wondering whether I had snagged a branch, and felt a klunk. Reaching to
the tip of the rod, I felt something furry. It was a bat! It must have
swooped in on my lure and been hooked. As a young man, in 1957,
I had caught a bat in the same way while fishing in the evening on a
canoe trip in Algonquin Provincial Park in Ontario.

I thought back to the enchanting books *Animal Treasure* and *Caribbean Treasure* by Ivan Terence Sanderson, then curator of the St. Louis
Zoo, about collecting specimens in exotic places, and the daydreams I
had had of emulating those field trips when I grew up. According to
Sanderson, the people on those expeditions would fire BB pellets into
the air, and bats would nail the pellets in flight, knocking themselves
out. Sanderson could simply pick them up to add to their collection.
Here I had done the same thing with a fishing lure.

Over my decades in television, I've learned that filming in another
country can be a huge hassle. No one wants to welcome into their community, or country, a crew that intends to portray them in a bad way.
People want to know the purpose of the film, what we intend to show,
who we will interview, and so on. Often we have to tiptoe our way
through government bureaucracy, red tape, demands for baksheesh,
and exchange of money in the black market. We usually have to oper-
ate in the local language to make arrangements for planes, hotels,
cars, porters, and so forth. When the crew comprises host, producer,
researcher/writer, cameraperson, camera assistant, soundperson, and
lighting person, along with forty heavy bags of luggage (some metal
trunks), a tough and savvy local agent is required to organize it all.

In Brazil, that individual was Juneia Mallus, who was as opinionated and tough as anyone I've ever met. She clashed frequently
with members of the crew, but she did a fabulous job. When we said
we needed to film an indigenous person who could articulate the

Paiakan

importance of the forest and show us through his or her community, Juneia knew who it should be: an extraordinary man she had worked with before—Paiakan, a Kaiapo Indian.

We were to meet Paiakan in the Kaiapo village of Gorotire, which was once reachable only by trails but now had a road from the outside. But "road" is a misnomer. The Amazon is a rain forest, and as we were driving our large truck in, rain converted the road into a slimy red slash through the forest. What was supposed to be an all-day drive turned into an agonizing day and night of grinding our way, slipping and spinning and slumping. John Crawford, our longtime soundman, turned into a heroic figure, driving during the entire ordeal.

I remember clambering out of the back in utter darkness and, scared stiff, creeping on hands and knees along the trunk of a tree, one of two tire tracks across a deep gorge. Somehow John guided that truck on those two thin trunks without slipping into certain death below. Horrific as the road was, it was nevertheless the opening for the influx of "civilized" products—white bread, candy, beer, liquor, tobacco—that pollute the community we were approaching.

Disgusted with what that road had done to this village, Paiakan pulled out and moved far into the forest to establish a new village where his people could continue to live traditionally. After a long search, Paiakan had found the perfect place on a low bluff overlooking a river filled with fish. He called the community Aucre (Ah-*oo*-cray), apparently named after the sound a certain fish makes when caught. About two hundred people had decided to follow Paiakan and live in Aucre. But he was to meet us in Gorotire.

It was early evening and we were relaxing in a hut in the village when Paiakan came by. He was husky, of medium height, with Prince Valiant–style, jet-black hair. He was controlled when he met us—not suspicious, but curious. Who were we and what did we want? All of our conversation had to be funneled through Juneia in Portuguese, the official language of Brazil, which Paiakan had acquired as a teenager and now spoke fluently. Juneia introduced him to all of us, but when he looked at me and heard my name, David, his face brightened in a broad smile. Perhaps he was showing respect because I was the host of the program? I learned later there was a more compelling reason.

While a teenager living at a Catholic mission, Paiakan was befriended by a Brazilian Japanese medical doctor named David, or "Davi" in Portuguese. This doctor went out of his way to help the Kaiapo and became a trusted friend. Paiakan said that encountering a second "Japanese" with the same name as his early mentor and friend seemed auspicious and more than coincidental. The Brazilian David had exhibited a great affection for the Kaiapo Indians; because of him, Paiakan trusted me. I have always felt grateful to Dr. David for making my entry into Paiakan's life so straightforward.

Juneia told us Paiakan's story, and it was remarkable. Paiakan's father, Chikiri, is a chief. For his first fourteen years, Paiakan had lived a totally traditional life, as his ancestors had done for thousands of years, hunting and gathering according to knowledge acquired and passed on for many generations.

But even the immensity of the Amazon rain forest was not enough to protect the Kaiapo from the encroachments of the brancos (Europeans). The Kaiapo could smell the fires and were beginning to see extensive gold-mining pollution in some of the big rivers. Paiakan realized he had to learn more about the encroachers. At seventeen, he went to the Catholic mission, where he learned Portuguese and some Brazilian culture. After he learned to write, he promptly wrote a book about the forest as his home. Paiakan could have moved to a city and become an urban Indian, but he had no desire to be assimilated. He wanted to learn enough to protect the traditional ways, and he moved back to his village.

Not long afterward, in 1985, the Kaiapo learned that a giant gold-mining operation had opened in their territory. I have heard many versions of what followed. Most agree on this story: Paiakan led a party of warriors to find out what was happening. For days the dozens of men traveled on foot, and finally they came to an immense clearing where thousands of miners were housed. Daunted at first, the warriors waited till late at night. They decided that one group would take control of the airstrip, where several light planes were parked; another group would take over the guard tower, which held men armed with machine guns.

The signal was given. Attack! Most of the guards were fast asleep, confident they had nothing to fear deep in the Amazon. The battle was brief. Shocked, confused, confronted with Indians in war paint, the guards surrendered. The Kaiapo turned on the floodlights and ran along the barracks, pounding on the walls to call on the workers to gather. Once the men assembled, the Kaiapo fired the guards' machine guns over their heads and told them to leave Kaiapo territory. I cannot imagine the turmoil those miners felt that night as they fled into the dark forest.

Kaiapo warrior policing the gold mine

The next day, some miners returned to try to retake the camp but were severely beaten by the Kaiapo, who held the camp for months. The Brazilian government was helpless, since the Kaiapo-controlled airstrip was the only access to the camp. Paiakan was invited to Brasília to negotiate with the government. Finally, he brokered a deal. The government desperately wanted to get the planes back but refused to shut down the gold mine.

It was a placer mine; the sandy soil was blasted with pressure hoses and filtered through screens, and then mercury was added to capture the gold. It is an ecologically invasive process that pollutes rivers with toxic mercury. Since the river was already polluted and spoiled, the Kaiapo decided they would permit the mining to continue on the conditions that they would receive a royalty of 5 percent on all gold recovered, that warriors would police the camp, that they would examine all goods flying in and out, and that there would be no women, firearms, or alcohol on the site.

We later filmed the mining site, and it was quite remarkable to see the warriors police the site, clad only in shorts, with bows and arrows as their weapons. There I met an elder whose hair was still jet-black. I was fifty-two and my hair had started to turn gray, but it was clear he was a lot older than me. He asked me how old I was, and I responded with a question, "How old do you think I am?" Back came his humbling answer: "Seventy?"

Paiakan had achieved an incredible victory. He became the acknowledged leader of the community; when he decided to move to Aucre, many people went with him. Paiakan had noticed that when he negotiated with government officials or miners, they would say one thing to him in private but another to the press or the public. This discrepancy angered him, so he bought a video camera to film all encounters with officials. Initially I thought it weird that this traditional Indian was fussing with a video camera, but soon I realized it was his insurance against the forked tongue of the brancos.

DARRELL POSEY WAS AN American professor at Oxford University and a leading cultural anthropologist who had lived with and studied the Kaiapo for years and was accepted by them. In January 1987, he invited Paiakan and his cousin, Kube-i, to attend a scientific conference in Florida. It was at that conference and on their first trip to a foreign country that Paiakan and Kube-i learned of Plano 2010, Brazil's grand scheme to build a series of dozens of massive dams in the Amazon rain forest, including several on the Xingu River. At a cost of US$10.6 billion, they would flood 18.7 million acres of forest, 85 percent of it Indian land. Paiakan's accidental discovery of Brazilian plans for his territory was reminiscent of what First Nations have experienced in Canada.

After the Florida meeting, Posey took the two Kaiapo to Washington, where they met American politicians to describe the new threat to their lands, looking for advice and support. The World Bank was considering a loan of $500 million to Brazil to build the dams, so Posey took Paiakan and Kube-i to World Bank headquarters to discuss the implications of the first dam, at Altamira, on the Kaiapo people. The media loved the two exotic Indians and gave them a lot of coverage.

Not surprisingly, the Brazilian government was enraged, and when Paiakan and Kube-i returned to Brazil, they were arrested for "criticizing Brazilian Indian policy" and for "denigrating the country's image abroad." The excuse used to arrest them was a Brazilian law that forbids foreigners from getting involved in issues of Brazilian interest. Here were two aboriginal people, whose ancestors had inhabited the forests long before there was a Brazil, being arrested as aliens.

Paiakan and Kube-i were arraigned for trial in the fall of 1988 in Belém. Meanwhile, Paiakan developed a plan to fight the dams. He decided that the Indian tribes who lived in the area to be flooded had to be informed and galvanized into protest. But how could this be done? They lived in some of the most isolated areas of Brazil, and many tribes were hostile to their neighbors.

Ironically, in a serious faux pas, Brazilians had chosen a Kaiapo war cry, Kararao, as the name of the first dam. It must have steeled the opposition. Paiakan wanted a motorboat to travel up the river to contact people and unite them in a fight to stop the dams. He wanted to coax those people out of the forest to roads and buses and transport them to the very site of the proposed dam near Altamira. There they would build a traditional village for the first gathering of the indigenous people of the Amazon. He had conceived of an event that would attract the world media and embarrass Brazil. It was a brilliant strategy, worthy of the most savvy Greenpeace stunt. This is what he had already cooked up when I met him in Gorotire.

THAT NIGHT, AS WE exchanged thoughts through Juneia, Paiakan was sizing me up.

The camera crew were to fly into Aucre in a couple of days, but Paiakan wanted to fly back to Aucre with his wife, Irekran, before the rest of the team. The extra flight would cost several hundred dollars. Nancy Archibald as the producer was worried about the cost overruns we were already racking up and refused to pay. I could see Paiakan and Irekran were anxious to go early, so I offered to pay the money and asked if I could go in with them. Nancy agreed, and the meeting broke up.

The next day, after some of the dancing staged by the women in Gorotire had been filmed, Paiakan, Irekran, and I took off for Aucre. As the plane leveled off, I had a moment of panic as I realized I would be spending the next days in a village where only Paiakan spoke any language other than Kaiapo and that was Portuguese, which I didn't understand. He had learned one English phrase: "Let's go, Dave." What if something happened and I couldn't communicate with anyone? I would be in the middle of an immense wilderness with no way to communicate with the outside world.

My panic quickly passed, however, as I was swept up in the wonder of the adventure, my childhood dream come true. After an hour's flight over endless, pristine forest, a clearing came into view. I saw an oval ring of huts by a stream, the Rio Zinho, "little river." A thin cleared track was our runway. We bounced along the stubble to a halt, and the plane was mobbed by what seemed like the entire village.

The women were naked except for beaded necklaces and bracelets, their bodies were painted with black patterns, and their faces were bright red with dyes from plants. Their eyebrows had been plucked, and a triangular area from their foreheads to the crown of their heads was shaved clean. Many of the men, whose bodies were also painted, wore flip-flops, shorts, and headdresses of brilliantly colored feathers. The naked children were painted and bore large holes in their earlobes from wooden plugs. None wore labrets (wooden disks inserted into the lower lip), but many adult men sported holes below their lower lips through which drool dripped. The women wailed in a high-pitched keening, eyes weeping and noses running, to let the arrivals know how much they had been missed. It was astounding to see people like the ones in Dad's magazines. Those had fueled my childhood dreams; these were the real thing.

I was an object of great interest, especially to the children, who had no inhibitions. They jostled about, pushing each other away and bumping into me as they tried to keep a frontline eye on me. Adolescent boys picked up the gear without being told, and we walked in the blazing sun toward Paiakan's hut. The inside of the hut was dark, enclosed by walls of sticks sealed with mud and covered with a thatched roof. A half partition divided the hut, with one side used for hammocks and the other for cooking and eating, and there we hung out.

Paiakan knew I was hot and sweaty. First things first—we walked along a path for a hundred yards until it fell steeply to the river. There women sat on the bank in the shade, putting dough balls onto hooks,

Kaiapo woman in Gorotire prepared to dance

which they threw out into the pool as bait to catch coarse-looking chublike fish called piau. Children dived into the same pool; others dipped metal pots into collecting pools, where clear water seeped out of the riverbank. The girls and women plunged into the pool and, cupping their hands, chanted and slapped the water in a rhythmic song.

It was overwhelmingly idyllic to my North American eye. The water was warm, but it was a wonderful relief from the humid heat. I did wonder about piranhas and learned the next day that people caught them in this same pool. The horrifying tales of piranhas attacking and consuming horses, reducing men to bone in a matter of minutes, turned out to be jazzed-up stories for the adventure magazines I'd loved. I'd also heard about the candiru, the tiny, parasitic catfish that homes in on urea leaking from fish and swims right into the unsuspecting anal pores. I knew the rumor that candiru may follow a trail of urine dribbling from human orifices and swim up urethras. Catfish have sharp spines on their pectoral and dorsal fins, and it is said that the pain of a candiru is beyond belief. Somehow I managed to suppress all such thoughts and just enjoy the scene.

Once my hammock was hung in Paiakan's hut, I wandered around the village circle, looking in doorways and waving at people lying in hammocks or working on chores. On some of the thatched roofs were tethered parrots that I suspect were the source of some of the feathers in headdresses. In the center of the clearing was a covered, wall-less structure where the men gathered to gossip, smoke, weave shoulder bands in which women carried infants, and create the feather ornaments. Their pipes were wicked-looking structures carved out of wood, with a straight stem opening out into a wider bowl where the tobacco was placed. The smoke must have rushed right into the lungs of the smoker. I was glad I had given up smoking a long time ago.

All around the village was forest. In the understory, useful plants such as bananas, pineapples, and cassava could be seen. Agroforestry is the deliberate modification of the forest by people, a practice that has gone on for thousands of years. When Europeans arrived in Africa, Asia, and the Americas, they found what they assumed were pristine wild forests. But it turns out these apparently natural forests had been modified. Villages would be built at the perimeter of wild forests. Over time, plants and trees would be gathered from the wild regions, taken to the villages, and deliberately planted in a perimeter zone to be used as needed. There could be hundreds of species in this zone, and that's why the diversity appeared to Europeans to reflect its wildness. Animals, too, came into the perimeter and were hunted for food. But the villagers knew it was the wild heartland that was the true source of their food.

I returned to Paiakan's hut as the sun approached the horizon. Inside, Irekran was cooking rice and beans in metal pots on the open fire, and in the center of the fire was a dead turtle just plopped on its back onto the coals. Irekran ladled rice and beans onto a tin plate as Paiakan grabbed a leg of the turtle, wrenched it off, and offered it to me. Clearly, it was considered the best part, as everyone watched me, anxiously anticipating an expression of gratitude appropriate to the honor. I smiled and bobbed my head, hoping they could see how happy I was. I had eaten snapping turtle before, when Dad had caught one and we killed and cooked it. As I remembered, the meat was very dark and . . . well, it was meat and it hadn't been too bad.

In the middle of the Amazon, I was hungry and any meat seemed fine. The only problem was that this leg was still pretty bloody and hardly cooked at all. Now, I'm Japanese and eat raw fish all the time, yet I couldn't help wondering what kind of parasites might be in a turtle in a tropical rain forest. But what really made it hard for me was the skin, which was covered in bumps and wrinkles that looked so . . . alive. And the claws, for some reason, really bothered me.

Nevertheless, I grabbed the leg by the claws and bit into the other end. Mmm, not bad. I really was hungry, and with the rice and beans it was great, but as soon as I finished the leg, a second one was plopped onto my plate—a real honor. I tried to attack this leg with the same gusto, only to have a third leg appear when I finished the second. That was it—I ate three legs and begged off the last one.

That night I lay in my hammock, listening to the steady thrum of insects and the chirps of frogs from the surrounding forest, the gentle snores and breathing of Paiakan's family all around me. I felt so far away from anything I knew. This was the realization of dreams I had held for forty years.

It had still been warm when we crawled into the hammocks, so I'd stretched out the thin sleeping bag I brought and lay on top of it. I fell asleep but woke up surprised to be shivering. The night had cooled right down, and I was so grateful to climb into the bag for the rest of the night.

The next morning, using sign language and gestures honed from playing charades, I found the latrine. It was a narrow, open pit that one straddled, partially hidden behind a woven screen. If you ever find yourself in a similar situation, don't look into the open pit—the image of a mass of writhing maggots will sear your brain.

That morning we ate rice and beans, and a fish someone had dropped off. Here in as remote a part of the Amazon as you could find, the impact of contact was obvious, from the shorts, T-shirts, and flip-flops to pots, knives, and fishhooks. Paiakan's hut contained the detritus of his trips to the outside world—plastic toys and his video camera. Still, this was as self-sufficient a way of life as one can imagine. A fractured limb, infected cut, or illness would have to be treated according to traditional knowledge and the medical skills available in the village. Without refrigeration, food had to be gathered daily; but that was a satisfying activity, and the food was fresh and chemical free.

It was frustrating to be so isolated by the barrier of language. Hand signals and smiles transmit only the most basic of information. I love charades as a game, but not as a way of life. I couldn't even ask important questions like "How is the fishing?" or "Are there jag-uars?" I was happy finally to hear a plane in the distance. Now one of the arrival committee, I scampered along with the other villagers to the airstrip and welcomed the crew.

After the CBC gang arrived, I had to write and memorize a couple of stand-ups while Juneia arranged for the Kaiapo women to perform a dance sequence in the clearing. It was a spectacular sight as the women, naked and painted from head to foot, chanted and danced in unison. At one point I looked over at Paiakan and realized he was directing them with hand signals. We interviewed Paiakan on-camera, asking him why he had moved his people here and what the forest meant to him, as Juneia translated his Portuguese for us. He was eloquent, and it was a very productive shoot.

Then Paiakan sat down with Juneia to talk to me about his plans to fight the dams. He asked me for help in raising money to take different tribe members to Altamira and to build the traditional village on the dam site. I had no choice but to promise I'd do the best I could. But if I were to raise funds, I realized a key question was: would he be willing to come to Canada himself? His presence would make all the differ-ence. Si: he would come.

Soon we were on our way out of the village, crossing a sea of green that extended as far as we could see on both sides of the plane. I vowed I would return for a longer stay. After nearly an hour, we began to see thin wisps of smoke, clearings, and huts and eventually landed near Redenção, the nearest settlement, which would have taken thirteen days to reach if we had canoed.

As soon as I could, I phoned Tara. She says I had a catch in my throat as I related the threats to the forest. "You have to do some-thing!" I told her. When she asked what, I told her about the Kaiapo and their charismatic leader, describing Paiakan's plan, his need for funds, and his promise to come to Canada to help raise money and the profile of the issues.

Kaiapo girls in Aucre before a *festa*

As I continued on my way for the remaining five weeks of the shoot, Tara sprang into action in Canada, organizing events in Toronto and Ottawa. In 1988, the Amazon was a hot topic. The scale of its destruction was on everyone's lips. With luck, Paiakan's visit would fuel public and press interest.

People were quick to lend a hand. In Toronto, Monte Hummel and the World Wildlife Fund offered support for a fund-raising event, and in Ottawa, Elizabeth May, who was now with the Sierra Club and had first rocketed into prominence fighting logging in Cape Breton, promised the same. Soon great plans were afoot.

The Amazon rain forest is immense. Although the ecosystem has been assaulted for decades by gold miners, loggers, peasants, and ranchers, most of it remains intact. As roads increase, however, at some point the integrity of the forest may become so diminished that it will no longer support its biodiversity.

On our shoot, we visited immense coal-mining operations where huge holes appeared in the forest. We visited the Balbina dam, which had flooded eight hundred square miles of forest and driven two tribes close to extinction, drowning untold numbers of animals and plants, yet silted up so rapidly that it was soon abandoned. A road through the forest is the greatest threat because it brings with it a flood of the landless poor, desperate to make a living and willing to destroy the forest to gain it. We interviewed representatives of the World Bank and the Inter-American Development Bank, who justified the need for roads to carry economic development into remote parts of Brazil.

After I left Brazil to return to Canada, our crew remained to interview Chico Mendes, the charismatic rubber tapper who had galvanized his cohorts to fight to protect the forest. Two weeks after we interviewed him, he was murdered. During the 1980s, over a thousand activists, including Mendes, Indians, and many Catholic priests, had been murdered in Brazil with impunity. But the murder of Chico

Mendes backfired. In death, Mendes's fame grew: he became a martyr, a worldwide symbol of the consequences of corruption underlying the destruction of the Amazon.

ON OCTOBER 14, 1988, Paiakan and Kube-i were to be tried for their visit to Washington. I flew down to Belém to witness the trial. The courthouse was ringed with young soldiers armed with rifles, pistols, shields, bulletproof vests, and clubs. Buses rolled up and out stepped hundreds of Kaiapo warriors in feathers and paint, carrying sticks, clubs, and bows and arrows. These men lined up in rows six abreast and advanced on the courthouse, beating the sticks rhythmically, marching in unison to their chants and periodic grunts. When they reached the soldiers, they lined up. Each warrior faced a soldier, menacingly staring him in the eye. The soldiers looked straight ahead, but if I had been one of them, I would have wet my pants.

Paiakan and Kube-i then gave speeches outside the courthouse, as the warriors gathered round them and sat down. An old Kaiapo woman began to scream at the warriors. Darrell Posey translated some of what she said: "I call upon you to take up arms, to kill the whites, slaughter them! I'm coming here to speak to you, to call upon you in the name of your mothers and your fathers, all of us older people. I'm calling upon you! I throw my words in your faces. Have I come in vain? You sit here while the whites are crushing us." The men sat there with their heads bowed. The same woman then turned to the soldiers ringing the courthouse and told them: "I am here to speak my anger at you! I am enraged with you. You sit there drawing maps of our land to steal it. But I tell you, we're going to beat you soundly in defence of our land!" Kaiapo women are truly ferocious.

Paiakan and Kube-i mounted the steps to enter the courthouse but were blocked for being "seminude." The judge ruled that they must dress to show respect for Brazilian law. When Kubei-i replied that they were dressed in respectful traditional attire, which gave them power, the judge said they must follow Brazilian formalities and should strive to become Brazilians. Darrell Posey muttered to me, "That would be genocide."

When the court wouldn't budge, Paiakan simply told the warriors they were leaving. He said that if the government wanted to try them, it would have to go to Aucre and get them. The Kaiapo men threw their drumming sticks onto the road, boarded the buses, and left without any interference from the soldiers. I picked up two sticks, which I still have as souvenirs of that encounter.

But no government officials would dare try to fly into the remote village, where they would be completely vulnerable. The case was eventually dropped because of the absurdity of the original charges.

PROTECTING PAIAKAN'S
FOREST HOME

I N   F E B R U A R Y   1 9 8 9 , we had arranged for air
tickets so that Paiakan could come to North
America. After a brief stop in Chicago, where he was a guest of Terry
Turner, a physical anthropologist at the University of Chicago, Paiakan
flew to Toronto for our concert to raise funds for the protest to be
staged at Altamira. Our translator was Barbara Zimmerman, a young
Canadian herpetologist who was working in the Amazon.

Tara had an audacious idea—why not invite the major multinational companies that did business in the Amazon to attend a reception before the concert to meet Paiakan in person and, in return, to
donate a thousand dollars? We would be asking companies that were
destroying the rain forest to give money to someone fighting to protect
it. We drew up a list of eighteen companies, from American Express to
the Bank of Japan, and I called the Toronto head of each company to
extend the invitation.

The Toronto reception was a gala event. The Elmwood Club
donated its elegant premises and exquisite Thai food. The CBC filmed
the arrival of the hosts—me, Paiakan, the Canadian writer Margaret
Atwood, and Gordon Lightfoot—and the well-heeled guests. Of the

eighteen companies, all but one sent a representative with a check. In one hour, we raised $16,500. That was a lot in the eighties. The only exception was the Bank of Japan. I had called the president, identified myself, and said, "I understand you have interests in Brazil and thought you would like to meet an Indian leader from the Amazon." After a considerable pause, he replied, "We have interests in Brazil, but we do not have interest in Indians."

The main event that night was the concert at St. Paul's Cathedral on Bloor Street. Dozens of volunteers had put up posters advertising it; when we got to the church, I was astounded to see a lineup extending around the block. More than three thousand people jammed that church, and the atmosphere was electric. A stellar list of people had agreed to appear: Margaret Atwood read a poem, and Gordon Lightfoot and a hot a cappella group, the Nylons, sang. The World Wildlife Fund had the terrific idea of selling certificates to "Guardians of the Rainforest" for twenty dollars a pop.

Ojibwa drummers sang, and then Gladys Kidd, an Ojibwa elder, addressed the crowd but looked directly at Paiakan: "The terrible thing that's happening is what we call raping the Earth. We had that happen here to us too. We do the best we can. I say that to you because I feel with my heart how it must be for you. The animals can live without us, but we cannot live without the animals. Give strength to one another, to our Kaiapo brothers, in your prayers tonight. In all the hall today you see the change come that they too can have peace in their hearts towards what is happening to them now—it will not happen if they work together. Meegwetch."

Paiakan appeared onstage in a shirt and pants, but his face was painted and he wore a brilliantly colored feather headdress. He looked spectacular. The grand room went silent as he spoke about his forest home, which had supported his people for so long; the threat the dam posed, and his need for our help. It was an incredible evening, and when it was over, we had raised more than $50,000.

We went on the next day to Ottawa and another gala event. Elizabeth May gave a brilliant speech, and once more Gordon Lightfoot performed. This time, he promised Paiakan he would go to the Amazon and sing for him. In Ottawa we also could try to exert pressure on government. Canada was a voting member of the World Bank, and we wanted our delegate, federal finance minister Michael Wilson, to vote against World Bank loans for destructive projects such as the dam.

At a press conference with Paiakan, a reporter asked, "Why do you wear feathers and paint?" Paiakan calmly retorted, "Why are you wearing a tie?" He knew what he was doing. The *Globe and Mail* in Toronto, the *Ottawa Citizen,* and the *Toronto Star* newspapers all featured color photos on their front pages. Michael Wilson got the message—he later told people he had received more mail and calls about the Amazon and World Bank loans than about any other issue in which he was involved. The Canadian public had responded magnificently.

By the time Paiakan left, after only a couple of days in Canada, we had raised $70,000. Cynics might say it was just the novelty and glamor of an Indian from the Amazon that prompted such support, or merely a response to assuage our own guilt about what we had done to First Nations. If that is true, I don't have a problem with it. But I also think the notion of the great rain forest filled with amazing creatures and people lifted our spirits and made us want to be part of its protection.

The Nature of Things program was broadcast as a two-hour special entitled "Amazonas—The Road to the End of the Forest," and it garnered a huge audience. The public's concern about the issue was building. Now the Altamira dam showdown was looming, and Tara began the difficult task of arranging our own trip all the way to Altamira, a frontier town deep in the Xingu valley of the Amazon. But Paiakan's visit had created enormous interest in the battle, and soon people were calling us to see whether we were going and then asking whether they could tag along. Before she knew it, Tara was juggling the logistics of travel, housing, malaria pills, shots, lists of what to take and wear—an enormous undertaking—for forty people! One of her priorities was to learn Portuguese to be able to pull the trip off.

We had a virtual who's who of the Canadian environmental movement traveling with us, including Elizabeth May of the Sierra Club, Peggy Dover of the World Wildlife Fund, Paul Watson of the Sea Shepherd Conservation Society, Jeff Gibbs of the Environmental Youth Alliance, Peggy Hallward of Energy Probe, Gordon Lightfoot making good on his promise, Guujaaw of Haida Gwaii, and Simon Dick, a Kwagiulth from Kingcome Inlet.

The British Columbia contingent flew to Toronto, where we met up with the eastern folk. At the airport we also met Rosie Mosquito, an Ojibwa-Cree from northern Ontario, and when we changed our plane in Miami, we were joined by Phil Awashish, the Quebec Cree who had become a hero when he learned of and sounded the alarm about Hydro-Quebec's plan to flood Cree territory.

We flew into Manaus, the Amazonian town that had flourished during the rubber boom early in the last century. We landed in the middle of the night and took taxis to our inexpensive hotel downtown, where we registered two to a room. We were all exhausted, but I was so impressed with Gordon Lightfoot. Here was a superstar who had his own jet to fly from gig to gig. I am sure he was accustomed to going to the airport in a limo and used to being taken care of, but here he was, one of the gang. A young man said to him, "Gord, you're bunking with so-and-so and there's your bag and here's your key," and Gordon hauled his luggage without complaint.

The next morning, Tara had arranged for us to visit the research station where Tom Lovejoy had studied the effect of forest area on the maintenance of biodiversity. It was called the Forest Fragments Project, a collaboration between the Smithsonian Institution in Washington, D.C., and Brazil's Insititute for Research in the Amazon. Lovejoy had made an inventory of the plant and animal species in plots of intact forest of one hectare, ten hectares, a hundred hectares, a thousand hectares, and ten thousand hectares, surrounded by cleared land, and then followed their fate over time. He found there was a direct correlation between size and biodiversity—the smaller the area, the fewer the surviving species—and that the rate of loss was inversely proportional—the smaller the plot, the faster the loss of species. His studies demonstrated that if biodiversity is to be maintained, very large tracts of wilderness must be preserved.

Our plan was to visit the lab site and stay overnight. An open truck picked us up as arranged and took us the fifty miles into the forest to the trail leading to the camp. As we entered the great Amazon forest, the impact of the road's existence became clear—it was a slash of dried red mud that animals, including birds, were reluctant to cross because they would be exposed and vulnerable; roads can be barriers to wildlife movement as much as fences are. And creeks were simply plowed through. As we wound along the road, it began to rain, a tropical torrent, and soon the truck was slipping and sliding up and down the hills as if we were on a carnival ride. Eventually we had to abandon the vehicle and walk. The rain was so intense that it drove straight through Tara's umbrella, to everyone's amusement.

Finally we reached the campsite. Our dreams of putting our clothes in a dryer were dashed. All we found was a concrete pad with a thatched roof and hammocks strung under that. Luckily a tarp covered a kitchen area, where a cook fed us caipirinhas (a delicious rum drink) and a magnificent meal of rice and tambaki, a large fish that eats nuts that fall into the water from the trees. I went out along a trail with my fishing rod and caught a couple of small fish, which I let go.

After dinner, Simon and Guujaaw picked up a plastic dishpan and thanked the cook by beating out a rhythm and singing feast songs from the coast of British Columbia. Several of the station's researchers joined us, including Barb Zimmerman, our Toronto translator and an expert on amphibians and reptiles, who had suggested the station trip in the first place. She took a group of us out late at night to look for frogs. It was very dark, and we shared tiny flashlights as we slipped and fell and cursed along the trail.

Barb was really impressive, finding the tiniest frogs on tree trunks and under fronds, but when asked about a bird that squawked away when we came along, or an epiphytic plant on a tree, her answer was, "Don't ask me, I'm a herpetologist." The reductionism of science demands this. But when I was in Aucre, every time I asked Paiakan about an insect, fish, or plant, he had a name for it and could tell a story about it.

From Manaus we flew to Belém. En route we spied a newspaper with a picture of Paiakan in a hospital bed! Had the gathering at Altamira been derailed by violence? Tara grabbed the paper and determined that Paiakan had appendicitis; he still intended to appear.

Our flight to Altamira was scheduled for 4:00 AM. Unknown to us, the airline was heavily overbooked because so many journalists wanted to go to the unprecedented protest at Altamira. We had reservations, but when all forty of us showed up more than three hours early, we were told there were only three seats left and the plane would take off as soon as it was full—two hours ahead of the scheduled time. I learned then that yelling in anger doesn't get you anywhere in Brazil. The people behind the desk simply melt away, leaving you fuming by yourself. I was devastated—all that planning, and here we were stuck in the Amazon. And only Tara spoke Portuguese.

It was decided that Rosie Mosquito, Gordon Lightfoot, and I would take the three remaining seats and Tara would try to charter a plane for the rest. As we flew off, I was sure I wouldn't see Tara again till I got back to Canada. After we had checked into our hotel and unpacked our luggage, I went downstairs and to my astonishment found Tara and the rest of the gang checking in. After we had left at two in the morning, Tara had found out where aircraft could be chartered, negotiated two small planes for thirty-seven people, collected the money from the gang for it, and landed in Altamira right on our heels. Her gift with language had paid off in spades.

Gordon Lightfoot and me on our way to the research station near Manaus

When we arrived at Altamira, everyone was abuzz with the news about Paiakan's emergency appendectomy only days before. I was sure that without him, the protest gathering could not possibly succeed. To our relief, he was there at the opening—gray and weak but still clearly the leader. He wore a striking headdress made of dark-red and blue feathers as he barked orders. It was a huge event, with some six hundred Kaiapo representatives and forty other tribes; hundreds of Brazilians, from officials at Eletronorte, the power company proposing to build the dam, to the National Indian Foundation (FUNAI), the Brazilian government organization for Indians; environmentalists and reporters from around the world, and hundreds of armed soldiers ringing the walls inside the building

The media were in a frenzy. Everything was so exotic that photographers and camera operators couldn't miss—just point and shoot. Each tribe of Indians wore its own characteristic patterns of body paint and headdresses of feathers, leaves, and grass. The meeting took place in a large building with a dirt floor covered in palm fronds. Soldiers in full gear lined the walls, and the various tribes sat on the floor in front of a large head table raised on a dais. After pouring in tribe by tribe with rhythmic chants that raised the roof, the Indians covered three-quarters of the floor in a large horseshoe around the table, and the onlookers, including us, and the media occupied the space between the Indians and soldiers.

Within the great hall, the officials from government and Eletronorte presented and rationalized their plans for Plano 2010 and the dams as best they could, but they were confronted with angry Indians and their Brazilian supporters including unions, rubber tappers, and human-rights organizations. An electric moment that no one who was there will forget occurred while an Eletronorte official was speaking: an elderly Kaiapo woman jumped to her feet, waved a machete, and began to harangue the Kaiapo warriors. I later learned she had asked whether the men there were fighters, and if they were, why didn't they kill these people who were oppressing them?

Even though I couldn't understand a word of her speech, it was clear that she was furious and was whipping the crowd up. The tension was unbearable; we bystanders were all very aware that we would be caught in any crossfire if violence or shooting broke out. To punctuate her remarks, the woman walked up to the head table, raised her machete at the Eletronorte official, and slapped his cheek with its flat side. A yell went up as the soldiers raised their weapons.

To his credit, the official didn't move a muscle. In the heat of that moment, I looked over at Tara and pointed to the floor; if violence broke out, we sure wouldn't make it to the doors. Paiakan exhibited his superb leadership skills as he stood slowly and held out his arms. Speaking softly and carefully, he calmed the heated crowd and eased the tension by saying that the woman's dramatic act was not aggression but theatrics.

To minimize contact with non-Indians and therefore reduce the chance that indigenous peoples would pick up a disease, a traditional village was built in the forest far outside town. Paiakan invited the Canadians to visit the village one night. It was wonderful. We were fed traditional food cooked on fires, and Guujaaw and Simon created a sensation when they appeared in full First Nations regalia, dancing, drumming, and singing.

I vividly remember the attendance of Pombo, a chief who went on to a political career in the Brazilian parliament but who died only a few years later. He had a headdress that resembled a woman's swim cap covered in feathers, and he gave it to Simon as we left. Raoni, the chief befriended by the English singer Sting, with the striking labret in his lower lip, was at the fireside along with Paiakan.

At one point, Simon brought out a bow and arrow, and when he raised it, the onlookers gasped; it was an aggressive act to raise a bow

One of the tribes at the Altamira demonstration

thus. When Simon let fly, I thought of all the people in the rest of the village who might be punctured by an errant arrow. Thunk! It went into a branch. Everyone in the group gave an appreciative grunt, while I exhaled in relief.

Simon and Guujaaw, two of the most outstanding First Nations traditional singers and dancers in all of B.C., wore carved masks on their heads and performed in front of Amazonian chiefs and warriors, who sat riveted. Guujaaw's face was streaked with black, and he wore a heavy animal fur. As he sang and drummed, sweat poured down his· face and body in the humidity. Later I met Simon standing in the shadows, tears running down his cheeks; this incredible contact had touched something deep within. He said his life had been transformed by that night.

Sting was scheduled to appear in solidarity with Raoni. All this excitement was the biggest thing ever to happen in Altamira. The rock star, a friendly man, stayed at the same two-bit hotel as our contingent.

Young girls waited outside for him, and when they spotted Jeff Gibbs, a tall, gangly young man from Vancouver, they'd scream, "Stingee! Stingee!" and surround him, begging for his autograph. Jeff happily signed for Sting, a huge smile on his face.

The event was a sensational success for Paiakan. It was raining the day the meetings ended, but when the tribes emerged from the building to dance and sing, the rain stopped and a rainbow spread across the sky. Even the most jaded reporter surely felt it was an auspicious sign. In celebration, the local men performed a special corn-planting dance outdoors.

The meeting was reported around the world, and under pressure from many countries, including Canada, the World Bank pulled its support from Plano 2010, bringing it to an end. Although the Amazon and Kaiapo territory remained under siege on many fronts, one threat, at least, had been defeated. After the meeting, Paiakan took off his headdress, which his mother had made for him, and gave it to me. It is another of my most prized possessions.

Because of his tremendous visibility and the success of the demonstration, Paiakan had been receiving death threats daily while in Altamira. We knew that in Brazil union leaders, Indians, and religious and civil-rights activists had been murdered with impunity. While in Altamira, Tara and I met late at night with a handful of trusted Brazilians concerned that Paiakan's life was in jeopardy. It seemed surreal; the death threats were serious, and here we were, coolly discussing ways to avoid Paiakan's assassination.

I marveled at the courage of the Brazilians present, who were surely putting their own lives in jeopardy by supporting Paiakan, while Paiakan himself showed no signs of fear or backing down. As long as he remained in Aucre, he would be safe, because the only way in was by plane on a tiny airstrip completely vulnerable to Kaiapo warriors. But in Aucre he also would be isolated. We spoke of setting up a fund so that when he needed to get out to Brasília or to travel abroad, he could call in a plane.

Press conference at Altamira. That's Sting standing, Paiakan seated looking up, and Simon
Dick in full regalia behind him.

Paiakan saying farewell to Tara and me at the Altamira airport

In the end, it was decided that Paiakan needed to get out of the country so that things could cool down. We asked him where he would like to go. "To Canada, to stay with you and Tara," was his reply.

WITHIN DAYS OF OUR return to Vancouver in March 1989, Paiakan arrived with Irekran and their three daughters, Oe, Tania, and baby Majal. Their body paint had faded, but the girls' heads still had a tri-angle of shaved hair, just growing in. In the chilly night temperature we had taken to the Vancouver airport clothing we had gathered from friends, but Paiakan refused to let his family wear anything used. Tara and I had prepared an apartment in the basement of our house for the family. But when Paiakan found out that the sheets were not new, he said they wouldn't sleep in the beds; our diseases were a very real haz-ard for them. New clothes and sheets became our first priority.

We had set a fire in the fireplace, and once the family was settled, we went downstairs to visit. We discovered that the little girls had

Demonstrating the headdress given to me by Paiakan at Altamira

dragged coals out of the hearth onto the bare wooden floor and were playing with them; we explained that wooden floors are different from dirt. When my father-in-law, Harry, went out the next morning for his usual early walk, he found the downstairs kitchen door wide open, one of the stove's burners red-hot, the television on, and all the lights blazing, but everyone apparently in bed.

Irekran and the girls spoke only Kaiapo, so all of our communication was through Tara and Paiakan speaking Portuguese. Paiakan's daughters and our girls got along famously, each learning many words and songs in the other's language. I have a vivid memory of Oe and Tania pedaling tricycles furiously along the sidewalks, Severn and Sarika running madly after them. I'd built our girls a playhouse high in the dogwood tree in the backyard, and Oe and Tania loved it, playing there for hours. They easily took to dressing up; we'd find Sari, Oe, and Tania sitting laughing in tiaras in the shower stall. Sarika took Oe and Tania to school with her as the best show-and-tell she'd ever come up with.

The whole family loved the killer whales then on display at the Vancouver Aquarium and returned again and again—six times in all—to gaze at those magnificent animals through windows that gave the public an underwater view from inches away. But our visitors' likes and dislikes were unpredictable. We took the family up Mount Hollyburn just outside the city, and while Irekran and the girls loved tobogganing and playing with snow for the first time, Paiakan sat in the car and smoked cigarettes.

The girls loved the sea and waded straight into it (in March!), but Paiakan and his wife always sat with their backs to it, which puzzled me. Then one day, as we were driving, our car drew alongside a wild river. All five of Paiakan's family flung themselves at the windows, everyone talking at once, pointing out the river's features in a flurry of excitement.

Oe *(left)* and Tania *(right)* with Sarika playing dress-up in the shower

We arranged for translators and took the family to visit as many different First Nations as we could. The first place we visited was Tofino, on Vancouver Island, where the Nuu-chah-nulth people were holding a meeting. As we flew across the island in a small seaplane, I pointed out the extent of clear-cutting below to show Paiakan we had our forest battles too. Gradually I realized he and Irekran weren't listening to me but were staring straight ahead, clearly uncomfortable. In the Amazon, it turns out, some pilots fly very close to the forest canopy; if there is a mechanical failure and there are no clearings to set down in, the plane can crash-land on the trees. Paiakan had survived three such crashes. But over Vancouver Island, we were flying very high to avoid the mountains, a couple of them more than seven thousand feet high. When Paiakan and Irekran looked down, they saw a lot of snow and rocks—not a very welcoming surface. After we finally landed, Paiakan announced, "Chiefs don't fly in small planes," which was baloney, but I wasn't going to argue. We ended up having to take a long bus ride and a ferry trip to return to Vancouver.

In Tofino, Paiakan was feted like a relative by the Nuu-chah-nulth. As he spoke through the translator about the struggle to protect his territories, you could have heard a pin drop. These were far from wealthy people, yet they collected thousands of dollars to help their brother from the Amazon. One old man hunted around in one of his pockets and finally came up with a hundred-dollar bill folded into a small square and obviously carefully saved for a long while. "He really needs it," was all he said as he threw it into a pot. Canadian First Nations people understood that the Kaiapo were going through what their own people had suffered and felt an instant bond with them.

At our cottage on Quadra Island in the Strait of Georgia, I showed them how we dig clams. Irekran and Paiakan loved looking for clams as a kind of game, but when I broke one open and ate it raw, they were revolted and lost interest in clamming. They wanted to eat only what they were familiar with—chicken, white-fleshed river fish, beans, farinha, rice, and bread, which they loved toasted. When we fed them halibut, they found the taste and texture a satisfactory substitute for freshwater white-fleshed fish.

But when we caught a small halibut on a fishing trip with a group of First Nations leaders, Paiakan was appalled. He'd never seen a flat fish, with both eyes on the top of its head, and found it monstrous—ugly and unappetizing. When I told him that was what he'd been eating, he never touched halibut again. At first, he and his family wouldn't eat salmon, either—too red.

Paiakan often surprised us. On one trip, we were driving up Vancouver Island toward Port Hardy and spotted a huge plume of smoke. As we drew nearer, we could see that an area of forest had been clearcut and the slash gathered into massive piles and set alight. Paiakan remarked, "Just like Brazil." Another time, having flown over large areas of clear-cut that were covered in snow and visible as a checker-board pattern from the plane, he said, "Brazilians destroy the forest because they are poor and uneducated. Why do Canadians?" When he first settled in our house, I drove him through downtown Vancouver, figuring he would be impressed with the cleanliness of the streets, the gleaming buildings, and the stores filled with goods. His response was unexpected: "To think all this comes from the Earth. How long can it go on?"

We took him to Alert Bay, home of the Kwakwaka'wakw people. On the ferry from Port McNeill on Vancouver Island to Alert Bay on Cormorant Island, several Kwakwaka'wakw kids kept coming by to look at Paiakan and shyly ask us who he was and where he was from. They could see he was an Indian, but he looked unlike any they knew. The boys were typical modern First Nations kids, dressed in jeans and runners with caps on backwards, and Paiakan imperiously ignored them. It seemed he could see that these youngsters were what the Kaiapo could become, and he did not like it.

When we arrrived at the ferry terminal in Alert Bay, we were met by Kwakwaka'wakw dancers in full regalia and led by our friend Vera Newman. We were feted in the spectacular communal "big house" and were again showered with gifts of money. (When I visit Alert Bay now, more than fifteen years later, people still ask about Paiakan.) We traveled to Haida Gwaii, where Paiakan was taken out on *Lootaas*, the canoe that was paddled from Vancouver to Haida Gwaii during the battle to save South Moresby. Everywhere we went, Paiakan made an indelible impression with his impassioned and articulate plea for help in protecting his forest home.

About three weeks after the family arrived, Irekran, a very severe-looking, imperious young woman, called our names and motioned us to approach. Paiakan translated: "Our children should be in Aucre studying. It's cold here. I miss my family. You promised to get us an airplane. Where is it?" Tara and I were nonplussed. Airplane? Where had she got that idea? As we racked our brains, we realized that back in Altamira, when we had gathered to discuss what to do about the death threats, one idea put forward was to establish a fund for Paiakan to use whenever he needed a plane to leave the village. Irekran must have interpreted this as a promise to buy a plane. To her, it appeared as if we just plunked down money whenever we wanted anything. A plane must have seemed a reasonable demand.

It so happened that I was scheduled to go to England the following week. There I called Anita Roddick, creator of the Body Shop empire, who had attended the Altamira gathering, met Paiakan, and been impressed by him. I told her about Irekran's demand, explaining that having a plane permanently available at Aucre would allow Paiakan to remain in touch and effective from the safety of the village but would have many other uses. It could be used to survey and police the vast area of Kaiapo territory, and it could transfer sick people and elders when needed. Anita had just had a meeting with her shop franchisees, where she had talked about Paiakan and his struggle, and the delegates had donated money from their own profits. Anita wrote us a check for US$100,000.

Toward the end of the family's stay with us, the ever-supportive gang at the Western Canada Wilderness Committee printed thousands of copies of a paper devoted to Paiakan and the issues in the Amazon. We joined with them and the Environmental Youth Alliance to hold several packed events at high school auditoriums. We all gave rousing speeches, and in the end, Haida leader Guujaaw got up to drum and sing and invited Oe and Tania and Severn and Sarika to accompany him. These wonderful events helped to raise more money for Paiakan's work.

After six weeks of living with us, Paiakan and his family decided it was safe to return home. They had raised thousands of dollars, made contacts with aboriginal "relatives" up and down the west coast of Canada, and would return with the promise of a plane soon to follow.

When we arrived at the airport, it seemed we had lived through a lifetime together, and to my surprise, Irekran began to weep inconsolably. In their society, there is a ritual kind of wailing that I had seen when Paiakan was welcomed home and when we witnessed a funeral, but this was different; I felt she really was sorry to leave us. We were soon all reduced to tears.

"Come and visit us," Paiakan begged, and we decided that would be a wonderful adventure. So we wished them well and promised we would travel down soon.

Meanwhile, in Canada, Tara discovered there was a whole catalog of used planes around the world and determined that a Cessna seemed the best choice. She also found a pilot named Al "Jet" Johnson, who had flown for decades with American Airlines, lived in Vancouver, and was a close friend of Sea Shepherd Conservation Society founder Paul Watson, who had gone to Altamira.

Tara contacted Al, and he offered to check a used plane we had found in Galveston, Texas. He reported that the Cessna Utility 206 was in good shape. It cost $50,000, which would leave enough to ensure a proper maintenance schedule. He recommended we buy it and have the seats pulled out so that extra gas tanks could be installed, and he would fly it to Brazil for us. Al is a true hero. In full hurricane season, he hopped and skipped across the Caribbean and along the north coast of South America, phoning in his adventures from cheap hotels in Guyana or Suriname. After navigating the plane through Brazilian authorities, he piloted it for Paiakan and the village for several months before finally returning to Canada.

A STEP BACK
IN TIME

TARA AND I DECIDED to go to Aucre the following summer. We believed Paiakan's invitation
was sincere, and the children already had a lot of wilderness experience
and were keen to go. But I was also worried. After all, Sarika was only
seven and Severn was ten—what if something happened to them? We
would be so far away from help. I knew Tara was as concerned as I
was, but she expressed only excitement and enthusiastically went about
arranging the myriad details of the trip. Our Haida friend Miles Richardson decided to join us, along with his girlfriend, Patricia Kelly, from
Chilliwack in the Fraser Valley, east of Vancouver.

After the Altamira protests, the Brazilian government was worried about troublemakers who might make contact with Indians and
get them all stirred up. We heard an edict might have been passed
requiring anyone wanting to visit an Indian village to first apply for
permission. We knew we would never be approved, so we decided to
ignore it and go in without official permission. We flew to Redenção,
a rough-and-ready frontier town where we had to find the plane we
had bought and a pilot to fly it.

The pilot we found flew us across the river and then mysteri-
ously landed the plane on a road, where he got out and walked away.
He reappeared with his girlfriend, who made one more person than
the aircraft could handle, so one of us had to be let off. Miles gallantly
offered to stay behind in Redenção, and although the pilot promised
to pick him up the next day, it was a pretty courageous decision. I had
flown into Aucre not speaking a word of Portuguese, but at least I
had Paiakan as a friend; Miles knew no one and ended up using
sign language to the few Indians who were around. He reached the
village, found a place to stay, had a meal, and got back out to meet the
plane next day.

After we left Miles, we flew over a sea of unbroken green for almost
an hour before an opening in the forest canopy appeared, revealing
the circle of huts I had visited just under a year before. We were a
great curiosity to the Kaiapo, especially our two daughters. Two
young boys hauled our bags as we were led to an empty hut and told
we could hang our hammocks there. When it became clear that we
didn't have a clue how to hang a hammock, the villagers dissolved in
laughter. It was the first of many amusements our ignorance provided
the community.

Like all the other huts, the one that was to be our home for two
weeks was made of mud plastered between vertical sticks and had a
thatched roof. The floor was dirt, and soon everything was covered in
a layer of red dust. The children, most of them naked except for strings
of beads around their necks, wrists, and ankles, crowded around to
watch our every move as we unpacked our bags.

Soon we were invited to Paiakan's hut, which was next to ours, and
treated to a meal of fish, beans, and rice. Sev and Sarika were happy to
be back with their friends Oe and Tania, who took them out to see the
river nearby. We learned to spend hours in that pool during the heat
of the day and never once even felt a piranha; Paiakan assured us

these fish were only a problem if water levels dropped—and they are delicious to boot.

We went to sleep that night refreshed by dips in the river, well fed, and only anxious for Miles to join us, which he did next morning. We had brought mosquito nets to wrap around the hammocks, as well as light sleeping bags for the early morning cold. After a couple of days of struggling with the netting, we gave up, as there weren't a lot of mosquitoes and Paiakan assured us it was the farmers and miners from cities who brought the malaria with them.

Each morning we woke up to find a row of faces staring at us. Children (and sometimes adults) would sit along the walls just watching—I guess we were their equivalent to early morning cartoons. All of our possessions were on the ground or in open bags and we never lost a thing, though we had many coveted items; everyone was delighted when we gave away much of our stuff before we left because it was too heavy for the plane.

We had to gather fresh food every day, a great experience for us because that meant we spent most of our time fishing. The first day, Paiakan took only Miles and me on a fishing expedition in the dugout canoe. But the females in our gang were very unhappy and demanded they be included. From then on, they were, although none of the women from the village accompanied us.

The Kaiapo were amused by my collapsible rod and tiny Seiko reel with four-pound test line, because my fishing gear was too light for the fish I might hook. I figured I'd show them; after all, a good fisherman is supposed to be able to land huge fish by playing them to exhaustion. On our first trip, I assembled the rod, put on a spinner, and cast into the murky water. *Blam, ping.* A fish hit and snapped the line. The tension was too tight, so I adjusted it, tied on another spinner, and cast—*blam, ping:* same thing. Hmm. The Kaiapos' eyes were crinkling in amusement, and when I cast for the third time and the same thing happened, the Kaiapo were roaring. Thank goodness they didn't know how to say in English "I told you so." So much for "civilized" technology, although they themselves did use nylon lines and metal hooks.

When I finally hooked a tucunare, that incredible fighting fish snapped my rod in two! I wasn't going to let it get away and began pulling in the line by hand, when wham, an arrow impaled my catch right behind the gills. I was too busy fighting the fish and hadn't noticed Paiakan as he raised his bow and shot an arrow. As far as I was concerned, I caught the fish . . . well, I hooked it, anyway.

Each time we made a trip, Paiakan took along Caro, a boy of about six. Caro would hand tools to Paiakan, jump out of the canoe to pull it to shore, or follow him into the forest to gather bait. He was obviously being taught in the very best way.

The river, Rio Zinho, was a wonder, narrowing to a swiftly flowing channel, widening out into long, deep pools, or becoming shallow with long riffles, each area containing a different array of fish. One day we paddled down the river to a wide, shallow area with rocks sticking out of the water. Paiakan got out with his bow and very long arrows. He carefully walked from rock to rock, staring into the clear water, and finally shot. The arrow had struck something. It waved about until eventually Paiakan carefully lifted an immense, snakelike fish from the water. It was an electric eel, capable of delivering a hefty electrical wallop that could be fatal to a small child.

Paiakan clubbed it repeatedly, then, making sure it didn't touch him or any of us, laid it in the bottom of the canoe. I don't know how long the dead animal takes to discharge its biobatteries, but it was quite a while before Paiakan touched it. The fish must have been close to six feet in length and four inches in diameter, and when Paiakan cut into it, I saw the flesh was milky white. Apparently it is a highly prized delicacy, but we didn't try any as it was divided among the elders of the village.

Paiakan *(right)* lifting an electric eel while Mokuka dispatches another one.
That's me on the top left, with Caro.

On one trip upriver, we came to a large, deep pool that must have been a hundred yards long and perhaps ten or more feet deep. We couldn't see the bottom. Paiakan drove the canoe into reeds along the bank and leaped out, accompanied by Caro. After a few minutes of thrashing and splashing, they emerged with a string of fish, each about six inches long. These, it turned out, would be the bait. They tied sixteen-foot lengths of thick line, with a large hook on one end of each, around pieces of wood that would act as floats. As we pushed off, Paiakan hooked a fish on each line and tossed the floats into the water as we continued upriver.

Hours later, on our way home, we came back through the pool and saw several of the floats buzzing around as if they were motorized. Beautiful catfish were hooked on the lines. And they too were delicious.

One of our longest trips was an all-day venture downriver. We would pull ashore to eat and then drift down. Paiakan had a small

motor on his boat but only a tiny can of fuel, and I worried about getting back upriver. At one point, we were caught in a tropical squall, and
we pulled in to a bank and huddled together while Paiakan cut down
several huge banana-like leaves to hold over our heads as umbrellas
until the rain passed.

For dinner, we got a fire going and Paiakan cut up a big tucunare
we had caught and put the pieces onto a large leaf. He squeezed a lemon
over them, put on some salt, then wrapped the leaf around the fish and
tossed it into the fire. Half an hour later, he opened the leaf to reveal a
steaming meal that was absolutely delectable. I told Paiakan that where
we came from, people would work for years to save enough money to
take a trip to spend two weeks doing what he and his people do every
day. He seemed amused, if not confused.

On our way back, as I had suspected it might, fuel became a real
concern. Here at the equator we were soon enveloped in the black of
night with a couple of flashlights whose batteries could go flat at any
time. As we putt-putted against the current, those flashlights reflected
off eyes in the shallows—crocodiles! Everywhere. Fortunately, this
particular species is quite timid with people. Miles has a great dislike
of snakes, and we'd heard of the giant anacondas lurking in the rivers.
Whenever we had to get out of the canoe in shallow, rocky stretches to
push the boat along, I felt bad for Miles, but he never complained.

We alternated between pushing and putt-putting along until we
finally ran out of fuel and had to paddle. Paiakan kept unnerving us by
gazing intently ahead and saying in Portuguese, "What happened to
the village?" There were no bright lights or search parties to greet us
when we finally turned a bend and recognized our swimming hole. It
had been a wonderful adventure, but I sure was glad to be back in our
hut, which had become home.

On one trip, we traveled far down the river to a place where sand-
bars arose in the water. We beached the canoe and Paiakan showed us

how to recognize places where turtles had laid their eggs. For my girls it was like an Easter egg hunt, and they scrambled along the sand looking for the telltale signs and digging deep down to find the buried treasure. "Don't take them all," we were told. "Always leave some to hatch."

Suddenly, Paiakan looked up and saw that the girls had wandered far away. He tugged my arm, clearly alarmed, and told me to call the girls to come back right away: "Tem onça!" We were in jaguar country. It was the first time I saw him express fear. Without alarming the children, we called them back. We found the boiled eggs to be chalky and unappetizing, but of course it's a matter of personal taste and experience; the Kaiapo love turtle eggs.

On another river trip, Paiakan and one of the young men stood on the bow of the canoe as we paddled along and with great expertise they cast a circular net. The net had weights along the edge; when it was cast properly, centrifugal force on the lead sinkers splayed the net into a perfect circle that trapped fish beneath it as it sank. A rope tied to the center of the net caused the weights to move toward each other as the net was drawn up; fish were entangled in the mesh. I tried several times but failed miserably to duplicate the cast. All of the schooling I had spent so long to acquire was useless here.

One day, we asked to walk through the forest. Irekran's brother, Diego, and a friend of his were assigned to accompany us. As we followed a path, we were struck by the number of trees bearing fruit or nuts. Diego pointed out other edible plants everywhere. As we walked, the painted bodies of our guides blended into the pattern of shadows and light and rendered them virtually invisible to our unpracticed eyes.

We were enjoying ourselves, eating bananas and mangoes, swinging on vines over creeks, or slicing pieces of certain vines to drink the water that gushed out of the cut end. But we were incredibly vulnerable. Our guides would appear and vanish, and if they had taken off for any reason, there was absolutely no way we could have found our way back to the village. There were moments when I wondered if Tara and I had been foolish to put our children in such precarious situations. But we weren't abandoned, and soon we were back in familiar territory, walking through the small clearings where plants were cultivated and farinha was roasted.

Before we had decided in which month to go to Aucre, we had asked Darrell Posey when there might be a festival or celebration. "Oh, go on down anytime," he advised. "They have celebrations all the time." Sure enough, we had been there for about six days when the women appeared with their bodies painted very dark and wearing only a sash of the kind they carry their babies with. For perhaps an hour, they danced around in rows on the grounds the huts were facing. We learned it was the start of a three-day celebration to honor women.

Next day, the women appeared in far more elaborate regalia, beads, and feather headdresses, and sang and danced for a longer period. On the third day, their adornments were spectacular, with feathers woven into wooden frames that towered over the women's heads. Elaborately painted, the women began to dance just before sundown and continued into the pitch-dark night. Then we were told in not-so-subtle gestures that it was time for us to bugger off, which we did. We felt privileged to have witnessed this amazing ritual.

After we had been in Aucre for about a week, Sarika asked Tara to take a sliver out of the bottom of her foot. Tara looked at it and called me over; a small volcano was erupting from Sarika's skin. Tara disinfected a needle and the area around the "sliver" and began to pick an opening to remove the object. She got it out and put some more disinfectant and a bandage on as Sarika went off happily. Tara held up what she had pried out—a small, fat worm. It was a parasite that apparently infects mammals during a certain time of the year. It sheds its eggs in the ground, and as animals pass by, the parasite attaches to the skin and

Oe and Tania with their aunt before a *festa* in Aucre

Sarika showing where the parasitic worm was in her foot

burrows in. I later heard of a German cameraman who had picked over seventy of them from his legs.

Earlier, I had stubbed my toe on a sharp stick projecting out of a wall. One of our biggest worries was getting an infection in a cut, so I sloshed on disinfectant and bound my toe tightly with tape. That night, the toe began to hurt, and by the second night, it was throbbing each time my heart beat. "Dammit," I thought, "it must be infected." Next morning, I tore off the bandage. The throbbing stopped; I had bandaged it too tightly. When I looked at the cut, it was healing well. But beside the cut under my toenail were three worms. Tara dug them out for me and I stopped wearing sandals.

Two days after we had arrived in Aucre, a woman had fallen from a roof and gashed herself very badly on a machete. We learned then that there was a radio phone in the village for emergencies, and frantic calls were made to send the plane in to take her out. After a day, the plane arrived and she was taken to Redenção, where she developed an infection and died. In a community of two hundred, an accident of this severity was upsetting to everyone.

About five days after our arrival, I woke early to wailing all around us. I woke Tara and suggested something bad had happened; perhaps someone had died. We got up and watched people streaming toward one of the huts, where a woman was screaming and trying to flagellate herself with pots and machetes—anything within reach. Other women restrained her and wailed with her. It turned out that an old man had died unexpectedly of tuberculosis. Next day we tried to be as inconspicuous as possible as the body was taken into the forest, where, we gathered, in the customary way it was left on a platform to be consumed by wildlife. I don't know the details of how his wife was dealt with, but somehow she was calmed, and the grounds were "cleansed" by a single male who walked back and forth for hours with a broom, sweeping away the spirits.

Two tragedies in a week were a lot for a small community to bear. After we had been in the village for some time longer, I woke in the night to shooting and yelling outside. It sounded as if people had been drinking and were now shooting wildly, though we had not seen alcohol or guns during our stay. Tara and I got up, and as we went to the door of the hut, there was Paiakan as if standing guard. "What's wrong?" we asked. He looked very grave and pointed to the full moon. "The moon is sick," he said, "and my people are frightened. They blame it on brancos [white people]."

I had no idea whether he meant that the conjunction of the two tragedies earlier in the week, and now the moon, meant we were being blamed, or whether it was Brazilians in general who were being held responsible for the disasters. We looked at the moon, and it was a strange orange-brown color with blotches on it. "Is it an eclipse?" wondered Paiakan. We couldn't tell; the moon looked distinctly odd.

"The people are chanting the moon back to health," explained Paiakan.

"Are we in danger?" Tara asked.

I expected him to reassure us, but his answer was, "*Não sei* [I don't know]." Now that worried us.

"Do you think people will calm down?" Tara persisted.

Again the chilling answer came back, "*Não sei.*" Patricia, Miles, Severn, Sarika, and I could claim "we're not brancos!", but Tara says she felt her white skin shining out of that hut.

What were the odds of going to the heart of the Amazon at the same time a lunar eclipse would occur? An hour later, Tara looked out and saw a clean white moon, a telltale bite out of one side. To the Kaiapo, such an extraordinary occurrence is filled with significance, indicating the order within their world has been disrupted and somehow has to be set right. Could these "signs"—the deaths and the eclipse—be punishment for something they had failed to do, or a portent of something extraordinary to come? In a worldview in which everything is connected to everything else, these occurrences cannot be dismissed as meaningless.

Thoughts surged through my head. The Kaiapo are famous for their ferocity. In 1990 two Kaiapo parties of warriors attacked illegal settlements in their territory and claimed to have killed thirty peasants; Raoni, Sting's friend with the plate-sized labret, had led one of the parties in Xingu National Park. In Gorotire, I had met a Brazilian nurse who loved the Kaiapo. She had been living in one of the villages for twenty years when a rumor spread there that white people had attacked a Kaiapo in Redenção. The villagers were so infuriated that they went after the nurse, who had locked herself in her hut. She laughed as she recounted the incident, but she had warned me: when there is a crisis, it doesn't matter how well received you've been; you are not Kaiapo.

Now, I have a curious trait. When confronted with an emotionally charged situation, I become sleepy. It seems to be some kind of defense mechanism, perhaps a way of avoiding further anxiety. In any case, I felt there wasn't much we could do but wait it out and hope things would be calm by morning. Normally I'm the worrywart, but I climbed into my hammock and went back to sleep. Tara lay there listening to bullets whiz past our thin mud walls. Boy, was she mad at me. But we survived.

Morning came. The girls woke up unaware of what had gone on. We ventured out cautiously, wondering what would happen. Superficially, life seemed to be normal as people went about cooking, fishing, swimming. We couldn't decide whether it was our imagination or whether the people were cooler toward us. Our idyllic stay in Aucre had come to a crashing end. We had planned to stay for a few more days, but some of the joy had gone out of it, displaced by our ignorance and fear.

When Paiakan announced that the plane was coming in to take him and Irekran and their children out of Aucre, we decided to leave too. This had been an experience of a lifetime, a step back thousands of years in time to the way humans have lived for most of our existence. We had reached across that huge chasm in friendship and had been accepted in return, yet the eclipse had brought each side back to the reality of how differently we perceive the world.

We had to lighten our packs for the plane and gave away T-shirts, flashlights, fishing gear, knives, whatever we felt would be useful. A young man who had hung around me on our fishing trips shyly gave me a feather necklace he had made. As we left, I didn't know whether the ritual weeping was just for Paiakan and Irekran or whether the Kaiapo also liked us and were wishing us the best.

Severn and Sarika didn't want to leave. It had been an enchanted experience for them, and they wanted to stay the full shot. But once again we were airborne, leaving Aucre and passing over that immense expanse of green.

After forty minutes, we passed a brilliant slash of red through the forest—it was a placer gold mine, and the destruction of the river was unbelievable. The water looked a foamy cream color. Soon we began to see smoke, at first small wisps here and there and then large plumes that blocked the sun—this part of the forest, home to the Kaiapo, was on fire. Sev, especially, became very agitated to realize her friends' habitat was being destroyed.

We stayed overnight in a motel in Redenção. In Aucre, money meant nothing. There, life depended on the skills and knowledge of the people, and the forest and rivers were abundant and generous. Suddenly we were thrown into a world where money was everything. After the mud hut and the Kaiapo children underfoot and the swimming and fishing, even this small town seemed noisy, polluted, and inhospitable. After a sad farewell to Paiakan and his family—who knew when we would see each other again?—we caught a plane to Cuiaba for a short visit to the Pantanal, a wetland fabled for its birds and crocodiles.

As we flew out of Redenção, Sarika complained that her eye was sore. It was red and bloodshot, and within minutes, a thick, milky mucus began to pour out of it. It was terrifying to watch the speed with which this infection developed. By the time we arrived in São Paulo, en route to Cuiaba, her eyelid was swollen shut. We rushed to a drugstore in the airport, where the pharmacist looked at her. I had expected him to jump back and shout, "Oh, my god!" or something equally dramatic, but he indicated it was a common problem and calmly handed us a tube of medicine. I was dubious, but we squeezed the medication into her eye, and within minutes the swelling began to decrease. In a few hours, her eye was free of infection.

While we were waiting for Sarika's eye to subside, Miles began to mock me about the parasites I had pulled out of my feet. How many had I had? Why had I worn sandals? He heaped scorn on me because I should have taken better care of myself. "Do you mean you didn't get any?" I asked. "You don't have any sore spots?"

"Of course not . . . " he responded, then stopped in midsentence. He plunked himself down on a sofa, tore off his shoe and sock, then saw the volcano between his toes. "Take it out, take it out!" he wailed. I could only laugh at this brave Haida warrior.

PAIAKAN BECAME A GLOBAL hero for his battle to protect his home. He was honored and feted in Europe and the United States. In 1990 he was elected to the United Nations Environment Program's Global 500 list of world environmentalists and, along with former U.S. president Jimmy Carter, received a prize from the Society for a Better World. I flew to New York to celebrate the award with him.

In 1992, an Earth Summit drawing participants from around the world was to be held in Rio de Janeiro in June, and as the date approached, we prepared to return to Brazil. Paiakan's renown had grown, and despite being a thorn in the side of those who would develop the Amazon, he was expected to play a central role at the summit. I heard the Tibetan religious leader the Dalai Lama had asked to share the stage with him.

We arrived in Rio and settled into an apartment on the Condado, just north of Ipanema. The night before the summit, Tara went out for groceries, only to see Paiakan's face on the cover of a national magazine with the words "O Savagem"—"the Savage!"—printed across his image. Paiakan was accused of picking up seventeen-year-old Letícia Ferreira in a car on the way to a picnic near Redenção and of attacking and raping her with Irekran's assistance and in the presence of their children. The sensational charges, described as "facts" in the most lurid language in the Brazilian news magazine, were announced by the young woman's uncle, the mayor of Redenção, who had campaigned on a virulent anti-Indian platform. Paiakan and his family had retreated to the safety of Aucre.

The whole thing stank to high heaven, but as a tactic to keep Paiakan out of the limelight, it worked brilliantly. At meetings of non-government organizations (NGOs) at the Hotel Gloria during the summit, Paul Watson and I shook our heads as one by one the spokespeople for environmental organizations distanced themselves from Paiakan.

In 1994, Paiakan was acquitted in absentia for lack of evidence. But years later, the charges were reinstated. I have pressed Brazilian lawyer Frank Melli, who is a staunch supporter of Paiakan's, to see whether Paiakan can be granted a pardon now that more than thirteen years have passed. He has been silenced far more effectively than if, like Chico Mendes, he had been martyred by assassination. In the meantime, we have set up a trust that will enable Paiakan's children, as is his wish, to go on to university so that they can be educated and work for their people if that is their goal.

When we had visited Paiakan in 1989, he mused that in Canada we pay our scholars and experts to teach at universities and pass on their knowledge to young people. "Our elders are our professors," he said, and told me he would like to have a Kaiapo university where elders could teach young people how to live in the forest. He wanted to show the forest could be valuable left standing. He wanted, for example, to establish a research station in a pristine area to which scientists would pay to come from the outside world; they would hire Kaiapo cooks and assistants, and they would both teach and learn from the Kaiapo.

Tara and I thought it was a great idea, and with the help of Barbara Zimmerman, the Toronto-born herpetologist who had worked in the Amazon for years and invited us to the Manaus research station, we began to set it up. To pay for it, we organized small, exclusive tours to Aucre and its fledgling station fifteen miles upriver, starting in 1990. People could experience a traditional Indian community and a tropical rain forest. Barb is a remarkable woman and scientist, the only person we could imagine who could pull off this research station project in so remote a place. She handled the Brazilian end of the visits, and Tara looked after the complex arrangements at home.

Severn with Iremaõ, Paiakan's son, at the Pinkaiti research station

Using the money brought in by these tours, the first scientific research station in the eastern lower half of the Amazon watershed was successfully established. After the David Suzuki Foundation was born, we transferred the project to the foundation. But it was a huge drain on Tara's time and energy, and when Conservation International, a well-funded American environmental organization that works to protect wilderness, offered to take charge of the project, we were happy to hand it over.

IN 2001, SEVERN RECEIVED a research grant from Yale University, where she was a junior, to study a species of tree in the Amazon rain forest in that same research station her mom and I had helped get going, now called Projeto Pinkaiti. With the funding of Conservation International and under the supervision of Barbara Zimmerman, the station was flourishing, with a steady stream of scientists and students from Europe and North America.

After hearing Sev's stories about being back in the Amazon, I decided to return to Aucre to see Paiakan while we were in Brazil filming for *The Sacred Balance*. Paiakan was heavier, and the village too had changed since my last visit. For some unfathomable reason, the thatched roofs had been replaced with metal. A dispensary with a concrete floor had appeared, staffed by a Brazilian who gave out medical drugs; a solar-charged television set was turned on for a few hours a night to show soccer while I was there, and a hut had been built for people who were coming and going to the research station upriver. In Aucre, I woke to the tap, tap, tap of metal devices being used to shell Brazil nuts for the Body Shop chain, which uses the extracted oil in its cosmetics. The plane we had delivered in 1989 still linked the Kaiapo villages together.

The cook for the camp at Aucre was a Brazilian who had a genuine affection for the Kaiapo and had been adopted by them as a Kaiapo, which is a tremendous honor and act of trust. To be adopted, he had to fast for a day, have his hair shaved off, and undergo an entire day of ritual dancing and painting.

Another big change was that Paiakan's daughters were being educated away from the village, in Redenção. Paiakan allowed mahogany trees to be selectively logged for the money he needed to keep the girls in town, and Juneia Mallus is disillusioned by this, but Barb Zimmerman believes such selective logging has a relatively small ecological impact. Paiakan still hopes to rally more outside supporters for preservation of the Amazon, but time has gone by and he has been stuck in the village, marginalized, forgotten by the media.

While I was there, Paiakan and I went fishing again. Unlike our summer visit of 1989, this one took place right after the rainy season and the river was quite high, flowing over the banks and into the forest. As we started off, Paiakan drove the boat right into a bush overhanging the river and began picking the walnut-sized orange fruit and dropping them into the bottom of the craft. When he had accumulated quite a large pile, he backed the boat away and, as we began our trip downriver, he told me to bait up with the fruit. If I hadn't known any better, I would have thought he was playing a trick on this gringo, and I was a little skeptical, but I dutifully pushed a hook through the skin of the fruit.

"Cast it out," he urged me, so I began to cast in a half-hearted way. I just couldn't imagine fishing with a fruit on my hook. What if someone saw me? Paiakan killed the engine, baited a hand line with another fruit, and began to throw it toward the trees along the river's edge. Right away he was hauling in a huge, flat, silvery fish. Well, I began to cast in earnest then and immediately hooked a fish, which broke my line. Paiakan caught three fish, while I hooked several and lost them all. We drifted down to a place where there were large rocks and pools; Paiakan jumped out and cast a hand net, pulling in several of the same species at each throw. In the end, we had ten beautiful fish, and once again I was awed by Paiakan's skill and knowledge. I caught no fish that day.

All too soon, my short visit was over, and I began to prepare to leave. Irekran offered to paint my body, which I had always hoped for, but I knew I would have to be filming again in a few days. "Not my face," I told her, with mixed feelings. Severn had been painted and I would love to have had that experience, but it would also have made me stand out and be subjected to stares in airports, which did not please me. So Irekran painted me up to my chin, with long, vertical stripes of dark-black dye. When I asked her how long the paint would last, she answered, "About ten days." Wrong. It lasted a month and created a buzz when I went to the gym back in Canada.

The day I left Aucre, I was wakened by a horrendous racket, which I learned was the pharmacist spraying insecticide around the village— malaria had come to this part of the forest. It seems there is no way to escape the forces of change, even in the deepest part of the Amazon.

Paiakan and me displaying his wife Irekran's paint job

DOWN UNDER

WHEN I WAS A BOY, another magical place I dreamed of visiting was Australia, home of the fabled duck-billed platypus. The platypus was the sort of creature that fired the imagination of an animal nerd like me, and I yearned to see a live one. With a flat, wide bill like a duck's tacked on to a furry body, webbed feet for swimming, and a poisonous spur on the male's hind legs, the platypus is an egg-laying mammal that suckles its young on modified sweat glands that drip milk onto hairs from which the young can lap it up. In North America, zoos might boast kangaroos or even a koala, but never a platypus.

In the 1960s, when I was starting out at the University of British Columbia, I met Jim Peacock, a brilliant young Australian doing groundbreaking work on chromosome replication in plants. He held a postdoctoral fellowship at the University of Oregon, and we would meet at conferences. We became friends. Unknown to me, he put my name forward for a position at the University of Sydney. Out of the blue, I received a request to apply for a genetics position. I was flattered to receive an unsolicited inquiry right at the beginning of my career, so I sent my very short curriculum vitae, hoping that at least I might be invited to visit and give a talk.

Instead, I was offered the position. I knew the university was the home of an eminent chromosome expert, Spencer Smith-White, which made the institution an attractive place to be. But my marriage was breaking up, and I could not imagine being so far away from my children, so I turned down the opportunity without even mentioning it to the head of my department to try to chisel a raise. I have often wondered what might have happened had I accepted that job.

In 1988, I finally went to Australia, and I immediately fell in love with it. The environmental movement was at a peak of energy and public support around the world, and Australia had recently established the Commission for the Future, a government-funded organization to look at the role of science in Australian society and its place in the country's future. It was a good idea, similar to the Science Council of Canada, which Brian Mulroney dismantled in 1993 during his second term as prime minister.

Phil Noyce (not the Aussie filmmaker of the same name) had been a science teacher who was recruited to the Commission for the Future because of his interest in communicating science to the public. He was young and keen and had encouraged the organization to invite me to give a series of talks in 1988. He would later become a close friend who convinced me of the importance of acting immediately to fight climate change. I had known humanity was affecting Earth's climate, but I felt it was a problem far in the future and that there were other, more pressing issues. Phil disagreed, and the evidence has piled up to show how prescient he was in believing action was urgent. (Tragically, he had an undetected congenital heart defect and died in the prime of his life, while playing tennis.)

I was delighted to receive the invitation and accepted. At last I would be going to Australia. What would I see? Because of the horrific discrimination endured by the Aboriginal people of Australia and the government's infamous "white Australia" policy of restricting immigration to maintain a Caucasian-dominated nation, I expected to have to search hard to see a person of color. In addition, the sexism of the country was well known, and perhaps that is why one of the most globally influential feminists of the time was an Australian, Germaine Greer. I was fully prepared to encounter bigotry, sexism, and anti-gay attitudes. I also thought there would be kangaroos and other marsupials jumping through fields and streets.

How ignorant I was. Like Americans arriving in Toronto to find a huge, modern city devoid of the expected igloos, I landed in Melbourne to discover a huge, sophisticated city of great diversity. I certainly did not expect to find vigorous Chinatowns in Melbourne and Sydney, as well as lots of Thai, Vietnamese, and Japanese restaurants. To my surprise, I discovered sophisticated, multicultural cities with plenty of ethnic diversity. There were no kangaroos in the cities, of course, but I did see them in the wild, where I learned they also gather in farmers' fields and graze openly. In the cities and in "the outback"—less inhabited, vast inland areas—there was an amazing profusion of birds in all shapes and colors—cockatoos, budgies, parrots. Even the "pest" birds like magpies are beautiful. And I'm not a great birder.

On one of my early visits to Australia, Phil took me to Phillip Island south of Melbourne, where fairy or little blue penguins *(Eudyptula minor)* still live in tunnels in the banks above the beach, and it is possible to listen to them making their gurgling songs in their nests. We can watch as they waddle down to the water's edge in the morning, hesitate, and then collectively plunge into the surf on their way to sea. In the evening they make their way back to their homes, walking past tourists without paying any attention. It's an impressive sight that reminded me of the way animals on the Galapagos Islands failed to recognize us as deadly predators and simply ignored us.

We had a similar experience in 2003 on Kangaroo Island off the southern coast of Australia. There we encountered an echidna; it and the platypus are the only members of that select order of egg-laying mammals, the monotremes. With a sharper beak and only two legs, the echidna carries a layer of thick, protective quills and makes a living by rooting about for grubs. When we spotted one, we jumped out of our vehicle; the creature ignored us as it dug into the side of the road—and we chalked up another amazing encounter.

I asked Phil if I could finally see a platypus, and I was rewarded at the zoo in Melbourne. I was taken behind the exhibits and shown an elaborate waterway constructed for the animals. I was able to watch them for as long as I wanted and saw them being fed their favorite food, a kind of crayfish called a yabbie. It was the realization of my child-hood dream and one of the great thrills of my life.

The Commission for the Future was determined to get its pound of flesh out of me, so Phil had arranged a heavy schedule of publicity events in addition to several formal speeches. It was virgin territory for me and for my audience. No one there had heard of me or my ideas, so I could spout off about all of my favorite subjects and be as opinionated as I wanted. It was very gratifying that people were tremendously recep-tive to my words. It makes sense—Australia is a country whose cli-mate and unique ecosystems encourage being in the outdoors, whether swimming, camping, or just firing up the barbie and chugging a few frosties from the Esky (translation: lighting the barbecue and drinking a few beers from the cooler). Water is a very real issue to everyone. I also suspect Australians were intrigued to hear a "Japanese" (me) who would slang the Japanese for their depredation of global resources like trees and fish. Whatever the reasons, there was a flurry of media interest in me wherever Phil had arranged interviews and news conferences.

The Australian Broadcasting Corporation (ABC) is as important to Australians as the Canadian Broadcasting Corporation (CBC) is to Canadians, but unlike Canadians, Australians fiercely support and defend the public broadcaster. After relatively small cuts were made to ABC's budget in the late 1990s, more than ten thousand people gath-

Quokkas, a type of marsupial, on Rottnest Island, near Perth, Western Australia

ered at a demonstration in Sydney to protest the loss of funding. In contrast, when the federal government made draconian cuts in the CBC's budget, only a couple of hundred people gathered in Toronto to support the corporation.

In Australia I was extensively interviewed on several local and national programs on ABC, none more important than the long-running *Science Show* hosted on radio by Robyn Williams. Robyn is an expat from Britain whose abilities in science communication have made him widely recognized and admired by the public, a kind of Aussie version of the late American astronomer-broadcaster Carl Sagan. I have come to know Robyn very well, as we have crossed paths often in Australia and North America. He has been the only host since the *Science Show* began to broadcast in the spring of 1974, and his program was a wonderful opportunity to talk about my ideas in depth.

By the time I had finished my first visit, I had not had time to get outside Melbourne and Sydney and so had still not seen any of the fabled wildlife of the continent. Nevertheless, I had fallen head over heels for the country and its people. Back home, it seemed everything I looked at triggered a memory of Australia. "Gee, in Sydney..." I'd say. Finally, Tara looked at me suspiciously and asked if I had a girlfriend back there.

As a result of that first visit, several groups invited me to return to give talks, and I was determined to go back with Tara. I was also approached by Patrick Gallagher, head of Allen & Unwin Publishers, an Australian company that had started out as a subsidiary of the English publishing house of the same name but in 1990 became independent. We have become good friends, and I have enjoyed a close relationship with the company. When I told Patrick I wanted to set aside some of my Australian book royalties to support Aboriginal and environmental groups in Australia, Patrick promptly offered to contribute 5 percent of the profits the company makes on my books to the fund.

Soon I was planning a return visit to Australia, this time to tour several cities to talk about my books *Metamorphosis* (my first autobiography) and *Inventing the Future* (a collection of columns I had written for newspapers). In 1989, Tara accompanied me to see for herself what had so impressed me with the country. We had a whirlwind tour through Melbourne, Sydney, and Canberra with lots of media interest. Sales of the books took off, and they became best-sellers.

Australia is as exotic as any place, yet people are familiar and speak English, so it is easy to get about and converse. Australians and Canadians share a colonial history and ties with Britain, and both are adamantly proud of not being American. In Australia, scores of young Canadians can be found working on farms or waiting on tables, and Australian accents can be heard all over the ski slopes of Whistler and Banff. People in both nations think of themselves (erroneously) as a country with a small population covering a vast area. In fact, much of Canada is covered in snow, ice, or rock, and that's why most Canadians snuggle along the southern border with the United States. Similarly, much of Australia is desert, so most of the population crowds into five major cities on the coasts. But nature and wilderness or the outback are a critical part of what people in the two countries value as part of our heritage and culture.

I once heard the Canadian communications theorist Marshall McLuhan remark that one difference between Americans and Canadians is that Americans will invite new acquaintances into their homes, but Canadians invite them to meet in a pub or restaurant, preferring to keep home for family and friends. I don't know how good a generalization that is, but I do feel Canadians are not nearly as outgoing and open as Americans. I have often been astonished to meet an American for the first time and be invited to stay at his or her home after a very short period of conversation. It is a quality I admire and appreciate.

In Canada, in contrast, we are far slower to extend such hospitality, but when we do, it seems more deeply felt and meant. Australians are much more open and gregarious than Canadians, but without the underlying assumption of superiority many Americans express. And the use of language by Australians is enthralling, from the contraction of words as in "uni" (university), "ute" (utility vehicle), and "servo" (service station) to novel terms like "larrikin" (hooligan) and "come the raw prawn" (attempt to deceive).

On that visit in 1989 with Tara, Phil Noyce and his wife, Georgina Tsolidas, accompanied us on a jaunt to the Great Barrier Reef. We flew to Cairns, the northernmost city on the east coast of Queensland. From there we traveled north by bus for another hour to the sleepy town of Port Douglas, where, a few years later, the wonderful Australian film *Travelling North* was shot. Port Douglas at the time was a tiny village with a few shops and a harbor where the *Quicksilver,* a large twin-hulled catamaran, is moored. It departs for the barrier reef daily, tying up at a permanent float at the outer reef. From there, tourists fan out to scuba dive or snorkel or just go down into a viewing area under the float.

Our first trip to the reef was heaven. We had never experienced such diversity of form and color, including dozens and dozens of species of coral—immense beds of purple stag coral with antlerlike branches, and huge domes of brain coral. There are giant clams with lips of green, pink, and purple, threatening to clamp onto unsuspecting divers the way they do in horror movies, and fish from immense groupers to parrotfish, pufferfish, and tiny clownfish hiding in the protective tentacles of soft corals. The Great Barrier Reef is truly one of the wonders of the natural world.

When we returned from our enchanting trip on the *Quicksilver*, we noticed an excavation site a block away from Port Douglas's Four Mile Beach with a sign saying an apartment building was soon to go up and one suite remained for sale. Phil, Georgie, Tara, and I bought it. Tara and I have enjoyed it ever since, an investment that represents our commitment to Australia as a second home. In the eight years I had lived in the United States, the idea of staying there permanently never entered my mind. But there in Port Douglas, having spent a wonderful day on the Great Barrier Reef, then walking the exquisite sands of Four Mile Beach in perfect weather, we seriously thought about moving to Australia. We have never regretted remaining in Canada, but we do feel privileged to be able to return to Australia again and again.

We fell in love with Port Douglas because it seemed a throwback to another time, when people moved at a slower pace. But when we returned a few years later, the town had been "discovered" and had undergone a major growth spurt that included a new Japanese-backed luxury hotel. Eventually the *Quicksilver* was sold to a Japanese company, and now high-end restaurants attract more tourists, and the feel of the place has changed. But the Japanese invasion and explosive development are just the latest assaults to change the area.

From December to March, the hot, muggy weather leads locals and visitors to spend a lot of time in the water. But you can't go swimming along Four Mile Beach, because of the "stingers"—poisonous jellyfish—some of which can incapacitate and even kill an adult human. Pictures of victims with stinger "burns" are pretty brutal, displaying open sores and wide swaths of red, swollen tissue. The only ocean swimming in the summer is in "stinger nets," which are strung out in the water and provide a haven from the jellyfish. It's not the way I had imagined spending time in the ocean.

Stingers were not a hazard in the past, because there were plenty of turtles that fed on them. But the turtles were "harvested" for their meat and shells, and at some point their numbers became so depleted that they could no longer sustain themselves, and they disappeared. Stingers and stinger nets now are just an accepted part of the hot season—but they didn't have to be. Let's hope the great interest of tourists in viewing turtles will help spur the reintroduction and protection of this species.

Two hours' drive from Port Douglas is the Daintree, a jewel of tropical rain forest that is easily accessible and delightful to explore. Yet in the adjacent lands around it, lots are being cleared and sold off for development. Every time I've visited the Daintree, I've been overwhelmed by the immensity of our ignorance and our arrogance in the way we treat nature. A few years ago, biologists "fogged" some of the canopy of the Daintree with pesticide, just as research entomologist Terry Erwin of the Smithsonian Institution had done in the Peruvian Amazon, and, like Erwin, they found thousands of species of insects that had never before been seen by humans. It is thought there must be tens of thousands of species in the Daintree yet to be discovered.

But remember, when a new organism—plant, animal, or microorganism—is collected, it can be "keyed out," meaning its taxonomic position is identified, and if it is new to science, it can be named. When a name is assigned to a new species, that does not mean we know anything about its numbers, distribution, habitat needs, or interaction with other species or even such basic biology as what it eats, how it reproduces, or when it matures. It is breathtaking, therefore, that even

though we remain almost completely ignorant of most of the species'
needs and interactions with ecosystems, we do not hesitate to destroy
those ecosystems to get a few "resources" that we find useful. We
should remember the story of the goose that laid golden eggs and realize that entire ecosystems like the Amazon and Daintree forests are
the goose. Only so long as they flourish will we be able to collect the
golden eggs.

BEFORE MY THIRD VISIT to Australia, I received a message that
someone named Peter Garrett, who sang with an Australian group
called Midnight Oil, had offered to do an event with me in Sydney
on my next visit. I wrote to ask Patrick Gallagher who this guy was
and whether he was legit. Patrick replied that he was a big name and
Midnight Oil was a very popular group, but the publisher seemed
hesitant about the idea of my doing an event with a rock band. His
reluctance gave me visions of trying to deliver a serious talk in front of
a screaming, drug-crazed audience interested only in hearing the rock
group. Uh-uh. I told Patrick to thank Peter but turn him down. Patrick
seemed relieved.

Huge mistake. I soon learned that Peter and the Oils were not just
big in Australia, they were huge! And they were on their way to con-
quering North America and Europe.

Peter was far more than just a performer; he was president of the
Australian Conservation Foundation (ACF), one of the largest environmental groups in the country, and he had run unsuccessfully for
the Australian Senate in 1984 for the Nuclear Disarmament Party, a
predecessor of the Greens. His fans were my kind of people. When I
first heard their signature song, "Beds Are Burning," demanding that
Australians confront the fact that the land belongs to the Aboriginal
people, I was blown away.

The song had the same impact on me as had another in 1988. First
I had received a call from a Bernie Finkelstein in Toronto. "Who are

you?" I asked. "I'm Bruce Cockburn's manager," he answered, "and Bruce asked if you would listen to a song he has just recorded." Kind of a weird request, but I did know Bruce Cockburn was a successful Canadian singer, and Bernie's office was close enough to the CBC for me to drop in. So I did, and Bernie put on a CD to play a brand-new Cockburn song, "If a Tree Falls." I cried when I heard it. It was powerful, and later, with the video, I knew it would be a hit. When Paiakan stayed with us, he loved Bruce's video of that song, even though he didn't understand the words.

Peter Garrett is an impressive sight. He must be six and a half feet tall, and he is lean and bald. When he performs, he's like a scarecrow puppet being manipulated by someone high above, arms and legs flailing about. I saw him onstage for the first time in Anaheim, California, and his rapturous reception by the audience showed me how badly Patrick and I had erred, but by then Peter and I had become good friends.

When he came to Canada in 1993 as the long battle over logging in the Clayoquot Sound rain forest on the west coast of Vancouver Island was heating up again, Midnight Oil volunteered to perform in the protest area. I was delighted to have the opportunity to introduce the band, and it was a marvelous concert, marred only by the nastiness of loggers who were there harassing the protesters and who screamed epithets and threatened the band as they left. (Eventually, more than nine hundred people were arrested before the Nuu-chah-nulth First Nation signed a resource management agreement with the British Columbia government.)

Because of the Australian public's tremendous response to my message of environmental stewardship, I had been urged by a number of people to start a David Suzuki Foundation Australia modeled on my Canadian foundation, but I resisted because I don't want to form a multinational organization. If our approach is useful and can be copied in Australia, there should be an autonomous Australian-created group based on similar principles.

On one of those early visits to Australia, I was told that a program called *The Couchman Show*, hosted by Paul Couchman, had asked that I appear as a guest. The Allen & Unwin publicist, Monica Joyce, was worried because she thought the show tended to be confrontational, and she suggested I talk to Couchman before deciding yes or no. I called and told Couchman that I was interested in dialogue, not in confrontational diatribes. "Oh no," he assured me, "we're not that kind of show. We like to have everyone offer their positions so we can have open discussion." I accepted the invitation.

Couchman had not leveled with me. The audience was stacked with businesspeople and economists, with a sprinkling of environmentalists, and the entire format was set up for confrontation. Because I had received assurance from the man himself, I was completely relaxed. An eminent economist shared the stage with me, and I presented my case that economics was fundamentally flawed because it excluded nature as a central part of its underpinnings (economists call it an "externality"). I probably said it a bit more forcefully than that.

Well, the economist launched into an attack on my position, egged on by Couchman. As the audience generously applauded the economist, I finally realized I had been set up. A few environmentalists in the audience tried to defend me, but we were overwhelmed by the onslaught against us.

In the end, the economist told me I didn't know what I was talking about, that the air and water were cleaner today than they had ever been. I exploded, "If you believe that, you are a fool!" I shouldn't have been so rude, but I had been under steady assault, and his statement revealed how ignorant he was. When it was over, I stomped over to Couchman and said, "You lied to me." He didn't care; he had generated his fireworks.

A year later, I met the Australian filmmaker Paul Cox at his home, and the first thing he told me was that he had watched me on *The*

Couchman Show and had been infuriated by the nonsense the economist spouted. He apologized over and over on behalf of Australians. I had long since overcome my anger, but I was glad there was support for my position among the viewers.

On another of those early visits to Australia, I received a request that I meet Green Party politician Bob Brown of the state of Tasmania. As an elected senator in the federal government, he has played an indispensable role in raising the profile of environmental and human-rights issues. We met in Melbourne, and as we strolled along the Yarra River at dusk, Bob suddenly stopped talking, looked intently along the riverbank, and pointed at something. It was a platypus. Thus my first sighting of a wild platypus occurred in a most unlikely environment, but I was delighted to think there was still room for the animals even in the middle of a city.

Bob wanted to know whether Lake Pedder, a pristine glacial lake in Tasmania's southwest wilderness that had been flooded in the 1970s to generate hydroelectric power, could be restored. Was it feasible? Did Tasmania need the energy the inundated lake supplied, and would the original values of that ecosystem be able to recover if the dam in the Tasmanian Wilderness World Heritage Area was removed? To study such matters, he needed money, and I offered him enough for someone to do the work. It was the early days of the David Suzuki Foundation, and I was pleased to be able to support an international project under our name.

The study showed that the energy supplied by the dam that had caused the flooding of Lake Pedder was a small part of the state's needs and could easily be given up without any economic disruption. The findings also suggested there existed sufficient residual vegetation and animal species around the lake to restore the original ecosystem if the water was permanently allowed to return to its natural flow. The study was released to the public, but, as with so many things in Tasmania,

Sarika and Severn posing with David Hudson's dance troupe in Queensland

tearing down a dam seemed a regressive step to the powers that be and the idea was rejected with hardly a thought.

One of our most memorable visits to Australia occurred in 1991, when my father had recovered from my mother's death in 1984 and had regained some of his great zest for life. Dad adored our children, and we invited him to join us on a trip to Australia. He was thrilled to go, and with his genuine curiosity and his skills as a raconteur, he captivated all those he met down under. He was enchanted with the trees, the flowers, the birds, and the people—a whole world to fill his insatiable appetite for new experiences and knowledge.

With Georgina and Phil in tow, we made our way to Port Douglas. There Tara bought an inflatable vest for Dad, and we took the family out to the Great Barrier Reef on the *Quicksilver*. Dad's arthritis had gnarled his limbs and digits, so he looked like a twisted gnome, but he didn't let it slow him as he hobbled onto the float. We fitted him with mask, fins, and snorkel to go along with his protective vest, and in he jumped, hand in hand with Sarika. There was Dad at eighty-one, holding onto eight-year-old Sarika, paddling over to one of the "bommies," a column of coral rising to the surface and easily encircled. I watched them swimming off and listened to their muffled exclamations through the snorkels: "Look at that!" "Over there!" "Grampa, Grampa, what is that?" It is one of my happiest memories.

SINCE THOSE EARLIEST VISITS, Tara and I have made several trips to Australia together, and during that time we have seen many changes. In the almost two decades since our first joint trip, the Great Barrier Reef has been changed by tourism, fishing, and the accumulation of effluents from cities, towns, and farmers' fields, which ultimately percolate through the reefs.

More recently, climate change has been responsible for coral bleaching over immense areas. Coral is more than one organism. An animal called a coelenterate, which is related to jellyfish, creates a hard shell around itself, a carbonaceous material we think of as the coral. The coelenterate harbors within it another species, a plant that provides energy through photosynthesis in return for the nutrition the animal captures. It's a classic example of symbiosis, a partnership in which both parts benefit from each other. The plants also confer color to the animal, and the Great Barrier Reef is a profusion of colors from purple to pink and green. The plant parts are extremely sensitive to temperature, and a rise in water temperature of just a degree or two can cause their death and hence the "bleaching" phenomenon of color loss. The animals can survive a season without their partners, but they then die if they are not reinfected with the plants.

Coral bleaching related to El Niño events unprecedented in their heat, duration, and shortened interval between are thought to be the basis for a global bleaching episode; El Niños are deviations from normal temperatures in the southern Pacific Ocean between South America and Australia. Coral reefs are oases of life, supporting a disproportionate abundance of life forms, and, as with tropical rain forests, disruption of their integrity represents a catastrophic threat to the ocean ecosystems of the world.

In 2003, when Tara and I again visited the Great Barrier Reef, it had visibly changed in both abundance of organisms and vitality. Dead stag coral littered the bottom, and the numbers and variety of fishes were noticeably diminished. (This is not a scientifically validated observation—it is subjective and anecdotal—but I think too much is at stake to ignore it.) Yet when we finally climbed back on the boat, the guides bubbled with enthusiasm, extolling the wonders of the reef and all its components. Part of that is their job; after all, we had paid a lot of money for the trip. But it is my impression that they really were enthusiastic and meant what they were saying.

Even in that short span since Tara and I had first visited this place in 1989, the degradation was perceptible to us. Because the guides had been working there only for a few years, however, they didn't have the same baseline for comparison. To tourists, the coral and fish are still dazzling in profusion and color, but I am sure an old-timer who has known the reef for decades will remember it in a state that no longer exists.

It was the same on our visit to the Serengeti Plain in Tanzania in eastern Africa. Our encounter with so many mammals filled us with wonder and delight that there still are such pristine areas with abundant wildlife—until we talked to some of the people who have lived there all their lives and remember a flourishing plain that no longer exists. Urban people like us live in such a degraded environment for wildlife that almost anything else looks rich and unspoiled. It's only when we dig deeper to find what the state of wildlife was decades or centuries before that we realize how much we are drawing down on nature's abundance.

ON THAT VISIT IN 2003, I was asked for the second time to be honorary patron of the Youth Conservation Corps (YCC), a program for youth who had dropped out of school but were unable to find jobs. The program gave them a stipend to spend six months a year learning how to rehabilitate the land, cleaning up soil and rivers, planting native species, making inventories of wildlife, and otherwise being trained for jobs in conservation. When Mike Rann had been minister for Aboriginal affairs in the Labor government of the state of South Australia in the 1990s, I met him, and we hit it off. I was asked to be the honorary patron of YCC, but when Labor was thrown out of office in 1993, the program was cancelled. Mike led the party back to power in 2001 and as state premier then resurrected the Youth Conservation Corps and asked me to return as honorary patron. I was delighted with the honor, and Tara and I attended a YCC event in Adelaide.

Once again, we were moved to see the dedication and enthusiasm of the kids. A young girl who seemed to have rings hanging from every part of her face and body enthused about her bird inventory: "I've seen twenty-five species right here in this field." A young man with tattoos on his face, arms, and legs and a bush of hair that exploded from his head exulted about how great it was to be out here in the country and to be paid for it. We were taken to a large area of degraded land where the trees had long been cut down, the land overgrazed by sheep, and the soil overrun by grass and brush. "This will be Suzuki Forest, named in honor of our patron," announced John Hill, the minister of environment. The Youth Conservation Corps will plant native trees on that land so that perhaps a couple of decades from now there will again be a young forest, one bearing the name of that Canadian bloke who used to visit Australia.

AYERS ROCK, THE LANDMARK familiar around the world as one of Australia's icons, is now known by its Aboriginal name, Uluru, and is an amazing sight. Imagine a flat desert, hot as hell; out of its haze looms a massive piece of rock that changes color as the sun makes its way across the sky. An Aboriginal woman offered to walk around Uluru with Tara and me. As when I was filming !San people in the Kalahari Desert, at first all I saw was scrub and sand. And as with the !San people, I was shown there was food aplenty. In Australia it's called "bush tucker," and this woman demonstrated great knowledge of it, pointing out tiny edible fruits and various nutritional and medicinal plants, as well as hiding places for insects and scorpions.

One of the terrifying aspects of globalization and economics is that this kind of knowledge is not seen as having value in a modern industrialized world, and what has taken thousands of years of careful observation, experimentation, and insight is being lost all over the planet in just a few generations and will never be recovered. This information is far more profound than current science, because it has been tested over time with the survival of those who possessed the knowledge.

During a book tour in the 1990s that took me to Brisbane, an Aboriginal man offered to take me on a short walk through the bush. I was delighted, and we drove to a nearby park. I was dressed in shorts and sandals, and as we stepped onto the trail, I looked at the leafy ground beside it and realized there were leeches waving their heads about a half an inch off the ground, just waiting for an easy victim. Fortunately, I evaded them as we searched for witchetty grubs, the white, fatty, larval forms of beetles that are much prized by Aboriginal people and eaten live or cooked. I was determined to eat a live one, but I must admit that I was not highly disappointed when the only grubs we found were "not the right kind."

In Adelaide after one of my readings, an elder who looked white approached me and introduced himself. He was Lewis O'Brien, a respected elder of the Kaurna people. He was very pleased because I had talked about the book I coauthored in 1992 with Peter Knudtson,

Aboriginal people in Arnhemland performing for *The Sacred Balance*

Wisdom of the Elders, which examined the congruence between aboriginal knowledge and scientific insights, and I talked about my respect for traditional knowledge and the way First Nations people had educated me about our relationship with Mother Earth.

In a simple gesture, Lewis said, "I want to give you a name—Karnemeyu. It means 'holy mountain'." Receiving a name is the highest honor I can imagine. It means far more to me than receiving an honorary degree from a university. What surprises me is that of the names I have received from aboriginal peoples, three have meant "mountain." Simon Lucas, a Nuu-chah-nulth from Ahousat on Vancouver Island, gave me my first such name, Nuchi, meaning "mountain," and the Blood Tribe near Lethbridge, Alberta, gave me the name Natooeestuk, meaning "sacred mountain."

I was browsing through children's books in a store in Australia and came across one of several books written by Percy Trezise, a white man, and illustrated by Dick Roughsey, an Aboriginal artist. As I read the book, I found this pairing of a Caucasian and an Aboriginal intriguing. I saw that Percy lived in Cairns, so when Tara and I were in the city, I called him. He invited us to drop in, and when we did, he was happy to talk about his life.

Born in 1923, Percy had grown up believing Aboriginal people were primitive, almost subhuman; that was the prevailing attitude of the day. When he was an adult, he met Dick Roughsey and quickly realized the artist was very talented. As he began to spend time with Dick, he learned the horrific cost of bigotry and became committed to showing the world that Aboriginal people are neither primitive nor unintelligent.

A professional pilot, Percy started to explore the northern parts of Queensland and to locate rock paintings all over the territory. These lands aren't empty; they are filled with evidence of thousands of years of unbroken use by the original inhabitants. By the time he died in 2005, Percy had contributed vastly to the documentation and preservation of Aboriginal culture and rock art and was an artist himself.

One of our greatest regrets was a trip Percy arranged for us that never happened. His son is a pilot, and Percy arranged for us to meet him and fly to one of the remote areas where Percy had documented and mapped hundreds of rock paintings. We were on the plane and strapped in when the announcement came that the weather was too inclement to risk flying.

BYRON BAY IS HIPPIE heaven on the east coast of Australia. I was met at the airport by a lawyer who was volunteering to help my book tour. On the drive into town, I casually mentioned that I had heard there were a lot of hippies and pot smoking in Byron Bay. Bam, he pulled a joint out of his pocket and asked if I wanted a toke. I turned it down, of course, but it looked as if Byron Bay was my kind of place. My talk was very well received, and we sold a lot of books. Before saying goodbye, the man who had picked me up handed me an envelope, which I shoved in my pocket and later threw into my suitcase.

The next day I had time to go snorkeling in the gorgeous bay that gives the place its name. The water was amazingly clear, and I spent most of my time simply floating among massive schools of sardines. There were turtles, seals, and lots and lots of fish. At one point I felt a burning across my cheek and after frantic wiping found an almost invisible tentacle of a bluebottle jellyfish. I ended up with a red line across my face, a small discomfort for a wonderful swim.

I forgot about the envelope from the man who had picked me up the day before and flew to Sydney to change planes to fly to Perth. As I got out on the tarmac, I noticed a sign warning that dogs were used to detect illicit materials. Then I remembered the envelope, so as soon as I got into the airport terminal building, I whipped into a men's room and threw it away. I came out whistling, and there was a dog! It approached my bag and immediately went at it. The dog's handler was a woman who recognized me and, pulling on the leash, said apologetically, "I don't know why he's so excited."

"Well, I did have some mangoes in there this morning," I suggested. "That must be it," the officer said, and she rather brusquely pulled the dog off my bag. Poor thing was only doing its job, but ever since, when I go to Australia, I ask my hosts how the mangoes are.

IN ALMOST TWO DECADES of visiting Australia at least twice a year, I have come to think of it as my adoptive land. It is a continent of extreme contradictions. Any tourist may be impressed with gleaming, modern cities, yet most of the country is virtually uninhabited by whites. Australia is an island continent where a rise in sea level as the planet warms will have an enormous impact. The climate, already tropical and subtropical, will grow increasingly warmer, but the federal government repeatedly refuses to act seriously to reduce its greenhouse gas emissions. Canadians envy Australia for its quantities of sunlight, yet the government fails to exploit this free, nonpolluting energy to make Australia a leader in solar technology as Germany and Denmark are with wind power.

Australia is a major exporter of wheat and rice, two crops that are not indigenous to the continent and require vast quantities of severely limited water. The flora and fauna of Australia set the nation apart with its unique biodiversity, yet exotic species, introduced accidentally or deliberately, continue to wreak havoc on local populations.

The history of Australia over the past two centuries has been one of decimation of the Aboriginal people, a deliberate attempt to eliminate them by killing or through assimilation, and a climate of racism has led to enormous problems for the survivors. But as the twentieth century ended, Australians overwhelmingly wanted justice and reconciliation for the Aboriginal people, and it is my sense that there is a growing appreciation for their knowledge and art.

Islands, even large ones like Australia, impose boundaries and acknowledgment of limits. Being bound together by the constraints of water, land, and biodiversity, Australians have an opportunity to confront the major issues of our time as a unified country. Unlike Canadians, who must constantly refer to or compare ourselves with our neighbors to the immediate south, Australians aren't as psychically hampered. The twenty-first century truly offers the chance for Australians to realize their future as the lucky land.

chapter ELEVEN

STARTING THE
DAVID SUZUKI FOUNDATION

IN MY EXPERIENCE since I had become swept
up in it in the late 1960s, the environmental
movement worked for clean air, water, soil, and energy, for a world rich
in diversity in which life flourished in abundance, and for sustainable
communities and a way of living in balance with the rest of the biosphere. But to achieve those goals, we often had to try to stop destructive activities.

So it seemed ironic that we were always fighting against things—
against testing underground nuclear explosives in Alaska, against drilling for oil in stormy Hecate Strait between Haida Gwaii and mainland
British Columbia, against further damming the Peace River at site c in
northern B.C. for hydroelectricity, against clear-cut logging, against
pollution by pulp mills. As the chief executive officer of a forestry company once wrote, environmentalists seemed "anti-everything."

As an academic with tenure at the University of British Columbia, a good grant, and a great group of students, I had a wonderful
life. I had tremendous freedom, no time clock to punch, and no boss
watching my every move. So long as I carried out my teaching and

administrative work and directed my students, I could spend most of my time having fun, though to me that meant spending seven days a week, often till 1:00 or 2:00 in the morning, at the lab. The freedom that academia offers enabled me to get involved in both civil-rights and environmental issues, and I began to throw myself into controversies.

In the 1970s, as host of both *Science Magazine* on television and *Quirks and Quarks* on radio, I was in a good position to explore a variety of issues, especially those related to race and the impact of modern genetics and technological advances on medical care. I spoke out on them, supported the peace movement, and opposed the proliferation of nuclear weapons and the Vietnam War. In British Columbia, it was impossible to avoid being drawn into environmental battles over pollution, clear-cut logging, and mining.

As an activist I operated in a helter-skelter fashion, getting involved when asked or when I saw something that triggered my interest. I could be useful by signing petitions, writing letters of support, giving talks to help raise funds or highlight issues with the public. But I was unfocused, helping out when the opportunity presented itself and acting as an individual.

Being high-profile brought some danger. When we were in the heat of the battles over logging, a bullet was fired through the front window of my home, my office was broken into twice to get at my computer; once, in Haida Gwaii, while I was jogging along the road outside the logging village of Sandspit, a truck was turned at me and I was driven into a ditch. Tara and I often felt very vulnerable and alone, and we worried about our children's safety.

During my fourth and last year (1978–79) as host of *Quirks and Quarks*, Anita Gordon had become the producer, and she continued in that role when Jay Ingram took my place. In 1988, with environmental concern making headlines, Anita asked me to host a CBC Radio series on the subject. I agreed, and we received the go-ahead to do five shows that were broadcast in a series called *It's a Matter of Survival*. Traveling to conferences in North and South America, Europe, and Asia, I interviewed for the program more than 150 scientists and experts from many countries and fields about environmental problems and how the world would look fifty years hence if we carried on with business as usual. Most of those interviews were conducted in an intense period of about four months, and I could suddenly see with crystal clarity that the very life-support systems of the planet were being destroyed at a horrifying rate and on a grand scale.

This new perspective galvanized me with a sense of urgency that has only increased over the years. The radio series conveyed the magnitude of the problem as well as the uplifting message that by acting now we could avoid the fate we were heading toward. The series evoked an incredible response. More than sixteen thousand letters came in, most ending with the plea, "What can I do?"

Until then, my standard response to such a query had been, "I'm just a messenger telling people about the crisis that is happening. I'm afraid I don't have all the solutions." But this time Tara said, "David, we've been warning people about the problems for years. This response shows we've reached a lot of the general public, but now people feel helpless because they don't know what to do. You've got to go beyond the warnings and start talking about solutions."

I didn't like assuming that responsibility, but I could see she was right. It's one thing to hear a dismaying report, but it's another thing altogether to track down experts, organizations, and articles that might offer answers. In raising the alarm, I now also had to provide something that would help people take action if they were so motivated.

This truth was brought home to me by another experience. Noam Chomsky, the famed linguist at the Massachusetts Institute of Technology and one of the strongest critics of American foreign policy, gave a talk to a full house at the Queen Elizabeth Theatre in Vancouver. I chaired the event, and like the audience, I was enthralled by his analysis and insights. But during the question-and-answer period, he refused to recommend courses of action, organizations, or even books to read, saying that people had to find the material and make up their own minds. That helped me to realize that Tara was right: by informing and alarming people, I had a responsibility to suggest potential answers.

As well, many of our friends were anxious about strains on our eco-systems and had begun to challenge us to lead an initiative, perhaps to found a new organization. With their help, Tara and I drew up a list of about twenty "thinkers" who were committed to environmental issues but who had diverse skills and points of view; we invited them to a weekend retreat to discuss whether we needed a new, solution-oriented group. About a dozen people could make it, and in November 1989 they gave us three days of their precious time.

We gathered in the idyllic setting of Pender Island, one of the Gulf Islands in the Strait of Georgia between Vancouver Island and the B.C. mainland. The lodge where we met was close to the ocean and had an orchard and paths we could wander while discussing ideas. Tara and I were pretty naive about how to run such a meeting; at first we had no facilitator or written agenda, only questions and a sense of urgency. Luckily, Vancouver writer Stan Persky, known for his incisive analysis and his expertise at meetings, took over as chair.

I talked about my sobering and motivating experience working on *It's a Matter of Survival* and the enormous public response it received. Then I asked two questions: "Is there a need, an important role, for yet another environmental organization? And if the answer is yes, what would its focus be and how would it differ from other groups?"

The brainstorming participants were outspoken and irreverent, leading to vigorous, productive sessions. We agreed that most orga-nizations we knew had sprung up as a result of a crisis—to oppose the spraying of a school yard with herbicide, to fight a factory polluting the water, to protect a treasured forest about to be clear-cut. But each crisis is merely a symptom or manifestation of a deeper, underlying root cause. Even if each crisis is resolved, we are no closer to long-term balance with our surroundings unless we get at the cause. An organization was needed to focus on root causes, so that steps could be taken to produce real change.

We agreed it should be a science-based organization. We would not do original research or give out research grants, but we would use the best scientific information available and hire scientists to help write or edit the papers we wanted to produce. Further, we would emphasize communication: we would learn how best to deliver this top-quality information to the public. Successful communication would be as important as the science itself. I have always believed this, which is why, as a scientist, I chose to go into television.

At the meeting on Pender Island, we also decided not to accept government grants or support—a decision that had enormous ramifications. Such support can become a substantial part of an organization's budget. But government priorities change easily; organizations are often told they could qualify for further grants if they would just shift their focus—and before anyone realizes it, the promise of continued funding is directing activities. We also decided that if companies offered us money, they would have to demonstrate a genuine commitment to environmental sustainability before we would consider accepting funds.

In the early days of the organization, the decision to abstain from government support made life difficult. We could have had several employees paid by Canada Manpower (the federal employment insurance system at the time) and grants to help us get up and running, but we chose to use only the money Tara and I were putting in. We stuck to that decision, and it gave us the freedom to speak out without worrying about jeopardizing our funding.

The group at Pender Island then decided the name of the organization should be the David Suzuki Foundation. I objected. It seemed conceited, and I was not in this endeavor to be remembered in perpetuity. It would also be an enormous responsibility to ensure that an organization carrying my name remained true to the values I believed in, as also shared and expressed by those at our retreat.

The counterargument was twofold. First, my profile in Canada had been built up over many years of working in science and the media and of speaking out, so my name would immediately tell people what the foundation stood for. If we named it the Pender Group, for example, we would be starting from scratch. Second, it might be possible to translate the reputation my work had created into fuel for the new organization. The viewers and readers who liked my work might send funds to support the initiative. It was a long debate, lasting many months, but in the end I had to acquiesce.

Miles Richardson, then president of the Haida Nation, was one of the first three board members, along with Tara and me. One of the strengths of the foundation from the beginning has been strong aboriginal input. Chief Sophie Pierre, the powerhouse administrator of the Ktunaxa-Kinbasket Tribal Council, attended the retreat with her little boy. Norma Cassi, outspoken young member of the Gwich'in First Nation of Old Crow in Canada's Yukon Territory, also joined us. A number of other key people had spent years working with First Nations communities.

By the end of the weekend, the Pender Island retreat had created a new organization. Now the challenge was to get it off the ground. But predictably, after the enthusiasm of the first gathering, everyone went back to their work. They were, after all, engaged scientists, lawyers, professors, and writers with far too much on their plates to begin with. Eight months later, nothing had happened.

Tara decided to get on with it. She met with a respected accountant to learn what had to be done, and she paid for a lawyer who by September 1990 had established our legal status as a charitable organization. Shortly after that, she found space for an office that was formally opened on January 1, 1991. Now the David Suzuki Foundation really existed.

The office was above an automobile repair shop and was cheap, but the gas and paint fumes seeping up through the floor each day must have been a serious health hazard. The roof leaked, the wastebaskets were populated with mice, and everything we had in the office—a raggedy collection of furniture and shelves—was borrowed or donated. From this bare-bones setting we were going to take on the world. It was a place where the original founding group could gather and where volunteers could drop in to work, which they did from the first day. We were gratified to see how willing people were to spend hours and days helping, but now we had to figure out what to do.

One of our first organizational arrangements proved unworkable, and it was my fault. At our founding meeting, we had decided to create a two-headed organization: an institute, which would carry out projects, and a foundation, which would have charitable status and raise funds for the institute. Each would have its own board. I had wanted to free the project arm from worrying about fund-raising so it could focus exclusively on its work, and I thought my best role would be to raise the money to get things done. The problem was that the institute board just wanted to bash ahead, and people became frustrated because we didn't have the money to do it, given that initially all the cash was coming from Tara and me. I didn't begrudge the money, but I wouldn't be able to provide enough for the projects we wanted to develop. I had to get busy helping the foundation raise funds.

Luckily, I was asked if I would like to raise money for a charity of my choice by joining a cruise from Vancouver to Alaska. I was to give lectures, and travelers would pay an extra, tax-deductible $125 to be part of our group. About 140 people signed up, and both Tara and I gave talks and promoted our new organization while discussing the environment. The ship had bars, restaurants, swimming pools, and a theater showing the latest films. Sarika was eight and still extremely shy, so I was surprised when we boarded the ship to see her scamper away with her sister and disappear for hours. She finally returned, breathless with excitement, clutching fistfuls of chocolate bars. "Daddy, Daddy!" she exclaimed. "There are stores with candy and it's all free. All you have to do is sign your name and room number!"

The trip was a delight, as we met people who were filled with enthusiasm and concern for environmental matters; many have remained our friends. Our efforts raised $18,000, which was a grand sum at that stage. But more was necessary; we had to use that money to find our supporters.

Over the years, thousands of people had written to *The Nature of Things with David Suzuki*. Many asked for transcripts, videos, or the names of experts: those requests were dealt with by staff. But many letters were addressed to me personally, asking a wide range of questions. I felt that if someone had taken the time to write a letter, he or she deserved a response. Usually I could jot a short note on a card, but often I wrote longer letters, always by hand.

All those people I wrote back to and the sixteen thousand who responded to *It's a Matter of Survival* made for a wonderful list of people we could approach for support. We met Harvey McKinnon, who had a long history of working for charitable organizations like Oxfam, and with his help, we drafted a letter reminding people they'd once written to me and asking for their support to find solutions to the ecological degradation of the planet.

The money we had raised from the Alaskan cruise paid for that first mailing. With the help of many volunteers, in November 1990 Tara sent out some 25,000 letters. What a learning curve that was! And then, just before Christmas, checks and cash began to come in, first as a trickle and then as a flood of full mailbags. Harvey said that in his fund-raising experience the returns were phenomenal.

Tara was both thrilled and appalled. It was one thing to pay for things with our own money; once donations were received, the responsibility was enormous. Having no experience in handling charitable donations, she had nightmares of losing track. We were also very aware that people had donated to us with faith that we would use their money effectively to carry out our mandate.

Within months of sending in forty- or fifty-dollar gifts, people were writing to ask what we had accomplished with their money. Our immediate needs were fund-raising software to track donations, computers to run it, and staff to keep all accounting accurate. We also had to increase our base of support by investing some of the funds in wider mailings. But our early supporters naturally wanted their money to go directly to projects that were protecting the environment. We had to come up with a creative solution that would bring quick results while developing the organization.

Tara and I had already been investing our own money to support Barbara Zimmerman, who was working in Brazil with Paiakan and the Kaiapo of Aucre to establish a research station in the Xingu River watershed, which drains into the Amazon River. The project helps protect a vast, pristine area, so we transferred this project to the foundation.

I had also been introduced to the Ainu of Japan, an aboriginal people who had held on to their culture through 1,500 years of Japanese occupation. Now they were close to losing their language and their last sacred river, the Saragawa. The river was to be dammed to provide energy for industrial development on the northern island of Hokkaido. Many felt the dam was not necessary and that it would threaten the salmon, a totemic species to the Ainu.

I was asked to help raise international awareness of this latest threat to Ainu culture, so Tara and I sponsored a visit to Vancouver by Ainu children and Shigeru Kayano, an elder in his sixties who was the youngest person still speaking the Ainu language. At one point, the Japanese translator broke down and wept as she listened to Kayano recount how he had been treated as a child by the Japanese. The event was packed and brought the audience to tears.

Remembering our experience with Paiakan and the successful protest against the proposed dam at Altamira, we suggested holding

Wearing my blanket from B.C. First Nations as I am feted by Ainu people in Hokkaido

a demonstration at the site of the dam on the Saragawa and inviting aboriginal people from other countries. This idea was enthusiastically accepted, and we ended up raising money to send delegations from several British Columbia First Nations communities: Alert Bay, Bella Bella, and Haida Gwaii. This project we also turned over to the foundation.

I had so looked forward to attending the demonstration and was disappointed when the date chosen for it coincided with a meeting of the International Congress of Genetics in Edinburgh, Scotland. I had agreed to be a vice president of the congress and to deliver a talk there, so I missed the gathering on Hokkaido. By all accounts it was a spectacular display as the First Nations from Canada danced and sang on the site of the dam. The event garnered a huge amount of media coverage. Unfortunately, it failed to move the Japanese government; the dam was built a few years later.

We were involved in other projects that became part of the foundation's early stable of accomplishments at little or no cost to the organization. Environmentalists and natives in western Colombia asked for help to protect the rich Choco rain forest, so Tara and I paddled a dugout up the Bora Bora River with a National Film Board crew from Canada to visit the people living in houses built on stilts and to produce a widely distributed program on the issues. In these ways, we demonstrated to our supporters that the foundation was actively engaged in significant projects, buying us time until the board could launch a well-thought-out slate of activities.

Tara had done a heroic job of getting the organization off the ground while learning everything from rules governing charities to board–staff relations, newsletter production, fund-raising techniques, and personnel issues. She had given up a prestigious teaching position at Harvard University to be a full-time volunteer for the foundation, but it took a huge toll. Whether at home or at play, she carried her work with her, an enormous weight of responsibility. I was still running around filming with *The Nature of Things with David Suzuki*, giving talks in different places, and raising money to support our foundation projects. Tara was stuck day in and day out with the nuts and bolts. She worked long hours, often seven days a week, coming home physically drained and psychologically burdened by worry.

Several times in those first twenty-four months, I told her, "Tara, let's drop it. You gave it a try, but it's just too much work. I can't do my share, and it's ruining your health." But she stayed with it, something for which I have enormous admiration and gratitude. The foundation became her baby, and she was going to nurture it and see it grow into an effective organization.

Gradually we raised enough money to hire staff. Board members rolled up their sleeves. Soon we could bite the bullet and hire an executive director to give the foundation leadership and get the new, board-directed projects up and going.

We received a number of applications and winnowed them to a shortlist that included Jim Fulton, the Canadian member of Parliament who had tipped me off about the struggle over logging in Windy Bay in Haida Gwaii. Jim had been a probation officer and as a candidate for the New Democratic Party (NDP) had stunned political commentators by wresting the riding of Skeena away from the Liberal cabinet minister Iona Campagnolo.

Skeena is all of northwestern B.C., a vast area the size of France. It's exhausting just thinking about how a politician can work in Ottawa yet serve such a huge riding three thousand miles away. Jim says he missed every one of his kids' birthdays while he was in office. Jim is a larger-than-life character. He is well over six feet tall and has a powerful chest and arms and a belly that could absorb any frontal attack. With his hair and mustache now turned white, he reminds me of those mountain gorilla males called silverbacks; like them, he commands respect by sheer physical presence.

But Jim also has a mischievous air about him, and he has delighted in childlike play both as a politician and as executive director of our foundation. Perhaps his most famous stunt as an MP came when, in an attempt to stop the spread of a virus infecting the sockeye salmon, the federal Department of Fisheries and Oceans had put a barricade in the Babine River, which drains into the Skeena, thus preventing the salmon from reaching their spawning grounds. Jim learned about it and drove to witness the fish smashing repeatedly into the barrier as they tried in vain to move upriver. He captured a large female sockeye, which was dying without reaching the spawning beds to complete her lifecycle. Jim put her in a bag and took her carcass to Ottawa.

There he donned baggy pants, slipped the bag down his pant leg, and smuggled it into the House of Commons. He rose during Question Period to query the minister of Fisheries and Oceans about the sockeye in the Babine, knowing the answers from Erik Nielsen would be bafflegab. As Nielsen waffled, Jim suddenly yanked the salmon out of his pants, splashing slime onto his NDP colleague Margaret Mitchell, who screamed and alarmed the

Jim Fulton, former Member of Parliament and now executive director
of the David Suzuki Foundation, at play

parliamentarians. Jim strode across the floor and slammed the fish onto Prime Minister Brian Mulroney's desk.

All hell broke loose. Some thought Jim had pulled a weapon. In the pandemonium, Jim walked out to address the waiting media. It was a sensational stunt he claims spurred Nielsen to act and let the Babine sockeye through to spawn. But it also led to the passage of "the Fulton Rule," which forbids a parliamentarian from carrying anything into the House that can be used as a weapon. Jim says he is proud of the fact that at the end of the species' next four-year cycle, the sockeye run in the Babine was one of the largest in recent history.

Jim was a serious politician and served his electorate well, as shown by his steadily increasing share of the vote through four elections. But it was on tough national issues—debates that lasted for years—that Jim really demonstrated his strength and vision of Canada.

In 1981, he successfully led the constitutional debate for the NDP in the House to secure the recognition and affirmation of aboriginal and treaty rights. For the next twelve years, Jim led the constitutional fight for the Nisga'a in Parliament, and today they have the first modern-day treaty in Canada.

Jim focused the battle on the floor of the House to save South Moresby, known to the Haida as Gwaii Haanas. It was his motion that was unanimously passed in Parliament and that triggered the release of $140 million to "seal the deal."

For five years, Jim debated Prime Minister Trudeau's decision to allow Amax Corporation to dump 100 million tons of toxic waste into Canada's pristine Pacific fishing grounds. Jim won, the dumping was halted, and the House ruled that the authorization of the dumping was an abuse of power. It was a remarkable story of tenacity and courage.

During the Gulf War, Jim exposed Canada's illegal production and testing of nerve gas at Defence Research in Suffield, Alberta. And long before Kyoto, Jim's work with Paul Martin and David MacDonald on climate change led to an all-party report calling for 20 percent cuts from 1990 levels of greenhouse gas emissions by 2005.

When Jim decided to end his political career after fifteen years, his departure was eloquently lamented by columnists and colleagues on both sides of the House.

I was incredulous but delighted when Jim applied to become executive director of our foundation. We had no track record as an organization, and we faced a huge challenge in raising the money to do our projects. I thought he was just checking around to see what possibilities were available, but he insisted he wanted the job. It was flattering that he would consider us, but I joked to him that if he had a gender change, the decision would be a slam dunk; I was committed to hiring a woman, and I told our board I favored a female candidate.

But during our deliberations, it became clear that Jim's track record as a committed environmentalist, his experience as a politician, the high esteem he commanded from First Nations and communities, his irresistible personality, and his exuberant energy made him the best choice. Our final decision was unanimous, and we were thrilled when Jim accepted our offer. We could pay him only a fraction of what he could command elsewhere, but when I apologized, he replied that he would get a pension from his years as a member of Parliament, and besides, "we have to be lifers on these issues."

By the time we hired him, we had already begun to acquire the financial support that enabled us to move to a new office on Fourth Avenue in Vancouver, in the heart of the Kitsilano neighborhood that had been a hippie magnet during the 1960s and '70s. It was an ideal location, and the building, built and owned by businessman Harold Kalke, is heated and cooled through geothermal heat-exchange pipes driven into the earth.

During the '60s and '70s, when I had an active genetics research program at UBC, the people in the lab worked and played together, a surrogate family. When I walked into our offices at the foundation, I felt a similar joy. Here were people earning a decent living wage and believing they were working toward a better world.

Jim came into the job with great vigor and soon launched projects as if we already had the money. I'm still hostage to my early years of poverty, but he had faith that we would raise the necessary funds. And he was right, but in the beginning, I was very nervous about all the spending. We were a brand-new, tiny organization with big plans; less than a year after opening our doors, we had a list of ten project areas we eventually wanted to cover.

If we were going to be effective in communicating with the public, we had to know something about what motivates people to change their behavior. After all, we would be going up against corporations such as the automobile, fossil fuel, forestry, and pharmaceutical industries, which spend billions on advertising and public relations. So we sponsored a conference in May 1995 and invited people who have studied and helped influence social change to share their insights; those talks were published as "Tools for Change," a document that has infused the way we do our work.

These days we are bombarded by media stories and headlines crying that the economy is the bottom line and should dictate the way we behave, our priorities, and our sacrifices. That never made sense to me—we know we are biological creatures, that if we don't have clean air, water, soil and energy, we cannot lead healthy, productive lives—so we commissioned John Robinson, head of the Sustainable Development Research Institute at UBC, to write "Living Within Our Means," which outlined humankind's fundamental needs and the real bottom line of sustainability.

AS WE BEGAN TO scope out our first project on fisheries, it became the model for later work. Salmon are iconic animals for aboriginal peoples on both the Pacific and Atlantic coasts of North America. If northern cod pulled Europeans to the shores of Newfoundland for five hundred years, the five species of Pacific salmon—sockeye, pink, chum, chinook (or spring), and coho—lie at the heart of Canada's coastal First Nations cultures, nourishing them physically and spiritually.

In thousands of rivers and streams along the west coast of North America, the return of salmon to their natal waters—in numbers that dwarf those of the fabled bison and passenger pigeons in the past and the caribou and wildebeest today—is one of nature's greatest spectacles. But salmon had disappeared from hundreds of rivers, and runs in many others were dropping steeply. Urban development, farming, logging, pollution, dams, and fishing had deeply affected populations that once flourished from California to Alaska; now they were maintained in large numbers only in B.C. and Alaska. As well, ocean-bottom trawling was destroying habitat crucial to marine biodiversity; a roe fishery to supply Japanese markets was devastating herring populations that were critical feed for many species, including salmon; salmon aquaculture was being touted as a replacement for wild populations.

We asked a group of distinguished experts to meet and discuss the nature of the problem, its primary causes and potential solutions. We then sought a more detailed analysis; Carl Walters, a world-renowned fisheries authority at the University of British Columbia, accepted our invitation to write a scientifically based evaluation of the state of Pacific salmon. Carl brought the analytic powers of computers to the fields of ecology and fisheries management and was known for his hard-nosed approach and fearlessness in telling it like it is. His report was extensively reviewed by scientists and fishermen before publication to ensure its accuracy and credibility.

The report, "Fish on the Line," concluded that salmon runs were in trouble along the coast of B.C. It put the responsibility for the problems on the Department of Fisheries and Oceans (DFO), indigenous peoples, and commercial and sport fishers—in other words, on everyone with a stake in the future of the fish.

With so much finger-pointing, it upset everyone, as expected. All interest groups knew the fish were in trouble, but none was willing to give up its share of the bounty. The report was criticized bitterly, and the media played up the angry critics. The David Suzuki Foundation had a major impact in delivering the message that the salmon runs were in trouble, and that there was clearly a need for a different management strategy. Now, what could be done about it?

In our next study, Lynn Pinkerton, today a professor at Simon Fraser University in Burnaby, B.C., and Marty Weinstein, adjunct professor at the UBC Fisheries Centre, both longtime workers in First Nations communities, identified common features in sustainable fisheries around the world. In all such cases, the resource was managed by the local fishing community, which not only was responsible for maintaining stocks but also was held accountable for their state, and the knowledge and experience of the fishers themselves provided the basis for the fishing practices. These findings were published in a report entitled "Fisheries That Work."

Canada attempts to manage its Pacific and Atlantic fisheries from faraway Ottawa in Ontario and relies on government experts who are not free to state the scientific evidence in public or to make recommendations based on it; government scientists are under intense political pressure to provide information and advice that support the government of the day. The observations and advice of those who make a living on the ocean and in rivers and lakes are rendered marginal or ignored. Such an approach on the east coast of Canada has been catastrophic—the cod fishery, for example, has long since collapsed—yet DFO has been unresponsive to the knowledge of local fishers.

"Fisheries That Work" was a good-news report, giving lots of examples of what works elsewhere and answers to outstanding questions. It was well received by local fishing communities, but the study received almost no play in the media. Crisis and confrontation make stories, but good news is deemed to be boring.

Undaunted, we funded a group of First Nations, commercial fishers, tourism operators, and environmentalists in the village of Ucluelet on Vancouver Island to apply community management of the local fish. The jury is still out on whether local management of species of salmon that migrate long distances can work when they are intercepted in the ocean. As a model for other projects, our fisheries studies provided a good one—do the analysis, look for solutions, then apply what was learned.

Since then, the foundation has funded numerous fisheries projects, including University of Victoria biologist Tom Reimchen's seminal work on the biological marriage between salmon and the rain forest; a province-wide DSF-sponsored inquiry on salmon led by the eminent B.C. judge Stuart Leggatt; a report on the DFO's policy of licensing the killing of spawning herring just for the roe; and a challenge to salmon farming.

THE GROWTH OF SALMON farms on the west coast of British Columbia has been cancerous. Today, production of salmon from open netpens dwarfs the number of wild fish captured. But these developments have been accompanied by numerous problems, and our foundation has played a major role in publicizing the dangers.

To many people, salmon aquaculture seems the marine equivalent of farming on land—use the ocean currents to slosh through nets that confine large numbers of animals whose growth is sped by regular feeding. The premise is that we can improve on nature with greater survival, faster growth, and year-round availability of the fish. But as we are learning from experience with cattle, poultry, and hogs, feedlots create enormous problems of disease, inhumane conditions, and waste.

But salmon aquaculture is wrongheaded from the very start. For one thing, unlike cows, sheep, and pigs, the fish are carnivores. They must eat fish. If we don't raise lions or wolves for food, why do we grow salmon? Food fish like anchovies, herring, and sardines, which people in South America eat, are being depleted to make pellets to feed salmon. As well, vast quantities of feces accumulate beneath netpens; diseases and parasites like sea lice explode and spread to wild fish, and large numbers of alien Atlantic salmon—also being raised in west coast salmon farms—escape periodically into the Pacific. Sea lions, otters, eagles, seals, and other predators attracted to the concentrated fish in nets have been legally killed by feedlot operators to protect their "crop." And the flesh of the farmed fish is contaminated with chemicals biomagnified from the feed fish, antibiotics, and dyes to color the flesh.

Aquaculture, like agriculture, must be a part of the food future for humanity, but it will be sustainable only when practiced according to principles that will ensure continued ecological, social, and personal health. Global health, environmental, and equity issues are poorly handled by advocates of salmon aquaculture, and chefs and the public in B.C. are catching on and showing signs of discriminating in their buying.

Ecological health also can be restored on a small, local scale. Salmon are at the center of one of our most gratifying projects, revitalizing the run to Musqueam Creek in Vancouver. In 1900, the area that now encompasses the city boasted more than fifty rivers, streams, and creeks, each with its own genetically distinctive races of salmon. Some waterways might have had fewer than a hundred spawners returning, others had hundreds of thousands, but together they supported millions of fish. The past century of human encroachment has meant creeks were filled in, streams diverted, and riverbanks cleared of vegetation and polluted as our needs trumped those of the fish. At the end of the twentieth century, only one stream in Vancouver still had wild salmon runs—Musqueam Creek.

The creek runs through the Musqueam Reserve on the west side of Vancouver, home of the Musqueam First Nation, but only a dozen or so salmon were making it back to spawn. In an area that is now heavily populated and includes many properties with riding stables, Musqueam Creek was under pressure from horses ridden through it, children playing in it, and the runoff from storm sewers and homes illegally hooked up to dump sewage into it.

In 1996, the David Suzuki Foundation was approached by the Musqueam people to help rehabilitate the creek. Willard Sparrow, grandson of the famous chief Edward Sparrow Jr., had become very concerned; in a way, the survival of that tiny salmon run seemed symbolic of the fate of his people. Could the old ways and the salmon they depend on be retained in an increasingly urban setting?

Nicholas Scapiletti was working for the foundation at the time and hit it off with Willard as the two of them began a campaign to raise money to clean up and protect "Vancouver's last salmon creek" and to educate people in the neighborhood. The Musqueam Watershed Restoration Project was begun to train Musqueam youth to care for the waterway, shore up its banks, create baffles to slow the water, plant trees along the edge, put up signs, and distribute informational flyers. Willard educated his people about the symbolic importance of the creek and got them to support a small group of stream keepers. Once, Willard was wading in the creek to check it when to his delight a woman on horseback spotted him and yelled, "Hey, the Musqueam are trying to bring the salmon back in that creek, so get out of there!" The neighbors had now taken ownership and pride in this small stream and were watching over it.

As Willard and Nick staged celebrations of the watershed, invited biologists to talk about biodiversity and nutrient flow, organized tree-planting days, and held salmon barbecues to mark the role of fish in our lives, the city and funding agencies found the restoration of Musqueam Creek irresistible. Not only did the duo get funding for the project, the city supported construction of a different kind of roadway in the surrounding area so that water could percolate back into the soil of the watershed instead of being sent down storm sewers to run into the ocean. The team even brought dead salmon from other runs and distributed them along the banks of the creek to return nutrients to the soil, as had happened naturally before "progress" intervened.

Musqueam Creek is on its way back to health; the number of returning fish rose to over fifty in 2004. Nature is incredibly generous when we give her a hand.

TARA WAS NAMED PRESIDENT of the foundation but was not paid for the long, often arduous hours she had put in to get it going. As projects were developed and staff began to pour out material, I was given credit for much of it because the organization carries my name, but in reality—as with the television shows I do—the foundation produces material through the hard work of a devoted team. Volunteers like Tara and me have been a crucial part of the organization's work and effectiveness; I have been amazed at the devotion and hours volunteers give, not just to us, but to so many important causes. They are part of the glue that holds society together.

As the foundation has taken on issues and projects, we also have become increasingly efficient in getting our message across. Our goal was to invest half of every foundation dollar in communication, since public education and awareness are crucial to our mandate of offering solutions. David Hocking, with long experience at Petrocan, came to us to head the communications team.

Having staff behind us also meant Tara and I were no longer feeling isolated or harried. If I was to talk to some special interest group or meet a political leader, the staff would often update background notes that made me so much more effective.

It is clear that the old ways of confrontation, protests, and demonstrations so vital from the 1960s through the '80s, have become less compelling to a public jaded by sensational stories of violence, terror,

Tara delivering a speech as president of the David Suzuki Foundation

and sex. We need new alliances and partnerships and ways of informing people.

When the foundation was started, we were imbued with the sense
of urgency implicit in the Worldwatch Institute's designation of the
1990s as "the Turnaround Decade." The decade came and went. The
world didn't change direction, but now the foundation has matured.
We have earned a presence in the media, influence within the political
and industrial community, and credibility with the public.

UP AND RUNNING

I N ITS EARLY YEARS, the David Suzuki Foundation (DSF) had to acquire a membership base that would support the projects we had planned. That meant we had to become adept at getting our message out.

We picked up experience in organizing press conferences and writing press releases, articles, op-ed pieces, and other documents, and the day came when the communications group, headed by David Hocking, established a Web site. I was slow to recognize the role the Internet would play in raising our profile, and I was nervous about committing the funds. Now I appreciate the importance of that investment.

Jim Hoggan, president of the largest communications and public relations company in western Canada, found our work interesting and worthwhile. He offered his expertise on a voluntary basis. He brought great integrity—he advises his clients that they should never deliberately lie, deceive, or cover up. Jim helped us develop the most effective ways to get our message out, and ever since he joined the board, he has devoted countless hours to our communication effort.

AS THE FOUNDATION BECAME more sophisticated and better equipped to tackle issues, we felt ready to take on some big ones. And of all environmental crises confronting us today, climate change looms as the largest.

Cited by the Canadian parliamentary all-party Standing Committee on the Environment as a threat second only to all-out nuclear war, global warming nonetheless can seem a slow-motion catastrophe that will not kick in for generations, and so it has been difficult to raise public concern about it.

Jim Fulton's political connections paid off when he persuaded Gerry Scott, a longtime strategist in the provincial New Democratic Party, to join us in taking on the foundation's climate change campaign. The challenge was to educate the public about what climate change is, what the scientific evidence is for its cause, and what the solutions are. Most environmental funding agencies were established to finance work on more immediate challenges such as toxic pollution, deforestation, or destructive developments. Global warming has implications on a much more immense scale, and it was extremely difficult to fund the project. I despaired over whether we could find the kind of money we would need to make a difference.

Stephen Bronfman of Montreal had joined our board in the early years. He became convinced that climate change was a serious issue and made a multiyear financial commitment to Gerry's group, becoming the largest individual contributor to the issue in Canada. Assured of this solid base of support, Gerry pulled together a small band of experienced and dedicated people and began to get the matter onto the Canadian public agenda. For such a small team, they carried out a remarkable series of studies and activities.

Gerry invited Ray Anderson, CEO of Interface, the largest flooring company in the world, to join our campaign to get industry leaders to start working to cut emissions and make money doing it. Ray stepped up to the plate and is now on the DSF board.

The group commissioned papers including "A Glimpse of Canada's Future," "The Role of Government," "Taking Charge: Personal Initiatives," "Keeping Canada Competitive," and "Canadian Solutions." But by far the most remarkable was "Power Shift," a study by energy expert Ralph Torrie, showing that with technology already commercially available, Canada could reduce its greenhouse gas emissions by 50 percent in thirty years.

We brought Dr. Joseph J. Romm to Toronto and Ottawa to talk about his 1999 book *Cool Companies,* which cited dozens of North American companies that had already reduced their emissions by more than 50 percent and remained highly profitable. Since then, the Rockefeller Brothers Foundation has begun to track "reducers"—companies, cities, regions, provinces and states that are making serious reductions in harmful gas emissions while saving tens of millions of dollars.

When *The Nature of Things with David Suzuki* broadcast a film by Jim Hamm showing many examples of opportunities to make money by reducing greenhouse gas emissions, the DSF put together a series of events in Toronto, Calgary, and Vancouver, with speeches, previews of the film, and exhibitions of energy-saving technologies such as windmills and then-unknown gas-electric hybrid cars. We knew we had to get on with demonstrating that there are alternatives to the polluting ways that are creating climate change, since neither governments nor businesspeople were leading the way.

It was hard work to get media attention until DSF employee Catherine Fitzpatrick had the brilliant idea of looking at the medical implications of burning fossil fuels. She concentrated on the direct effects of air pollution—not the spread of new diseases in a warmer world or starvation from drought and failing crops, but the direct, day-to-day, physical effects of air pollution on people. If we couldn't get attention for climate change as a monumental threat, we could bring attention to the more personal costs of burning fossil fuels.

Sharing a joke with Gerry Scott when he was director of climate change work
with the David Suzuki Foundation

This strategy worked. Using government data, the doctors and scientists Catherine commissioned produced a report entitled "Taking Our Breath Away." It found that air pollution, much of it from burning fossil fuels, was prematurely killing sixteen thousand Canadians a year. A plane crash killing all occupants is a great tragedy, but imagine a full jumbo jet crashing in Canada every week: you get an idea of the magnitude of these preventable fossil fuel–induced deaths from pollution.

And every fatality is just the tip of an immense iceberg. For every death, there are many more serious lung problems requiring hospitalization, including surgery. For each hospitalization, there are many more days lost from school or work, then many more with reduced productivity because of low-grade problems of bronchitis and asthma.

"Taking Our Breath Away" was the first DSF report to be translated into Canada's other official language, French, as "À couper le souffle." Doctors recognized the significance of the report, and English- and

French-speaking physicians supported our call to reduce air pollution. Federal and provincial medical societies also signed on to our initiative to reduce greenhouse gas emissions for health reasons.

One of the first people to buy in was Dr. David Swann, chief health officer for the province of Alberta. I was stunned when he was fired for taking this position. This is Canada, yet here was Alberta behaving like some tin-pot government vindictively punishing a public servant for deviating from the government line. Dr. Swann fought back and eventually won reinstatement, but he soon left public service in the province. Taking a stand on climate change in Alberta took courage.

In concert with other organizations, Gerry commissioned papers that looked at the impact of climate change on Canada's national parks. Jay Malcolm, a forestry professor at the University of Toronto, concluded that global warming would dismantle the species balance of our most prized parks: some species could adapt to higher temperatures, but others would have to move to remain within a viable range.

A 2004 DSF study, "Confronting Climate Change in the Great Lakes Region," looked at the hydrological implications of climate change on lakes Superior, Michigan, Erie, Huron, and Ontario, which constitute the largest area of fresh water on Earth. The report concluded that the effects would be catastrophic.

The Nature of Things with David Suzuki did a series of programs on global warming, including a two-hour special. Polls showed that Canadians were becoming increasingly concerned about climate change, and I like to think that both the David Suzuki Foundation and *The Nature of Things* played an important part in increasing that awareness and concern.

The evidence of climate change is now overwhelming, and to me nothing is more compelling than the cover story in the conservative *National Geographic* magazine in September 2004. Presented on a fold-out page, the 400,000-year record of carbon dioxide concentrations in the atmosphere, teased from the Antarctic ice by researchers, reveals a curve that in about 1990 suddenly soars above the highest level found in all that time. That curve then leaps straight up.

But personal observations, even if anecdotal and not statistically significant, are compelling too. When Tara and I camped above the Arctic Circle in June 2005, we saw and heard firsthand evidence of shrinking glaciers, melting permafrost, and newly arrived plant and animal species. Arctic peoples speak of global warming as a well-established fact that has changed their habitat and already threatens their way of life.

Yet, despite the overwhelming consensus of climatologists and the most painstaking assessment of scientific literature in history, in 2005 the media continued to treat climate change as if it is a controversy, as if there is still doubt. They give far more space than is warranted to the small number of "skeptics" who deny global warming is occurring. This is tragic.

Accepting that the danger is real, society can look for solutions. Reducing greenhouse gas emissions means buying time to switch to alternative, nonpolluting energy sources and enjoying the direct benefits of a cleaner environment, better health, and the conservation of valuable, nonrenewable fossil fuels. If by some miracle the crisis passes, those nonrenewable fossil fuels will still be there, our homes and businesses will be more efficient, and our environment will be cleaner. Acting on climate change is a win-win situation, whereas doing nothing will make the corrective measures much more difficult, much more expensive, and perhaps too late.

After the Earth Summit in Rio in 1992, an intergovernmental negotiating committee was established to meet and work out a framework within which the climate convention could be assessed. In 1995, the Conference of the Parties (COP) to the United Nations Framework on Climate Change was established to meet annually in a different country. At the meetings, terms of the protocol were refined, progress assessed and scientific information updated. The first COP meeting in North America was held in Montreal from the end of November to early December 2005.

Thousands of delegates, NGO participants and press attended, and DSF was a prominent participant. In addition to ten staff members, eight board members took part in the meetings in different capacities. Staff worked diligently to make our position known: the Kyoto process must carry on, emissions in the industrialized nations should be cut by 25 percent by 2020 and 80 percent by 2050 if we are to minimize the consequences of the buildup of greenhouse gases. It was gratifying to see that there was no longer a debate about whether climate change is happening or whether we should reduce our emissions. The big questions were how, and how much by when.

Stephen Bronfman, as a board member, sponsored a breakfast for businesspeople concerned about climate change. More than four hundred people attended to hear another board member, Ray Anderson. As a very successful businessman, Ray could speak to the audience as one of them and his message of "doing well by doing good" resonated strongly with the audience.

Soon after being elected, George W. Bush indicated that he would not ratify Kyoto and wanted to ignore the entire process. By the Montreal meetings, the Protocol had been ratified by enough countries to make it international law. The large U.S. delegation in Montreal had no official status but actively worked to derail the Kyoto Protocol as a failure and to recruit other countries to its plan to seek new, cleaner technologies that would reduce the need to cut back on fossil fuel use. As representatives of the most powerful nation on Earth, the U.S. contingent had a lot of clout, but the country is also the world's biggest emitter of greenhouse gases and therefore has a big responsibility, as Prime Minister Paul Martin stated in his opening address. In the end, despite the American pressure, the rest of the world united to back the

Kyoto process and continue the path toward much deeper cuts. It was a crowning achievement for the delegates and may very well be looked back upon as a watershed moment.

MANY OF US IN the David Suzuki Foundation cut our teeth on battles over the future of British Columbia's forests. From South Moresby and Stein Valley to the Khutzeymateen and Clayoquot Sound, one forest after another in pristine areas had become threatened, sparking a public outcry. It seemed natural for the DSF to be involved in forestry issues.

Taking the cue from our work on fisheries, we first asked the question, what is the economic position of forestry in the province today? Even though the number of jobs and relative contribution of tax revenues from forestry were steadily declining, the media continued to widely report that forestry contributed fifty cents of every tax dollar in British Columbia's coffers. Dr. Richard Schwindt and Dr. Terry Heaps, economists at Simon Fraser University, agreed to do an analysis of the forest industry, and we published it in 1996 as "Chopping Up the Money Tree." They showed that the province's economy had become much more diverse than it was fifty years earlier, and that British Columbia's revenues from forestry were about five cents of every tax dollar.

The rant that environmentalists damage the economy and threaten jobs did not reflect reality. Forestry jobs were being lost, but the volume of wood cut was steadily increasing. The province's chief forester was well aware that logging practices greatly exceeded the renewable level. Huge machines were replacing men and working tirelessly and with deadly efficiency, aided by computers. Worse, despite legislation to prevent the export of raw logs, more and more were being shipped to other countries where high-quality jobs were created to process that wood. Every raw log exported cost B.C. jobs and economic potential. The DSF did an analysis showing that Washington State created two and a half times more employment per tree than did B.C., and California five times more.

It bothered me that Canadians, who have some of the best wood in the world, purchase finished products from Scandinavia. I don't believe we are so backward that we can't develop our own lines of wood products, using our own materials. We should use our precious raw logs far more conservatively and ensure that every tree cut creates a maximum number of jobs.

Jim Fulton recruited the dean of arts at UBC, the distinguished scholar Pat Marchak, to perform an exhaustive analysis of forestry in British Columbia. She ended up writing a book in 1999 with Scott Aycock and Deborah Herbert, *Falldown: Forest Policy in British Columbia*, widely considered the authoritative document on the subject. Pat concluded that a reduction in the volume of wood cut was needed because the current levels were not sustainable. She recommended that the use of wood be diversified to generate more jobs per cubic yard.

Could an ecoforestry code be established that might allow logging while maintaining the integrity of the forest? In 1990, DSF staff member Ronnie Drever wrote a report published as "A Cut Above," which outlined nine basic principles of what has since come to be called ecosystem-based management (EBM). Although parks and other protected areas, if sufficiently large and interconnected, can help somewhat to protect the biodiversity that sustains our economies, the future is bleak unless land outside parks is developed carefully and sustainably through EBM.

Even before "A Cut Above," we knew it was possible to log extensively in a sustainable fashion. Vancouver Island forester Merv Wilkinson has logged his forest selectively since the 1950s and removed the equivalent of his entire forest, yet has more board feet of timber growing now than before he began. In Oregon, the family-owned company Collins Pines has been in forestry for 150 years and today does some US$250 million in annual business, yet its forests are considered among

Canadian icon and hero Merv Wilkinson demonstrating
sustainable forestry at his Wildwood farm

the most pristine in the state. Thousands of employees earn a living from those forests, and the company remains globally competitive though all logging is carried out selectively, not through clear-cutting.

But forest companies whose shares are publicly traded on the stock market are driven by the need to maximize return for their investors. There is little incentive to practice sustainable forestry when to do so would mean restricting the volume of trees cut annually to perhaps 2 to 3 percent—nature's annual increase in size. Clear-cutting an entire forest and putting the money in investments would generate double or triple the interest; investing the cash in forestry in Borneo or Papua New Guinea could make perhaps ten times the return. Or the money could be put into something else, like fish, and when they're gone, into biotechnology or computers. Money can grow faster than real trees.

One result of the pressure on forestry companies to reduce their cuts is that increasingly they "high-grade," logging the most valuable species and ignoring the rest. It's a worldwide problem. In the Amazon, mahogany has been high-graded throughout much of the vast forest. Today in British Columbia, it's clear that companies are high-grading cedar at an unsustainable rate. Cedar occupies such a central place in coastal First Nations culture that the DSF commissioned two studies, "Sacred Cedar" in 1998 and "A Vanishing Heritage" in 2004, that showed how little cedar is being left for traditional use in totem poles, canoes, masks, and longhouses.

We also published a report on culturally modified trees (CMTs), which are trees that have been used by First Nations cultures on the B.C. coast over the millennia. Partially carved canoes emerging out of logs can be found decaying on the ground, and cedar trees still stand that reveal long scars where bark was stripped for clothing; some show vertical house planks have been removed without killing the tree. CMTs are precious artifacts that testify to First Nations occupation and use of the land long before the arrival of Europeans.

In addition to the report, called "The Cultural and Archaeological Significance of Culturally Modified Trees," we initiated an archaeological training program that enrolled dozens of representatives from eleven coastal villages to become CMT technicians. This generated jobs for First Nations communities, as forestry companies, required to inventory and protect these artifacts, hired such trained personnel to identify CMTs within their logging domain on government land.

WE WANTED THE FINDINGS from our reports to reach a wider audience, and in 1994 the foundation met with Greystone Books, a division of Douglas & McIntyre, the highly respected B.C. publisher. The DSF and Greystone would copublish books meant for a wide audience, and although profit was not the foundation's primary goal, we hoped the books would find an audience big enough to make them relatively self-sufficient. By 2005 we had published twenty books on a wide range of issues. It's been a lot of work, but it has been very satisfying to me to have authored or coauthored ten of them.

As the foundation grew, it seemed to me we needed a different kind of book, a philosophical treatise that would define the perspective, assumptions, and values that underlie our activities. As I began to write it, it forced me to consider matters more deeply. *The Sacred Balance: Rediscovering Our Place in Nature* brought the fundamental issues into sharp focus for me. To my surprise and delight, the book became a number 1 best-seller in Canada and Australia and continues to sell. As with other books, I signed over my royalties, so that book alone has brought the foundation close to CAN$200,000 to date.

THE CORNERSTONE OF THE foundation is its relationship with First Nations peoples and communities, and that has remained strong through the years. We understood that the First Nations along the coast of what is now British Columbia have occupied the land for millennia, and that the traditions that had evolved in their relationship with the land would tend to make them better stewards than governments and companies. We also knew that since treaties had never been signed, coastal First Nations should have sovereignty over their land.

Miles Richardson, one of the DSF's founders, is a very political man, having been president of the Haida Nation for twelve years before being appointed chief treaty commissioner for B.C. to encourage progress on treaties between Canada, B.C., and First Nations. Miles is a big man, literally and figuratively, with a formidable intellect, a huge zest for life, and a relish for facing its most difficult problems. He likes to remind us that as human beings we possess foibles, idiosyncrasies, weaknesses, and beauty. He more than anyone has tried to teach me to revel in the here and now and take pleasure in what I am doing in the moment.

When, in 1998, an opportunity arose for the DSF to work on coastal issues in B.C., Miles urged us to look at forming relationships with local First Nations communities so that we could work together and find ways of protecting forests and fish while creating sustainable ways to make a living. With chronic levels of unemployment in Native communities reaching well above 50 percent, even those who have taught us much of what we know about Mother Nature become so deprived of employment and income that they must accept the sacrifice of much of their surroundings. Having cleared the readily accessible trees in the south and around Prince Rupert, forest companies now coveted the rich forests of remote communities in the central and north coast and Haida Gwaii.

In the winter of 1997–98, Jim Fulton asked Tara to step into a staff position. He knew she was the only person who could be the foundation's "diplomat" and establish relationships with the eleven small First Nations communities within the temperate rain forest of the central and north coast and Haida Gwaii. The territory of these communities represented a quarter of all the remaining old-growth temperate rain forest in the world. He believed the best and right way to protect the forests and fish was to work with First Nations to help realize their sovereignty over the territory. Tara and I didn't have the vision Jim and Miles did, and we couldn't clearly understand how the nations would unite, but Tara subordinated her misgivings and began to travel alone into each community to meet the leaders, elders, and families in the villages.

Long before these first forays, Tara (and our family) had already established deep friendships in two of these villages, Skidegate and Bella Bella, as well as Alert Bay and others to the south. We had been adopted by two families and had long felt a responsibility to make a contribution to their villages.

In many First Nations communities, a schism has been created between traditional chiefs, who inherit their position, and the chiefs and band councils elected under rules imposed by the Department of Indian Affairs. We were well aware the traditional chiefs would be supportive, whereas elected councils had to prioritize jobs and development. But we didn't want to exacerbate community division, so we decided to go through the "front door"—the elected councils—hoping to meet the traditional chiefs and elders later with each council's blessing. We wanted to be completely open and forthright in our dealings with each community. In the past, environmentalists had enlisted the support of individual band members to fight to protect certain areas, but when the battle was over, the Native people sometimes had to deal with debt and ill will left behind. Many band councils were understandably suspicious of our motives.

Tara visited these remote villages to explain what the David Suzuki Foundation was and to explore partnerships in areas of common interest. We made no secret that our concern was the conservation of the old-growth forests, but we also acknowledged First Nations sovereignty over them and our willingness to work with First Nations to gain recognition of their rights. We hoped our science, fund-raising activities, and contacts might be useful.

In general Tara was made welcome and treated with respect, but she was sometimes berated by the councils. Once, when she had returned from a trip and I was quizzing her about the experience, she burst into tears as she recalled the loneliness, the pressures, and the humiliation. One band council member had chastised her: "Greenpeace and all you goddamned environmentalists..." Many First Nations are understandably wary, having watched a succession of do-gooders like us too often abandon them with promises unfulfilled.

Many of the communities situated in the rain forest in the mid- to north coast of British Columbia are extremely isolated, some reachable only by boat or floatplane. Often they suffer from chronic high unemployment and thus are vulnerable. To secure a small medical center and the promise of a handful of jobs, a community may have to sign agreements that will allow a company to liquidate their forests in a matter of years. One of the most pernicious practices Tara observed in the late '90s was what government and company employees called "consultation." Forced by the courts to consult First Nations, a company representative would fly into a community, call or bump into a few people and chat about their families, health, and local gossip, then call that a consultation.

Visiting the villages makes one re-examine concepts of wealth and poverty. I once visited a remote village of some two hundred people. When my plane landed, dozens met me at the dock. That night my hosts put on a feast in my honor. Tables sagged under platters piled with salmon, crab, halibut, herring roe, bannock, moose meat, eulachon, clam fritters, dried seaweed, and desserts. After dinner, the head of the band council opened the speeches by saying the band was poor and required money to buy things the people needed; that was why they had allowed logging in their territory.

When it was my turn to speak, I pointed out that in my affluent neighborhood of Vancouver, where there were probably three times as many people in one block as there were in that village, after twenty-five years I knew fewer than twenty of my neighbors by name. There was a park half a block away in which I didn't allow my children to play alone. Our home and car had been broken into several times. Even with thousands of dollars, I said, I could never have bought a feast like the one they had prepared for me. They were rich in what we had lost—community, land, and resources.

Yet Canadians have no right to tell First Nations they should live in some romanticized version of a museum-like state, frozen in time. These are twenty-first-century people who need boats and motors, computers and plane tickets. Can they protect their traditional values and their surroundings while finding ways to sustainably generate income for the things they need, in a manner acceptable to them? The decisions are theirs.

Although conservation was a serious issue to all the villages, jobs—community economic development (CED)—were the first priority. We accepted this challenge and set about turning ourselves into a CED organization, opening a DSF office in Prince Rupert and hiring Jim MacArthur, and then Sandy Storm, to run it.

AFTER EXTENSIVE RESEARCH for a CED model, we learned of a program called Participatory Action Research (PAR) that we thought might be of interest to the First Nations on the coast. For more than half a century, the program has been used successfully by peoples as diverse as Inuit in the Arctic and Sami in Russia.

PAR is based on a bottom-up philosophy whereby the knowledge, expertise, traditions, and skills within the community form the basis of its economic development. One of the first steps in the process is to hold community workshops to determine what people see as the community's strengths and what they want the community to be a decade or two later. Next, projects are identified and priorities developed. Soon, traditional mapping is used to determine how new jobs can be built from old. The PAR approach identifies a job here, another there, until collectively they add up to a significant number and help to keep the money circulating within the community. A PAR-trained worker is sent to live for up to three years in the community that is seeking a strategy for economic development. He or she gets to know the people, identifies their skills, abilities, and needs, then works with them to find opportunities and solutions until the adviser is no longer needed.

Michael Robinson, current chief executive officer of the Glenbow Museum in Calgary, Alberta, has had a lot of experience with PAR and advised us in a series of workshops on the method. Tara began to discuss the PAR process with elders and leaders, taking other advisers into the villages with her. She developed an all-female team that besides herself included an economist and former head of the Vancouver Stock Exchange, Ros Kunin; a lawyer and now judge, Jane Woodward; a PAR expert, Joan Ryan, and a politically experienced First Nations member from Yukon, Lula Johns. People began to refer to them affectionately as the Spice Girls.

As Tara became a familiar visitor in the communities, we began to learn what priorities each village had. The first community to which we sent a PAR worker was Nemiah, a village on the east side of the coastal mountains. The Xeni Gwet'in (Nemiah) people's territory in the drier Chilcotin Plateau includes the headwaters of some of the richest sockeye runs on the coast. Nemiah is about a four-hour drive on dirt roads from the town of Williams Lake.

Several people applied for the PAR position, and the band chose Roberta Martell, a garrulous, energetic, and tough young woman who had the drive to achieve all we and the community had hoped for and more. One of her first recommendations was to establish a community-owned laundromat in Nemiah. She started a community garden to provide fresh vegetables and organized the building of two straw-bale houses that were cheaper, more energy efficient, and of better quality than the kinds of homes built for the community under government

The PAR team in Nemiah. *Left to right:* Roberta Martell, Bonnie Meyers,
Maryann Solomon, and Francy Merritt.

cost allowances. She recognized the tradition of horse riding presented
an economic opportunity to establish trips for tourists.

Roberta's greatest achievement was to recognize three young
women who had the energy, vision, and connections to continue the
process of economic development after she left. A film was made about
the Nemiah project and broadcast internationally.

WHEN JIM FULTON ASSIGNED Tara to be a diplomat, he spoke
of the need for coastal First Nations to unite in recognition of common values and goals if the fish and forests of B.C. were to be sus-
tained. Both Tara and I knew such an initiative would have to come
from the First Nations themselves, and while Tara worked on community economic development issues, we watched to see if it would be
forthcoming. Tara knew our limited resources could not create jobs on
the necessary scale: we hoped leverage could come when a powerfully
united coast met with government.

In British Columbia, most First Nations are represented in what's called the B.C. First Nations Summit; delegates meet in Vancouver regularly to discuss issues of mutual interest. In the fall of 1999, timing our overture to coincide with a summit meeting, we invited leaders from the communities Tara had been visiting to meet us and each other to discuss some forestry information. Almost all accepted our invitation.

At the meeting, Art Sterritt from the Gitga'at community of Hartley Bay, and Gerald Amos of Kitamaat village, seconded by several others, commented on the novelty and significance of the gathering and suggested the DSF call a conference of all communities in the central and north coast and Haida Gwaii. We were delighted to do so. We invited the eleven communities, plus Nemiah, to a two-day meeting at the Musqueam Reserve in Vancouver in March 2000 and raised the money to pay all expenses. Members from all twelve communities attended.

After a prayer and welcome from the Musqueam hosts, each attendee made a statement about what he or she was most concerned about and hoped might result from this gathering. To commemorate the millennium, the meeting was called Turning Point. As these tremendously competent elders and leaders spoke, it was clear they had open hearts, and I felt they were desperate to be heard by us. Discussions ensued, and there were tribal differences about historical disagreements and overlapping territory, but all continued work to define various challenges and ponder a unified approach. One discussion group drafted the powerful declaration:

Declaration of First Nations of the North Pacific Coast
PREAMBLE
The North Pacific Coast is a rich, varied and fragile part of the natural world.

The connection between land and sea with people has given rise to our ancient northwest cultures.

We recognize this life source is under threat like never before and that all people must be held accountable.

This united declaration is the foundation for protecting and restoring our culture and the natural world.

We are the ones that will live with the consequences of any actions that will take place in our territories.

DECLARATION

We declare our life source is vital to the sustenance and livelihood of our culture and our very existence as a people.

The First Nations of the North Pacific Coast inherit the responsibility to protect and restore our lands, water and air for future generations.

We commit ourselves:

· to making decisions that ensure the well-being of our lands and waters.

· to preserving and renewing our territories and cultures through our tradition, knowledge and authority.

· to be honest with each other and respectful of all life.

We will support each other and work together as the original people of the North Pacific Coast, standing together to fulfill these commitments.

The DSF attended Turning Point in a supportive role, providing funding, organization, research, and contacts. We made it clear that while we believed the land belonged to the First Nations communities and supported their struggle to have that ownership recognized by government, we wanted the forest and marine ecosystems in which they dwell to remain healthy and productive in perpetuity. People have lived there for thousands of years and need those resources to make a living; parks that exclude First Nations use of the land are not a solution. Our outlook differed from those of environmental groups who just sought more "acres" of parks and protected areas.

We organized and funded many more Turning Point conferences. We brought in First Nations people whose land claims had been settled, to speak of what happened after. As the union strengthened, we worked hard organizing countless separate meetings with forestry companies, mayors of coastal communities, tourism operators, loggers, truckers, government officials, and other environmental groups, who all began to recognize and support the power of the Turning Point process and participants.

The New Democrat provincial government was under pressure to come to some kind of accommodation because the forestry companies knew that until land-title issues were settled, logging in the central to north coast forests would be increasingly contentious. On April 4, 2001, Premier Ujjal Dosanjh signed two documents, one of which set in motion negotiations with the provincial and federal governments and the Turning Point communities on what was termed a government to government to government basis. It was an acknowledgement that the First Nations and the "stakeholders" had legitimate rights.

As the Turning Point organization grew in strength, the foundation's role diminished, and eventually it was time to disengage ourselves. In September 2003, in a formal celebration in Skidegate village on Haida Gwaii, we were thanked and farewells were made. The DSF received a drum, symbol of the heartbeat of the people, and we gave each community a gift of fossilized cedar leaves, a symbol of tenacity and survival.

The foundation moved on with its many other projects, but Tara and I had made friendships and developed relationships that continue today and that we will cherish for our lifetimes.

A POSTSCRIPT LED TO one of the most painful episodes of my adult life. When the David Suzuki Foundation agreed to complete independence for Turning Point from our list of projects, the major funder of that initiative expressed a reluctance to transfer its funds directly to Turning Point. We had worked closely with the Lannan Foundation for years, but Turning Point was a newly independent organization without a track record; the funder wanted to continue contributing through DSF.

We would be responsible for how those funds were used by Turning Point. Jim knew this was not wise and asked the funder to give directly to Turning Point, but this was not an option. Reluctantly, we agreed to handle the funds and carry out "due diligence" with Turning Point.

When we initially set ourselves up as a double-barreled organization in 1991, the project-based institute arm had chafed under the limits imposed by the fund-raising foundation arm. Now DSF staff found themselves in the position of being like the hated government "Indian agents" of the past, giving the money but making Turning Point jump through hoops as required by Revenue Canada.

Unfortunately, we were in the midst of the long, drawn-out federal audits of every dime of our spending that have plagued us in recent years and cost the DSF over $100,000. We had to be equally demanding of Turning Point. Moreover, we had to ensure the funder's wishes were carried out.

Inevitably, this arrangement led to an explosive confrontation and a formal severing of ties between our two organizations. For DSF, it meant relief from the burden of legal responsibility for those funds and being the bad guy demanding accounting, but the bitter resentment at the role we played is a painful legacy of what remains one of our proudest achievements.

PERHAPS THE MOST FREQUENT question I'm asked after I give a speech is, "What can I do?" We used to say, "Think globally and act locally," but in my experience problems seem so immense that individuals contemplating them feel insignificant and helpless. The slogan disempowers, rather than motivates. The eminent philosopher-priest Thomas Berry suggests that to be effective globally, we must think and act locally, and I agree.

In the late '90s, the DSF contacted the Union of Concerned Scientists, an influential group of scientists in the U.S. who had developed a list of suggested activities to reduce our ecological footprint. We worked with them to modify their suggestions, numbers, and analysis for Canada.

Each of us affects nature—air, water, soil, energy, other species—through what we eat, how we move about, and where we live. Focusing on food, transportation, and housing, the Union of Concerned Scientists and the DSF came up with ten of the most effective things individuals can do. When I first read the list, I threw it aside and exclaimed, "Come on, get serious. This is too easy!" But Ann Rowan, who was heading the project, showed me the scientific rationale underlying each suggestion and convinced me.

We called these ten steps the Nature Challenge and asked Canadians to make a commitment to implement at least three of them in the year ahead:

1. Reduce home energy use by 10 percent

2. Choose energy-efficient home and appliances

3. Don't use pesticides

4. Eat meat-free meals one day a week

5. Buy locally grown and produced food

6. Choose a fuel-efficient vehicle

7. Walk, bike, carpool or take public transit one day a week

8. Choose a home close to work or school

9. Support alternative transportation

10. Learn more and share information with others

We kicked off the project at events in six Canadian cities: Toronto, London, Montreal, Winnipeg, Calgary, and Vancouver. Each event was sold out, thanks to performances by comedians, musicians, and other celebrities, including some in the media. Tara and I both spoke, and we tried to sign up as many people as possible to do their bit to make a difference. It's working: the current number as I write is more than 140,000, including dozens of mayors, entire city councils, and premiers—with thousands of constituents signing on, no politician could refuse to do something concrete as well.

THE DSF INITIATIVE FOR which we have the highest hopes is Sustainability Within A Generation (SWAG), the name adopted from the title of a report we commissioned in 2003.

David Boyd is a lawyer who headed the Sierra Legal Defence Fund in Vancouver. He is now an adjunct professor at the University of Victoria in B.C.'s capital city and a writer who covers environmental issues from a legal standpoint. His book *Unnatural Law* explores the way different countries have legislated environmental protection. Though polls indicate the environment is the major concern of Canadians, Boyd found Canada ranks near the bottom in related legislation and performance: it is number 28 out of 30 nations in the Organization for Economic Cooperation and Development. Only Belgium and the United States rate lower.

The DSF contracted David to write a document suggesting how society might achieve sustainability in areas such as waste, energy, food, and water. He cut through divisive issues and came up with a remarkable report that arose from a simple question: what kind of country do we want a generation from now? Do we want a land where the air is clean and there are no longer epidemic levels of asthma? Of course. Do we want to be able to drink water from any lake or river? Naturally. Do we want to catch a fish and eat it without having to worry about contaminants? Sure. Everyone agrees with these goals, so now we have consensus and a target that gives us direction.

If we know that in the long term we want to achieve sustainability, it is helpful to choose a target date. David chose the year 2030 and then divided society's needs into nine areas:

Generating genuine wealth

Improving efficiency

Shifting to clean energy

Reducing waste and pollution

Protecting and conserving water

Producing healthy food

Conserving, protecting, and restoring Canadian nature

Building sustainable cities

Promoting global sustainability

In Boyd's analysis, it is possible to achieve sustainability in each area if we begin to work toward it immediately and aim to reach concrete targets set within specific time frames. The report "Sustainability Within A Generation" has garnered a positive response; when Jim Fulton and I presented it to Canadian prime minister Paul Martin in February 2004, we learned he had already read it and enthusiastically embraced it. He promised to try to exceed our targets in all areas but one—energy.

We had recommended that subsidies to the fossil fuel industry be stopped. The prime minister admitted frankly that such a step would have huge political ramifications in oil-rich Alberta and couldn't be taken. But he did promise to try to level the playing field for renewable energy sources, to which he did commit a billion dollars from the sale of the government-owned oil company, Petro-Canada. After our meeting, the prime minister sent the document to senior bureaucrats with instructions to see how the recommendations could be embedded in government infrastructure, which would ensure that even with changing governments, the basic goal would remain in place.

David Boyd was appointed in 2004 on a contract to advise the Privy Council of Canada, a high-powered body of advisers to the

The Board of the David Suzuki Foundation. *Left to right:* Severn, Wade Davis, me, Mike Robinson, Tara, Peter Steele, Ray Anderson, Stephen Bronfman, Jim Hoggan, and Jim Fulton. *(Absent: Stephanie Green and Miles Richardson.)*

government, where he met regularly with senior civil servants. Politicians change, whereas bureaucrats remain; if civil servants embrace the principles of "Sustainability Within A Generation," they could help shift government infrastructure and attitude.

I also presented the report to the Federation of Canadian Municipalities in Ottawa to a very positive reception. The Australian Conservation Foundation is now writing an Aussie version of swag.

In November 2005, John deCuevas, a colleague of Tara's when she taught at Harvard, invited a group of thirty-five funders, scientists, environmentalists, and activists to meet us for a dinner and then spend the following day in discussion at Harvard's Faculty Club. I presented "Sustainability Within A Generation," which was embraced with enthusiasm. The group recommended that the DSF document be Americanized, and two researchers have been hired to work on this. The group wants to put together a blue-ribbon panel of scientists, economists, athletes, celebrities, and politicians to be ambassadors for swag.

"Sustainability Within A Generation" has been a galvanizing and unifying focus within the foundation because all of our projects are tied to the goal of sustainability within its 2030 time frame.

WHEN THE RADIO SERIES *It's a Matter of Survival* was broadcast in 1988, I was overwhelmed by the speed with which the planet was undergoing human-caused degradation. Since the foundation opened its doors, the signs of danger have been rising.

Human beings are not specially gifted in speed, strength, size, or sensory acuity compared with the other animals we evolved with on the African plains. Our great evolutionary feature was our brain, which conferred memory, curiosity, and inventiveness that more than compensated for our lack of physical attributes. Foresight, the ability to look ahead and recognize both dangers and opportunities, guided us into the future. That was what got us to this moment in time, when we are the most numerous, powerful, and demanding mammal on Earth.

We have been repeatedly warned that we are on a dangerous path. We must not turn our backs on the core survival strategy of our species by subordinating ecological concerns to the demands of the economy, political feasibility, and personal ambition.

The battle to save Mother Earth remains urgent and must continue.

chapter THIRTEEN

RIO AND
THE EARTH SUMMIT

I N 1991, SOON AFTER we had established the David Suzuki Foundation, we heard that the Earth Summit was to be held in Rio de Janeiro in June 1992. The American zoologist Rachel Carson in 1962 had published her ground-breaking book *Silent Spring*, about the unexpected consequences of pesticides, and the environmental movement had grown spectacularly through the 1970s and '80s.

The Earth Summit was meant to signal a profound shift, the realization that henceforth humankind couldn't make important political, social, and economic decisions without considering the environmental consequences. But by the time of the meetings, environmental concerns were already giving way to economic priorities.

The period between *Silent Spring* and Rio reflected the evolution of a remarkable grassroots movement. Greenpeace had been born in 1970 in Vancouver as a result of protest against an American plan to test nuclear weapons underground on Amchitka Island in the Aleutian Islands, off the Alaska Peninsula.

In 1962, there wasn't a single department or ministry of the environment on the planet. Carson's book put the word "environment" on everyone's lips, and the movement had grown so explosively that by 1972 the United Nations was persuaded by Canadian businessman and international environmentalist Maurice Strong to hold a major conference on the environment in Stockholm. The American scientists and educators Paul Ehrlich, Margaret Mead, and Barry Commoner were there, as was the English economist and conservationalist Barbara Ward, along with Greenpeace and thousands of environmentalists concerned about species extinction, pollution, and disappearing habitat.

The United Nations Environment Program was established as an outcome of the Stockholm meetings, and environmentalists took up causes from whales and seals to polluted air and vanishing forests and rivers. The spectacular postwar economic growth had come at a cost that people recognized only after Carson's warning shot. Technology and human activity have consequences for our surroundings, and we had ignored them for too long.

For most of our species' existence, we have been profoundly local and tribal, spending most of our individual lives within a few tens of square miles and coming into contact with perhaps a couple of hundred others in a lifetime. But now we were emerging as a global force. Now we had to consider the collective impact of all of humanity, and it was a difficult perspective to grasp and accept.

When Tara and I had visited the village of Aucre deep in the Amazon rain forest in 1989, we had left a small plastic bag of garbage in our hut, assuming it would be buried after we left. When I returned a decade later, that bag was still there. Throughout their existence, the Kaiapo had lived with materials that were totally biodegradable and so could be left where they were or tossed into the forest to eventually decompose. When plastics and metals began to appear in the Amazon as the Kaiapo made contact with the outside world, those materials were strewn around just like the banana skins of old.

In the twentieth century, human beings had become so numerous and our technological prowess so powerful that we were affecting the biophysical features of the planet on a massive scale. Yet we still thought as local animals. It was almost impossible for the average person to grasp the idea of millions of acres of forest being destroyed, billions of tons of topsoil being lost, toxic pollution of the entire atmosphere, and a massive spasm of extinction. The environmental movement had to come up with catchy ways of representing the bigger picture so people could relate to it—the Amazon as the "lungs of the planet," cute and cuddly baby seals, charismatic animals like whales or gorillas.

The movement grew as local communities began to grasp the consequences of using air, water, and soil as toxic dumps and belatedly recognized the value of wilderness and of other species. By the late '80s, grassroots concern had pushed the environment to the top of the list of public concerns to such an extent that Margaret Thatcher, the ultra-right-wing Conservative prime minister of Britain, was filmed picking up litter and declaring to the camera, "I'm a greenie too." In Canada, newly reelected Progressive Conservative prime minister Brian Mulroney demonstrated a sudden commitment to the environment by appointing his brightest star, the mesmerizing political novice Lucien Bouchard, as minister of the environment and raising the portfolio to the inner cabinet.

In the United States in 1988, Republican political candidate George Bush Sr. promised that, if elected, he would be "an environmental president." Australia's Labor government was led by Bob Hawke and then by Paul Keating during this period, neither of whom had any record of interest in the environment. But the public was concerned, and Keating was forced to appoint as minister a champion of the environment, Ros Kelly, whom I met and admired over the years.

As their records in office demonstrated, it was public concern about the environment that generated the declared environmental commitments by politicians, not any deeply felt understanding of why the issue was important. When economic difficulties set in, the environment disappeared as a high priority and the environmental movement was forced to struggle to keep matters on the political agenda. To the jaded media, the environment was an old story. Indeed, some revisionists, such as the American writer Gregg Easterbrook, the Danish political scientist Bjørn Lomborg, and former Greenpeace president Patrick Moore, began to argue that the environmental movement was beating a dead horse, that it had been so successful that it was time to move on to other issues such as the economy.

If 1988 was the peak of public concern, interest continued to be high enough in 1991 to make the Earth Summit a highly anticipated event. It would be the largest gathering of heads of state in history, but I was skeptical that such a huge meeting would accomplish much. My daughter, Severn, had other ideas.

When we had returned from our trip to the Amazon in 1989, Severn had been so upset after seeing the rain forest under assault by farmers and gold miners that she had started a club made up of her grade 5 friends who shared her concern about forests. They would gather at our house to have tea and talk about what they might do. They called their club the Environmental Children's Organization (ECO) and soon were giving talks at their school and then at other schools as word of their existence spread. They began to make little salamanders and earrings out of Fimo clay and sold them to raise money.

Somehow Severn heard about the Earth Summit and asked whether Tara and I were going. I answered that we weren't and asked why she was curious. "Because I think all those grown-ups are going to meet and make decisions and they're not even going to think about us kids," came the answer. "I think ECO should go to remind them to think about us."

Tara and I had been involved in a number of international issues, but we had not worked with international organizations such as the United Nations, around whose official Conference on Environment and Development the broader Earth Summit had evolved. Without even reflecting on Severn's idea, I rejected it: "Sweetheart, it's going to be a huge circus with lots of people. Rio will be hot and polluted. Besides, it will cost a lot of money." Then I promptly forgot about Sev's hope.

That summer, we had a visit from Doug Tompkins, an American who had started the clothing company Esprit with his wife, Susie Russell. When the marriage broke up, Susie bought him out and left him with a considerable chunk of money, reputed to be in the hundreds of millions. Flying his own plane, Doug travels the world looking for opportunities to invest in groups fighting to protect large areas of wilderness, and he personally buys large tracts of land to protect.

Somehow he had heard about Tara and me and the newly formed David Suzuki Foundation, so he flew to British Columbia with deep ecologist Bill Duvall and visited us at our cottage on Quadra Island for two days. During that time, unknown to Tara and me, Severn told Doug about her idea of taking ECO to Rio the following year. He was more enthusiastic than we had been and told her, "That's a good idea. Write to me about it." She did, and one day a couple of months later, she said, "Hey, Dad, look," and held up a check for US$1,000 from Doug Tompkins.

I was astonished. I was also pleased with her initiative in writing on her own, and for the first time, I reflected seriously about her idea; I realized she could be on to something. I talked it over with Tara, and we decided it might be worth going to the Earth Summit if children could call attention to the long-term implications of what was being decided by grown-ups. So we went back to Sev and told her we realized she had a good idea and that we would support her by matching every dollar ECO could raise. That meant she already had $2,000.

Severn and Sarika and the other ECO girls plunged into projects to raise money, gathering and selling secondhand books, creating and selling their Fimo salamanders, and baking cookies. But all that brought in only small change. Jeff Gibbs of the Environmental Youth Alliance, that young man who had cut his teeth in environmental activism in high school, took ECO under his wing and helped the girls publish a series of ECO newspapers with articles the youngsters wrote about the environment. Jeff also suggested a major fund-raising event at which the kids could tell people what they wanted to do. It was scheduled for March 17, 1992. With a great deal of help from Jeff, Tara, and others, the girls booked the Vancouver Planetarium, made and distributed posters, and called members of the press and urged them to cover the event. Parents, relatives, and friends, of course, were recruited to attend.

The event was packed. Tara had the inspiration of including a blank check in the package of material left on every seat, thereby removing the excuse "I didn't bring a check with me." The girls had all prepared talks to go along with a slide show about the environment. They said they wanted to go to Rio to be a conscience to adults, and they asked the audience to help them. It was a powerful presentation because the girls spoke from their hearts, and their very innocence and naïveté touched a chord. During the break, an older man leaped onto the stage, held up five checks for $200 each, and announced he was so inspired that he would donate them if others would match them. People began to fill in the blank checks. Dad anted up $200.

The girls ended up with over $4,700 from that one event, which they had hoped might raise $1,000. Raffi Cavoukian, the well-known children's troubadour, had moved to Vancouver; he had become very interested in environmental issues and wrote a check for another $4,000. Somehow a Toronto philanthropist who supports women's issues heard about the girls and sent another check for $4,000.

In all, the girls had raised more than $13,000, which Tara and I had to match—enough money to send five ECO members (including, of course, Severn and Sarika) and three parents (Tara, me, and

Patricia Hernandez, the Spanish-speaking mother of one of the other girls) to Rio.

Although I was now planning to go to the summit, I remained skeptical about what the meeting itself would achieve. In December 1991, I interviewed conference coordinator Maurice Strong for *The Nature of Things with David Suzuki* and expressed my skepticism. He was irrepressibly optimistic, saying the conference couldn't fail because the future of the planet was at stake. When I pressed him, he responded, "If it does fail, it must not be allowed to be a quiet failure and recede unnoticed from memory."

The Earth Summit was heralded by Carlo Ripa di Meana, environment commissioner of the European Union, as a chance "to make decisions, obtain precise and concrete commitments to counteract tendencies that are endangering life on the planet." But in order to ensure U.S. president George Bush's participation, the proposed Treaty on Climate was watered down from a target of a significant reduction in greenhouse gas emissions to merely "stabilizing 1990 levels of emissions by 2000." This caused Ripa di Meana to boycott the meeting because, he said, "by opting for hypocrisy, we will not just fail to save the Earth, but we will fail you." So things were not looking good.

Once it was known that Tara and I were going to Rio, we were asked to become involved in some of the deliberations leading up to the event. For years, hundreds of groups and thousands of people had been attending Prepcom (Preparatory Committee) meetings in different countries to draft documents to be presented to and signed by leaders at Rio. The signings would be merely formalities and photo ops, because all the wording would have been worked out beforehand.

To persuade all countries to sign on, the wording in the documents had to be fine-tuned to avoid offending signatories—oops, can't talk about overpopulation to the developing countries, don't mention family planning lest it scare off the Catholic countries, mustn't raise the issue of hyperconsumption in the industrialized countries. Documents on forests, water, air, and so on were drafted, passed through many hands, edited and reedited, rewritten many times.

By the time I was called in to one of the meetings in Vancouver to look at a forestry document, people were spending a great deal of time arguing over whether there should be a hyphen here or a comma there or whether it should be "the" or "a." Maybe I'm being unfair, because I went to only one meeting and abandoned further attendance as a waste of my time. I know lots of people who invested huge amounts of energy in the process, and thank goodness there were people willing to do it.

For me, the important thing was not in all of the picky details but in an overarching vision that would establish the real bottom line: that we are biological beings, completely dependent for our good health and very survival on the health of the biosphere. At the David Suzuki Foundation, we felt one contribution we could make at Rio would be such a statement or vision, so I began to draft a declaration that would express an understanding of our place in the natural world. As I began to work on it with Tara, she suggested it should be like the American Declaration of Independence, a powerful document that would touch people's hearts. "How about calling it the Declaration of Interdependence?" she suggested, and it was instantly obvious that was what we were drafting.

Tara and I went back and forth with our efforts and then recruited Raffi, our Haida friend Guujaaw, and the Canadian ethnobotanist Wade Davis, to contribute. At one point I kept writing the cumbersome sentence, "We are made up of the air we breathe, we are inflated by water and created by earth through the food we consume." That was what I wanted to express, but I wanted to do it in a way that was simple and inspiring. As I struggled with the lines, I suddenly cut through it all and wrote, "We are the earth."

That was the first time I really understood the depth of what I had learned from Guujaaw and other aboriginal people. I knew we incorporate air, water, and earth into our bodies, but simply declaring that's what we are cut through all the boundaries. Now I understood that there is no line or border that separates us from the rest of the world.

There is no boundary—we are the earth and are created by the four sacred elements—earth, air, fire, and water. It follows that whatever we do to the planet Earth, we do directly to ourselves. I had been framing the "environmental" problem improperly—I thought we had to modify our interaction with our surroundings, regulating how much and what we remove from the environment and how much and what waste and toxic material we put back into it. Now I knew that wasn't the right perspective, because if we viewed ourselves as separate from our surroundings, we could always find ways to rationalize our activity ("too expensive to change," "it's only a minuscule amount," "that's the way we've always done it," "it interferes with our competitiveness," et cetera). But if we are the air, the water, the soil, the sunlight, then how can we rationalize using ourselves as toxic dumps?

This is what our final document was:

Declaration Of Interdependence

THIS WE KNOW

We are the earth, through the plants and animals that nourish us.

We are the rains and the oceans that flow through our veins.

We are the breath of the forests of the land and the plants of the sea.

We are human animals, related to all other life as
descendants of the firstborn cell.

We share with these kin a common history, written in our genes.

We share a common present, filled with uncertainty.

And we share a common future as yet untold.

We humans are but one of thirty million species
weaving the thin layer of life enveloping the world.

The stability of communities of living things depends upon this diversity.

Linked in that web, we are interconnected—
using, cleansing, sharing and replenishing
the fundamental elements of life.

Our home, planet Earth, is finite; all life shares its
resources and the energy from the Sun,
and therefore has limits to growth.

For the first time, we have touched those limits.

When we compromise the air, the water, the soil and the variety of life,
we steal from the endless future to serve the fleeting present.

THIS WE BELIEVE

Humans have become so numerous and our tools so powerful
that we have driven fellow creatures to extinction,
dammed the great rivers,
torn down ancient forests, poisoned the earth, rain
and wind, and ripped holes in the sky.

Our science has brought pain as well as joy;
our comfort is paid for by the suffering of millions.

We are learning from our mistakes, we are mourning our vanished kin,
and we now build a new politics of hope.

We respect and uphold the absolute need for clean air, water and soil.

We see that economic activities that benefit the few
while shrinking the inheritance of many are wrong.

And since environmental degradation erodes biological capital forever,
full ecological and social cost must enter all equations of development.

We are one brief generation in the long march of time;
the future is not ours to erase.

So where knowledge is limited, we will remember
all those who will walk after us,
and err on the side of caution.

THIS WE RESOLVE

All this that we know and believe must now become
the foundation of the way we live.

At this Turning Point in our relationship with Earth,
we work for an evolution from dominance to partnership,
from fragmentation to connection, from insecurity to interdependence.

I believe the final Declaration of Interdependence is a powerful, moving document that sets forth the principles that should underlie all of our activities. We had the declaration translated into a number of languages including French, Chinese, Japanese, Russian, German, and Spanish, and took copies to give away in Rio, one of the first tangible products of the David Suzuki Foundation.

As we were doing this and setting up the foundation office, Tara was organizing ECO's involvement in Rio and the logistics of hotel, food, travel, shots, and so on. As the time to leave approached, I was increasingly anxious and worried, but the girls saw the trip as an adventure and opportunity. They were so innocent. Despite my concerns, we took off in a state of excitement and hope. I had to fly to Europe at the end of the conference, but Tara had arranged for the children to have a post-Rio reward of a visit to the Amazon.

We landed in Rio, and, as I had feared, it was hot and the air was heavy with pollution from the traffic. I still tended to worry about details—where would we stay, what about food, how would we get around, what about toilets—but Tara is the one who makes those arrangements. My children just ignore me—"Oh, Dad, stop being so anal" is the way they put it. Tara had arranged for an apartment overlooking the fabled Copacabana Beach, but we had too much to do to enjoy the resort.

Tens of thousands of people arrived in Rio de Janeiro to attend the Earth Summit, which included the official UN conference, housed at Rio Centro and ringed by armed guards demanding passes to enter;

the Global Forum, for hundreds of nongovernmental organizations (NGOS) from all over the world; and the Earth Parliament, for indigenous peoples. Each conference was many miles away from the others. I don't doubt that this was a deliberate decision to keep the NGOS and indigenous people as far away from the official delegates as possible, if for no other reason than to minimize the contrast between well-heeled representatives staying at fancy hotels and the rabble like us on minimal budgets staying in the cheap parts of town.

With such distances between summit events, the media had to make decisions about what to cover, and usually Rio Centro was where they hung out because telephones, fax machines, and computers were set up there. As it was, the fun and excitement were to be found among the NGOS, whereas the delegates in business attire were trapped in long, serious, and deadly boring deliberations behind closed doors, completing the final wording of documents to be signed later, when the world leaders arrived.

It was a circus. I hated it. The city was uncomfortable and overrun with cars, and everywhere we went, there were crowds of people trying to be seen or heard. If you're not anal like me, Rio is a wonderful place to visit. The beaches are lovely (although the water is polluted and best left alone), the sun always shines (although it has to make its way through the haze) and there are nightclubs and restaurants galore. We went to churrascarias, amazing places where meat is brought out on skewers and one can fill up on enormous servings of food while children outside beg for leftovers. As in all big cities, but especially those in developing countries, the contrast between the world that tourists inhabit and the extreme poverty in slums is difficult to accept. To prepare for the conference, Brazilian authorities had forcibly removed street people from downtown Rio so that the official delegates wouldn't have to confront the contrasts.

The girls had brought three issues of their newspaper and among them spoke English, French, and Spanish. ECO had registered as one

The ECO gang in Rio. *Left to right:* Michelle Quigg, Severn, Raffi, Sarika, Morgan Geisler, and Vanessa Suttie.

of the thousands of NGOs and applied for a booth where they could display their papers, posters, and pictures and meet people. Tara and I had been asked to speak at a number of NGO events, and before the end of our presentations at each session we would say, "I think you should hear from the ones with most at stake in all that's going on here" and bring the girls onstage to make short submissions.

The media began to hear about them by word of mouth and went to their booth for interviews. It was a good story to have these cute girls speaking so seriously and passionately. David Halton from CBC took the girls to a favela, where street people lived, and interviewed them for a long story. Jean Charest, Canada's newest federal environment minister, visited the booth to talk to the girls, but they were frustrated because they felt he was more interested in telling them things than in listening to them. The girls were articulate, passionate, and telegenic, and their plea to be remembered while delegates made big decisions affecting their world was so simple and undeniable that it cut through all the rhetorical flourishes and political posturing.

At one of the events at the Earth Parliament, I gave a short talk and then yielded the stage so that Severn could also make a speech. I didn't know it, but in the audience was James Grant, the American head of UNICEF, the United Nations Children's Fund, and he was so moved by Sev's remarks that he asked her for a copy of them. He told her he was meeting Canadian prime minister Brian Mulroney that evening and wanted to give him that speech in person. I never heard whether he did or not, but we learned later that Grant had run into Maurice Strong and told Maurice he should give Severn an opportunity to speak.

The next day, Tara and the girls were scheduled to leave Rio to take their trip to the wilderness camp in the Amazon. But in the morning, we received a call from Strong's office inviting Severn to speak at Rio Centro in a session for children. Three other girls, representing various youth groups, had been selected ahead of time to speak, and now Strong added Sev to this group. One girl was from Germany, another from Guatemala, and two, including Sev, were from Canada. Each was to speak for no more than three or four minutes.

The call from Strong's office was exhilarating. The trip to a camp in the Amazon would have to be postponed, a huge undertaking in Brazil, but Tara went ahead and began to make new arrangements. Severn had had the inspiration more than a year before to go to Rio and make a plea. The girls had worked like demons to raise money, publish papers, and attend the meetings. And now they were to speak to the delegates.

What could she say? I was overwhelmed with the immensity of the opportunity and the challenge of compressing the important issues into a short talk. I began firing off ideas about points I thought she should make in her speech on pollution, wildlife, future generations. Sev said to me, "Dad, I know what I want to say. Mommy will help me write it all down. I want you to tell me how to say it."

We didn't have much time. Sev wrote out her speech on a piece of paper, adding words and phrases in the margins as all of us offered our critique. I had no idea how she would be able to read the scribbling. We rushed out to grab cabs, and as we careened through the streets of Rio, I made Sev go over her speech several times, trying to help her smooth her delivery and remember which words should be emphasized, just as my father had done for me when I was a boy.

The conference center was air-conditioned, with only a murmur of background noise—a stark contrast to the vibrant colors, smells, and sounds of the Global Forum. We entered the conference room, an immense hall that could have held thousands but contained only a few hundred people; it looked almost empty. Sev was last on the list. The other girls made their presentations well, pleading for better care of resources, wildlife, water, and the poor—the kind of statements adults could feel good about listening to and in response could promise they were doing their best.

Finally, it was Sev's turn. She was twelve years old and had not had time to prepare thoroughly, and I was scared stiff—but I hadn't given her enough credit. She has a mother who is a superb thinker and writer, and Sev herself had been listening to us, absorbing our concerns and solutions, thinking about her life and her surroundings, and she spoke simply, straight from the heart. Here is what she said:

Hello. I'm Severn Suzuki, speaking for ECO, the Environmental Children's Organization.

We are a group of twelve- and thirteen-year-olds trying to make a difference—Vanessa Suttie, Morgan Geisler, Michelle Quigg, and me.

We raised all the money to come five thousand miles to tell you adults you must change your ways.

Coming up here today I have no hidden agenda, I am fighting for my future.

Severn speaking to the plenary session of the Earth Summit in Rio de Janeiro
(taken from video)

Losing a future is not like losing an election or a few points on the stock market.

I am here to speak for all generations to come; I am here to speak on behalf of the starving children around the world whose cries go unheard; I am here to speak for the countless animals dying across this planet because they have nowhere left to go.

I am afraid to go out in the sun now because of the holes in the ozone; I am afraid to breathe the air because I don't know what chemicals are in it; I used to go fishing in Vancouver, my home-town, with my dad, until just a few years ago when we found the fish full of cancers; and now we hear about animals and plants going extinct every day—vanishing forever.

In my life, I have dreamed of seeing the great herds of wild animals, jungles and rain forests full of birds and butterflies, but now I wonder if they will even exist for my children to see.

Did you have to worry about these things when you were my age?

All this is happening before our eyes, and yet we act as if we have all the time we want and all the solutions.

I'm only a child and I don't have all the solutions, but I want you to realize, neither do you—you don't know how to fix the holes in our ozone layer; you don't know how to bring the salmon back in a dead stream; you don't know how to bring back an animal now extinct, and you can't bring back the forests that once grew where there is now a desert—if you don't know how to fix it, please stop breaking it!

Here you may be delegates of your governments, business-people, organizers, reporters or politicians, but really you are mothers and fathers, sisters and brothers, aunts and uncles, and all of you are somebody's child.

I'm only a child yet I know we are part of a family, 5 billion strong; in fact, 30 million species strong, and borders and governments will never change that.

I'm only a child yet I know we are all in this together and should act as one single world toward one single goal.

In my anger, I am not blind, and in my fear, I'm not afraid to tell the world how I feel.

In my country we make so much waste; we buy and throw away, buy and throw away; and yet northern countries will not share with the needy; even when we have more than enough, we are afraid to lose some of our wealth, afraid to let go.

In Canada, we live the privileged life with plenty of food, water and shelter; we have watches, bicycles, computers, and television sets.

Two days ago here in Brazil, we were shocked when we spent time with some children living on the streets, and here is what one child told us: "I wish I was rich, and if I were, I would give all the street children food, clothes, medicine, shelter, love, and affection."

If a child on the street who has nothing is willing to share, why are we who have everything still so greedy?

I can't stop thinking that these are children my own age, that it makes a tremendous difference where you are born.

I could be one of those children living in the favelas of Rio, I could be a child starving in Somalia, a victim of war in the Middle East, or a beggar in India.

I'm only a child yet I know if all the money spent on war was spent on ending poverty, making treaties and finding environmental answers, what a wonderful place this Earth would be.

At school, even in kindergarten, you teach us how to behave in the world—you teach us not to fight with others; to work things out; to respect others; to clean up our mess; not to hurt other creatures; to share, not be greedy.

Then why do you go out and do the things you tell us not to do?

Do not forget why you are attending these conferences, who you are doing this for—we are your own children.

You are deciding what kind of a world we will grow up in.

Parents should be able to comfort their children by saying, "Everything's going to be all right," "We're doing the best we can," and "It's not the end of the world."

But I don't think you can say that to us anymore.

Are we even on your list of priorities?

My dad always says, "You are what you do, not what you say."

Well, what you do makes me cry at night.

You grown-ups say you love us, but I challenge you, please make your actions reflect your words. Thank you.

I was absolutely floored. It was a powerful speech, delivered with elo-
quence, sincerity, and passion. The audience was electrified. All of
the presentations in the convention hall were broadcast on monitors
throughout the building, and I am told that when Sev began to speak,
people stopped what they were doing and gathered around the television sets to listen to her. Severn received one of only two standing
ovations given during the entire conference (the other was for President Fidel Castro of Cuba, who also gave a powerful speech).

When she left the stage to come to us near the middle of the auditorium, her first words to Tara were, "Mommy, could you hear my heart
beating?" As she sat down between us, a member of the American delegation rushed over to shake her hand and congratulate her. "That was
the best speech anyone has given here," U.S. senator Al Gore told her.

The speech was filmed and is archived with the United Nations. I
have a copy of it and have shown the video dozens of times to audi-
ences attending my talks; each time, I am moved by its simplicity and
power. The repercussions of that speech had a huge impact on Sev's
life. Canadian journalist and human-rights activist Michelle Landsberg
wrote a column about it, and the speech has been printed verbatim in
dozens of articles and translated into several languages. John Pierce of
Doubleday contacted Severn about writing a book based on it, which
she did in 1993; the book is called *Tell the World*. She was interviewed
again and again, offered opportunities to host television programs,
and invited to give speeches. She received the United Nations Environment Program's Global 500 award in Beijing in 1993.

It was all pretty heady stuff for a twelve-year-old, and I began to
worry about what this would do to her sense of herself. I stopped worrying the next year, when she was invited to appear on *The Joan Rivers
Show* in New York. "Dad," Sev told me, "I hope it's okay, but I'm not
going to do this. I have to study, and I want to make the basketball
team." She had her priorities right.

AGENDA 21 IS THE 700-page tome adopted by 178 governments at Rio; essentially, it was a blueprint for the world to achieve sustainable development. The cost of this massive shift from a focus on the economy above all else to an inclusion of environmental factors was estimated to be $600 billion a year, although the cost of not doing anything was not estimated and would have been many times greater. The developing world was expected to put up $450 billion of it, a sum that represented 8 percent of their collective gross domestic product (GDP), and the industrialized nations were expected to cough up the remainder, a mere 0.7 percent of their GDPs. Before the Earth Summit was over, developed countries were already complaining that their contribution was impractical, and the target of 0.7 percent of GDP has not been reached by any of the major industrial nations such as the United States, Canada, and Australia, even though the goals set in Rio in 1992 were re-affirmed at the Johannesburg Earth Summit in 2002.

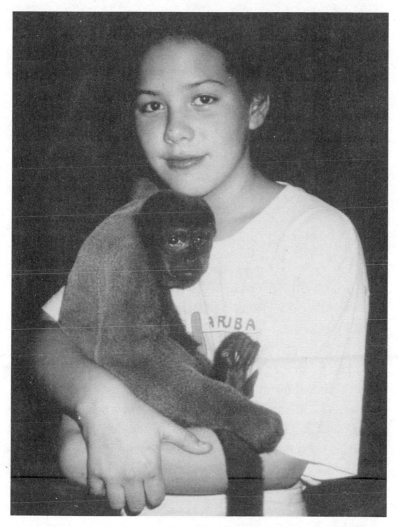

Sev and woolly monkey at the Ariau Jungle Towers on the Amazon

chapter FOURTEEN

PAPUA NEW GUINEA

I N 1992, A MAN who was working in Papua New
Guinea asked if he could drop by my house in
Vancouver. Shortly after he arrived, Nick Fogg asked to go to the bathroom and stayed there for an inordinately long time, audibly ill. When
he emerged, gray and weak, he told me he was having a malarial flare-
up. Nevertheless, he managed to ask me whether I'd be interested in
visiting the South Pacific country.

Nick worked for CUSO (formerly Canadian University Services
Overseas and still known by the old acronym), a nongovernmental
international developmental organization, and despite his alarming
condition, I was immediately interested because I'd heard so much
about the island nation from Richard Longley, the main researcher for
the television series *Science Magazine*.

Richard was trained in England as a botanist and had taught for a
number of years in Papua New Guinea. Long before I became involved
in the TV program *The Nature of Things*, he was the contact person for
CBC producer Nancy Archibald when she made a film there for that
series. Richard eventually moved to Toronto, where he was hired to

do research for the new series *Science Magazine*. In that capacity, he visited the University of British Columbia, where he interviewed me, and later I ended up being asked to host the show.

I had seen Nancy's program on Papua New Guinea, which showed some of the incredible variety of people and animals living on the island of New Guinea north of Australia. To bird-watchers, Papua New Guinea is famous for its fabled birds of paradise. I was thrilled with Nick's invitation, and I made the visit to Papua New Guinea in 1993. It is an awesome place, more than 80 percent of it covered with high mountains and deep valleys. At one point we flew into a large valley, where I could see five airstrips carved into the hills within a six-mile radius; the villages they serve are only a few minutes apart by air, but the valleys and dense forest between them take days to cover on foot. The isolation imposed by the rugged terrain has resulted in a profusion of cultures and over seven hundred languages, about 45 percent of the world's total.

Not long ago, neighboring tribes raided each other and practiced cannibalism, which perpetuated a terrible disease called kuru, for years thought to be hereditary. Famed population geneticist Theodosius Dobzhansky wrote a paper in *Science* magazine describing kuru as a disease caused by a dominant gene. However, Stanley Prusiner had earned a Nobel Prize in 1997 by showing that kuru was caused by a "slow virus" related to the prions causing BSE (mad cow disease) and the human counterpart, Creutzfeldt-Jakob disease. Kuru, or "laughing disease," was so named because its victims suffered facial muscle contractions that gave the appearance of a grotesque smile.

Kuru was transmitted primarily to children and women, who tended to be given the highly infective brains to eat while the men ate the preferred muscles, which carried far fewer of the causative agents. Christianity had ended the cannibalism and intertribal wars, and although I didn't like the way the religion had come to

Party greeting me at the airport in Port Moresby, Papua New Guinea

dominate Papua New Guinean cultures, it was hard to decry the abo-
lition of the killing.

Nick had arranged for Indigenous Environment Watch, a group of
native and nonnative environmentalists, to issue a formal invitation,
which I immediately accepted, and the next time I was visiting Australia I flew in to Port Moresby, the capital of Papua New Guinea. When
my plane landed and taxied toward the terminal, I peered out to see a
crowd of children holding up flags and a large sign of welcome. "Must
be a politician or someone important," I remarked to my seatmate.

Imagine my surprise when the plane stopped and I saw that the
sign said "Welcome Doctor Suzuki"! As I walked from the plane to
the airport terminal, a man painted yellow and wearing an elaborate
feather headdress, boars' teeth piercing his nose and hanging from his
neck, and a grass skirt, and a bare-breasted woman who was also elaborately painted, greeted me and, dancing, led me to a room where I was

waved through customs without a question. Then I was led to a car and whisked into town. Wow, wish I were met like that everywhere. It was just a hint of what was to come.

Papua New Guinea had been claimed by a succession of countries during the colonial period of the nineteenth century, from Holland and Britain to Germany and Australia, and received full independence from Australia only in 1975. Real European contact with the establishment of permanent European outposts and diplomatic relations goes back little more than a century, and many tribes had been contacted by white people only within the past few decades. In Port Moresby, I met an anthropologist named Nicholas Faraclas, who had worked and taught at the University of Papua New Guinea for many years. He has a great affection for the people and in 1997 wrote one of the most powerful pieces about them that I've read. Here is part of what he said:

> Imagine a society where there is no hunger, homelessness or unemployment, and where in times of need, individuals can rest assured that their community will make available to them every resource at its disposal. Imagine a society where decision makers rule only when the need arises, and then only by consultation, consensus and the consent of the community. Imagine a society where women have control over their means of production and reproduction, where housework is minimal and childcare is available 24 hours a day on demand. Imagine a society where there is little or no crime and where community conflicts are settled by sophisticated resolution procedures based on compensation to aggrieved parties for damages, with no recourse to concepts of guilt or punishment. Imagine a society... in which the mere fact that a person exists is cause for celebration and a deep sense of responsibility to maintain and share that existence.

Such a place is not fiction, says Faraclas:

> When the first colonisers came to the island of New Guinea, they did not find one society that exactly fit the above description. Instead, they found over one thousand distinct language groups and many more distinct societies, the majority of which approximated closely the above description, but each in its own particular way. These were not perfect societies. They had many problems. But after some one hundred years of "northern development"... nearly all of the real developmental gains achieved over the past 40,000 years by the indigenous peoples of the island have been seriously eroded, while almost all of the original problems have gotten worse and have been added to a rapidly growing list of new imported problems. ("Critical literacy and control in the new world order," in *Constructing Critical Literacies*, edited by Sandy Muspratt, Allan Luke and Peter Freebody)

Nick Fogg had arranged for me to be flown to remote areas in the mountains and on the coast to meet people who were living traditionally but were under threat from illegal logging of their land. After staying overnight in Port Moresby, I was flown up into the mountains to Kokoda, where we landed on a grassy field. When the plane taxied to a stop, we were surrounded by a group of men wearing full body paint and spectacular regalia festooned with feathers, shells, and pigs' tusks. I was taller than all of them, but two of the men grabbed my legs and lifted me up on their shoulders. I was taken totally by surprise, and as I tried to twist upright, I threw my back out. I had a camera hanging around my neck and tried to get it into position as I struggled to stay upright without making my back hurt worse.

These two fellows were unbelievably strong and ran—not walked fast, ran—sweating and grunting as the others running along with us drummed and sang. I was bouncing up and down, feeling very, very uncomfortable, suffering jolts of pain up my spine while also trying to take pictures of this unique experience. The men ran all the way to a village about half a mile away, never once indicating I was too heavy or stopping for a rest. It was a wonderful relief to be put down.

In the village was a large outdoor stage where people gathered for meetings and entertainment. An elaborate dance with drumming and singing was performed for me, and then speeches were given in pidgin, which Nick translated for me. The people understood what the logging of the forest meant, a loss of their identity and traditions, but they also needed money for medicine and clothing like T-shirts and shorts. I gave a speech about what was happening around the world and how precious the forest was to this community. I emphasized that the people must retain control over their land and develop a community economic strategy that would allow them to generate an income without destroying their surroundings. I gave the speech in sentences that Nick translated into pidgin. The speech seemed to go over well, and I stayed overnight in a structure that was built above the ground on posts. Even there, what was impressive was the commonality of our humanity—these were people with whom I could laugh, eat, and communicate—yet I couldn't imagine the way they looked out at the world; culturally, it was as if we came from different parts of the universe.

Nick had arranged for a visit to a series of remote villages, which we reached by boat, plane, or jeep. Each village I visited entertained me with performances and plays the people had made. One play portrayed the arrival of Europeans, and the caricatures of the aliens were sidesplittingly funny. The performers were dressed in homemade costumes, and the white man was depicted as a clown, ordering the locals around and not having a clue about the tricks being played on him. I found it hilarious that the pompous visitor was so full of his own self-importance while the Papua New Guineans simply humored him, knowing he was a fool.

In one village, the inhabitants lined up to greet me after I had passed through a gate made of branches and leaves, signifying I had been welcomed onto their land. I shook hands along the line until I reached a young man who was covered from head to foot with what looked to me like a white fungal growth. I took a deep breath and shook his hand, assuming that whatever it was on his body must not be readily transmissible or he wouldn't have been there. Fortunately, my hand didn't develop any tropical rot and fall off.

In each village, I was treated generously, feted, and fed traditional foods. In one community, chicken, yams, and other root vegetables had been covered with leaves in a hole and a fire lit on top. Hours later, the meal was excavated and served—delicious.

Everywhere I went, people were spitting. This is disconcerting, because the spit is red from the eating of betel nuts, which also stain and etch cavities in the teeth. Nick told me the nuts—the seeds of betel palm—induce a pleasant buzz, but I was leery and never tried it. I wish I had, but I didn't want to stain my teeth. I was even more worried that to activate the drug in the plant, it has to be combined with a strong alkali that can burn the mouth. I didn't want to do that to my tongue or cheeks.

What you do is chew the nut to make a fibrous paste and then flatten it onto your tongue. The alkali formed by crushed, burned clamshells is placed onto the bed of betel nut on your tongue. You fold the flattened betel nut around the clamshells, using your tongue and the roof of your mouth so the alkali doesn't burn anything, and then the whole mass is chewed and mixed. The mixture turns red and the active ingredient is created. The big question is, how did people ever figure out such an elaborate process?

Like the Kaiapo in the Amazon, the people in these remote villages were almost completely self-sufficient. *The Nature of Things with David Suzuki* broadcast a two-part series based on a remarkable exchange

Trying out the drum given to me by people in the Kakoda Mountains in Papua New Guinea

between a tribe in Papua New Guinea and a Salish First Nation com-munity in British Columbia. First the Canadian group went to Papua New Guinea for several weeks, and the following year the Papua New Guinea group visited B.C. One of the Papua New Guineans com-mented that everything they had received while they stayed in B.C.— food, clothing, gifts—had to be bought with money that had to be earned. "When they visited us," he said, "everything we used came from the land."

Nevertheless, the products of the industrial economy were visible in every Papua New Guinea village I saw, from metal pots and pans to woven cloth in shirts and pants to radios and chain saws. I kept think-ing how different it must have been to go there in the 1950s and 1960s. That's when biologists like the Harvard ant expert E.O. Wilson, and the University of California (Los Angeles) bird authority Jared Dia-mond had studied in these wild lands. Having become an independent nation, Papua New Guinea must find a source of revenue for the government and bring the benefits of education and medical care to very remote communities. The challenge is to decide whether traditional customs and practices have value in a global economy and, if they do, how to protect them while generating incomes.

Ecotourism seemed to be an obvious potential source of revenue, since millions of people are avid bird-watchers and birds abound in the tropical forests. As well, the surrounding seas are crystal clear and teeming with fish, turtles, and coral. But I couldn't see how development of infrastructure—buildings, water, food, beds, blankets, and so on—and personnel could be organized without a huge disruption in traditional ways. In most villages, I slept above the ground on a platform covered with a floor of branches, and in one lovely location I slept right beside a glistening-white, sandy seashore. There would be enough people willing to rough it as I did, but it would be difficult to ensure there was food and first aid for cuts and infections, bites, and possible accidents.

I had been treated with great honor and respect and given gifts in each village as if I were royalty. After this tour of the villages, I returned to Port Moresby, where Nick had arranged for me to meet environmentalists. Many had fought against logging and mining, but there was great frustration because of the corruption of government officials. I couldn't figure out why people spoke so openly to me of their problems and asked me for advice, until I learned that there was some television reception in the city from Australia and that radio was big in the country. I learned that some of my programs and interviews had already been broadcast in Papua New Guinea.

In a speech in Port Moresby at the university, I suggested that by any objective assessment of natural resources—intact forests, abundant wildlife, clean water and air, rich oceans—Papua New Guineans must rate among the wealthiest people on Earth. The World Bank and transnational corporations were pressing them to adopt their ideas of progress and development; according to them, Papua New Guinea seemed poor. If Papua New Guineans could keep the World Bank and the International Monetary Fund (IMF) off their backs, I said, they could define what development means to them in a way that fits their culture and thus chart their own way into the future.

My remarks were covered by the media, and on my last night in Port Moresby, I received a note in my room from Ajay Chibber, World Bank division chief for Indonesia and the Pacific Islands. He had heard a broadcast of some of my remarks about the World Bank and was most upset; he said I was completely misinformed and demanded to see me to set me straight.

At six o'clock the next morning, I met Chibber and Pirouz Hamidian-Rad, a senior economist in the East Asia department of the World Bank. Chibber waded right in and said, "You and I are well off. We don't have the right to deny the poor people of the world an opportunity to improve their lives." I agreed, but I asked who is really "poor" and how we define "improvement." I suggested that the World Bank was forcing the so-called developing world to accept its definitions, that global economics overvalues human capital while ignoring the services of the natural world as "externalities." That's why forests and rivers, for example, which have provided a living for people for millennia, have economic value as defined by people like Chibber only when humans "develop" them by cutting down the trees or damming the rivers. I suggested there are other ways of measuring wealth and progress, to which Chibber retorted, "People around the world are better off now than they have ever been. There's more food than ever before in history, and it's because of economic development."

Chibber's statement encapsulated the belief that has concentrated wealth in a few hands while creating ecological degradation and poverty for many from Sarawak in Malaysia to Brazil to Kenya. I told him that leading scientists were warning about ecological disaster, to which he responded: "Scientists said twenty years ago there would be a major

Typical regalia

famine and large numbers of people would die. It never happened. They often exaggerate." So he wrote off scientists as lacking credibility. I wrote about him in a column, which I later included in my book *Time to Change,* and was gratified to learn years later that he had been removed from his position after my visit, though he went on to other World Bank posts.

The problem with groups like the IMF and World Bank is that everything is viewed through the perceptual lens of economics. Where people and communities have lived well through subsistence agriculture, fishing, and forestry for thousands of years, revenues are not generated for governments or corporations. By economics measures, countries that subsist traditionally become "developing" or "backward" and therefore "poor." An example of the consequence of conventional economic "progress" is described by Richard J. Barnet and John Cavanagh in *Global Dreams: Imperial Corporations and the New World Order:* "Sabritos [the Mexican subsidiary of Frito-Lay, owned by PepsiCo] buys potatoes in Mexico, cuts them up and puts them in a bag. Then they sell the potato chips for a hundred times what they paid the farmer for the potatoes."

After I returned to Canada, I soon received another invitation to Papua New Guinea, this time from women in a town called Wewak in East Sepik province. They were concerned about the loss of their forests and rivers and asked if I would visit. I am a sucker, and so I arranged to go to Papua New Guinea again on my next trip to Australia, in 1994. On that trip, I met Meg Taylor, a remarkable lawyer who later became the Papua New Guinean ambassador to the United States, Mexico, and Canada. She straddles two domains, traditional Papua New Guinea and the aggressive world of industry. I could sense the pull of each sphere on her, which perhaps reflected her background. Meg's mother was a Papua New Guinean, and her father was an Australian, the first white man to cross the island of New Guinea

on foot; it is hard to imagine the difficulties he must have encountered, given that each valley is so cut off from the next that all evolved
different languages and cultures. Meg remains a force in Papua
New Guinea, but she has to weave her way between the traditional
values of the country's cultures and the economic demands of industrialized nations.

In East Sepik, the women were desperate to retain their cultural and
traditional ways and were upset because some of the chiefs were being
lured by alcohol, women, and bribes to sign away their timber for a pit-
tance. The money from cutting the trees wasn't reaching the ordinary
people, and the forests were being stripped. I could only offer them
suggestions on how communities might develop small-scale economies
and relate to them the impact that I had seen Western economic development have on aboriginal people in Canada, Australia, and Brazil.

I was intrigued by Papua New Guinea, because it has one of the
largest intact tropical rain forests left on the planet and is still occupied
by the indigenous people who own the forests by law. The question is
what will happen in the coming years. I promised to help by sending
money from a fund I had set up in Australia from the profits of my
books there. The women didn't ask for much, but they wanted a chance
to develop markets for their traditional products.

These are the people whose men once wore amazing penis sheaths
of many sizes and shapes, and these, I am sure, would be a tourist attraction. Papua New Guineans are excellent carvers, and if their costumes
and feather, shell, and ivory necklaces and armbands could be sustainably made, they would be able to generate an income. I was introduced
to a man who had developed a "walkabout" sawmill, a setup so light
that a pair of men can carry it into the forest and mill a tree on the
spot. The lumber can then be carried out manually, and it is valuable
enough to make the effort worthwhile yet have a negligible impact on
the forest. I kept remembering those two men who carried me on their
shoulders as if I were a feather.

Dressed up to entertain

I felt there were alternatives to simply clearing the entire forest for those trees that have high market value, which is what Malaysian and Japanese companies are doing. We have to find ways of getting the money for that wood directly to the people who live in the forests. The resources belong to them, and they have the greatest stake in exploiting them in such a way that the forest will remain in perpetuity for future generations. If the head offices of the logging or mining operations are in Tokyo, Kuala Lumpur, or New York, profits are drained to them, leaving little but dribs and drabs for the people who will have to eke out a living with what is left.

In Wewak, I was taken by motorboat several miles out to sea to a small island. As we slowed and approached the beach, my hosts pointed into the clear water. Below I could see the carcasses of trees lying on their sides. "Those were once on land," I was told, "but the water has risen and that's why they are there." Was it thermal expansion of the water due to global warming, they asked me, but I didn't know. I was taken snorkeling in wonderfully clear and warm waters that were filled with fish, and I was thrilled to follow a large sea turtle that swam below me and gradually sank deeper and deeper until it disappeared. Eco-tourism was a pretty sure bet here, I felt.

Throughout my visit, my emphasis was not that the people should stay frozen in the past. They must decide on the importance of their traditions and the attraction of economic growth. One of the pilots of a small plane Nick had arranged for me on my first visit had huge holes in his nose and ears, where he clearly wore large plugs in his off time. In the pilot's seat, his appearance seemed rather incongruous, but Papua New Guineans have computers, video cams, and all the other accoutrements of modern society. The question is whether they will slavishly follow the path of globalization, which is reducing cultural and biological diversity all over the world, or whether they will keep their culture and knowledge as the basis for finding a sustainable future.

William Takaku, environmental activist, artist, and actor,
who starred in the movie *Friday* with Pierce Brosnan

In my talks, I reiterated the priceless nature of their traditional knowledge, lore painstakingly acquired over thousands of years and, once lost, never recoverable. My message resonated strongly with the young activists I met, but not with the non-Papua New Guineans, who were there for the economic opportunities.

I was scheduled to meet various businesspeople, politicians, and other important folks for a breakfast on my last day. I was placed next to the governor general, a physically imposing Papua New Guinean who had no pretensions and was down to earth in his conversation with me. While he was eating, I looked at his profile and realized I could see through the cartilage of his nose between his nostrils. He must at some time have worn a nosepiece.

I was also scheduled to give a talk that would be broadcast live across Papua New Guinea, a terrific opportunity, because radio was (and is) still the principal means of communication. I gave what must have been an unusual, even radical, speech about the need for the people to decide for themselves what matters most to them and to protect that above all else. They shouldn't allow officials like the World Bank people to set the agenda for them. My talk was met with great enthusiasm.

Unknown to us, as my speech began, an Australian who was in mining in Papua New Guinea became so incensed that he drove to the radio station that was beaming my speech, walked in, and pulled the wires out of the console, stopping the broadcast! Blithely ignorant of this, I went to the airport after the broadcast and left the country. I heard only later that inflamed listeners called in, many saying the expat should be killed, and that he was subsequently kicked out of the country. In April 2005, I attended a conference of Pacific countries on tourism, held in Macao, where a Papua New Guinean came up to me and said, "I was there at your speech that morning." Apparently it has become legendary.

chapter FIFTEEN

KYOTO AND
CLIMATE CHANGE

HUMAN BEINGS HAVE become so powerful
that we are altering the chemistry of the very
atmosphere that sustains us. Scientists have speculated on this possibility since the nineteenth century, but for the average person, it has only
recently become a matter of concern.

We tend to assume that the atmosphere reaches the heavens. But air
within which life can exist is only five or six miles deep; many of us can
easily run that distance. When I interviewed Canadian astronaut Julie
Payette for the film series *The Sacred Balance,* she said that each time
she circled the planet on her voyage in space she could see with every
sunrise and sunset the thin layer just above the earth—the atmosphere.
"We were way above it," she said. "Below that thin layer is where life
flourishes and above it, there is nothing; it's a vacuum."

If we were to reduce the planet to the size of a basketball, the
atmosphere would be thinner than a layer of plastic we use to wrap
sandwiches. And that is what we pour our effluents into every time
we drive a car and every time our factories send pollutants through
their smokestacks.

More than three billion years ago, plants appeared and began to photosynthesize, taking up carbon dioxide and combining it with water and energy from the sun to begin the process of carbon chain formation, which generates all of the molecules necessary for life. A byproduct of the chemical reactions in this process was oxygen. Before there were plants, the atmosphere was toxic for animals like us, since it was heavily laden with carbon dioxide and devoid of oxygen. Plants created the oxygen-rich atmosphere on which we depend and removed the carbon dioxide generated as part of respiration to keep the amount of carbon dioxide in the atmosphere at about 280 parts per million (ppm). But for more than a century, modern industrial activities have generated so much carbon dioxide from burning fossil fuels that all the plants on land and in the oceans can't keep up with it, and carbon dioxide has been accumulating in the atmosphere.

The fundamental mechanism of global warming is not contentious. Naturally occurring molecules such as water, carbon dioxide, methane, and nitrous oxide reflect infrared or heat waves. These molecules in the atmosphere act in the way glass on a greenhouse behaves, allowing sunlight to pass through but reflecting heat; hence these molecules are called greenhouse gases. On Mars, which has a very thin atmosphere, temperatures ricochet between the boiling heat of day and the freezing cold of night because there is no blanket of greenhouse gases to keep the heat on the planet. In contrast, Venus is permanently covered with a thick cloud of carbon dioxide, so surface temperatures are in the hundreds of degrees. Earth has had just the right combination of greenhouse gases in the atmosphere to stabilize temperatures between day and night and enable life to evolve and flourish.

Careful studies conducted in Hawaii for over fifty years have registered the unequivocal rise in atmospheric carbon dioxide levels from 280 ppm in preindustrial times to the present 362 ppm, a 32 percent increase. The upward curve in the rate of increase suggests that if we carry on with business as usual, we will double the concentration long before the end of the century. These studies also suggest that if we were to cut all our emissions by half overnight, thereby bringing our annual emissions to a level that can be reabsorbed by all photosynthetic activity within the biosphere, it will still take *hundreds* of years before the temperature changes from what we have already added to the atmosphere will level out, first in the air, then on land, and finally in the oceans. In other words, we have already set in motion an experiment with Earth that will not be fully played out for many, many more generations of humans.

Since the mid-1980s, I had known that the buildup of greenhouse gases such as carbon dioxide might be on a scale sufficient to affect our climate. But I thought there were far more pressing immediate issues, like toxic pollution, deforestation, and species extinction, and that climate change was a slow-motion disaster that would not really kick in for generations. It was only in 1988, when I first visited Australia, that Phil Noyce, my host, convinced me it was an urgent issue that needed action now. In the autumn of that year, climate experts from all parts of the world, who were gathered in Toronto for a major conference on the atmosphere, warned that the threat of global warming was real and called for a reduction in greenhouse gas emissions of 20 percent in fifteen years.

That year, the World Meteorological Organization and the United Nations Environment Program established the Intergovernmental Panel on Climate Change (IPCC), made up of hundreds of climatologists from many countries, to monitor the state of global climate. Sadly, hindsight reveals that had governments responded and met that challenge beginning in 1988, the air today would be cleaner, people healthier, and fossil fuels more plentiful, and we would be saving hundreds of billions of dollars and be well along the path to achieving an emission level that could be absorbed by the biosphere.

At the height of global concern about the environment, governments and nongovernmental organizations planned the 1992 Earth

Summit in Rio de Janeiro. The countries attending the summit agreed to stabilize greenhouse gas emissions at the 1990 levels by 2000, but most countries, including Canada, merely called for "voluntary compliance" with the targets. In the meantime, the fossil fuel industry launched an aggressive campaign to discredit the very idea that human activity was influencing climate, and the use of fossil fuels and thus greenhouse gas emissions continued to rise.

In 1995, to film for *The Nature of Things*, I attended a conference on climate organized by the Intergovernmental Panel on Climate Change in Geneva. Hundreds of IPCC climatologists from more than seventy nations had painstakingly assessed thousands of scientific papers on weather and climate, and they concluded in 1990 in their first major assessment that global climate was warming, and that the change was not part of a natural cycle. In 1995, the IPCC's second assessment concluded that "the balance of evidence suggests a discernible human influence on global climate." Though it seemed to me a pretty tepid conclusion—in the global arena, delegates are under enormous scrutiny and pressure from groups like governments and industries—this was a powerful warning. The IPCC's third assessment, released in 2001, was even stronger.

In Geneva, I was deeply moved by two delegates I met there. One was a Kenyan farmer who said traditional farmers used the cyclical appearance and disappearance of different plants as the cues to start plowing, planting, and harvesting, but they were having difficulty because these wild indicator plants seemed to be out of phase. Here was a scientifically uneducated farmer, dependent on external signals for his livelihood, reporting signs that climate was changing. I also encountered a South American Indian who told me that even on the equator, where there are not the traditional seasons that we know, plants were behaving in strange, never-before-seen ways.

Unfortunately, these traditional people did not have PhDs and were not fluent in the jargon of science, and like the people living on tropical coral atolls threatened by rising waters and the Inuit of the Arctic reporting on melting permafrost, they were paid little heed.

The IPCC continues its work, especially refining computer models and carefully refuting the arcane objections (satellite readings fail to confirm ground level measurements, sunspots are the primary cause of warming, models have no basis in reality, et cetera) of a handful of nay-sayers, most of whom are funded by the fossil fuel industry. Overall, the enormous undertaking by the IPCC has merely made the warnings of 1988 stronger and more urgent.

Most climatologists believe the evidence is overwhelming that the atmosphere is warming unnaturally, that humans are the major contrib-utor to this warming, and that immediate action is needed to counter the effects. Sadly, the renowned science-fiction writer Michael Crich-ton, author of *The Andromeda Strain* and *Jurassic Park,* has recently published a sci-fi thriller, *State of Fear,* based on the premise that envi-ronmental extremists are creating ecological crises to frighten people into supporting them. It is a preposterous thesis that seems to legitimate the idea that climate change is not real and does not require action.

There have been other books that purport to disprove climate change, many of them written by ideologues who dismiss environ-mentalists out of hand or who have a vested interest in industry. Gregg Easterbrook was an environmental writer for *Newsweek* and other publications, so his suggestion that environmentalists had been so successful that they had achieved most of their goals was taken very seriously, though it was refuted by many eminent ecologists and experts. Academic Bjørn Lomborg's book *The Skeptical Environmen-talist* has been embraced by right-wing think tanks like the Fraser Institute in Vancouver and business organizations. Again, a great deal of effort has had to be made to counter Lomborg's claim that the state of the environment is far better than environmentalists acknowledge.

One of the remarkable aspects of the IPCC work is the consensus of all but a handful of climatologists. Very few new ideas in science achieve such agreement among the overwhelming majority of experts. Consider biology—evolution is the fundamental basis on which our interpretation of life on Earth rests, yet there are hundreds of people with PhDs in biology who believe in the biblical version of Creation and deny evolution. Complete, 100 percent agreement is seldom achieved in science, so when most climatologists agree about something, their conclusions must be considered compelling.

Crichton ends his novel with a rant of his personal opinions, complete with references and footnotes that give the illusion he is writing a scientific treatise. He argues from examples in the history of medicine where consensus has proved to be wrong to discredit the IPCC conclusions. For example, doctors once universally believed that pellagra was the result of bacterial infection when it was actually a dietary deficiency. Physicians used to believe that deliberate bleeding cured a variety of problems and that ulcers could not be caused by bacteria. But in the world of medicine, as Harvard Medical School director Eric Chivian points out, doctors are trained to intervene when the evidence may not be absolute but where the dangers of not acting become too perilous. For example, one cannot be absolutely sure of a diagnosis of appendicitis before operating, because the risks of peritonitis and fatal septicemia from a ruptured appendix are too great. This is comparable to the need to act on global warming—except that here, as Chivian says, "we're dealing with the lives of billions of people."

Some opponents of reducing greenhouse gas emissions accept that the climate is changing, but they argue that we need a higher level of certainty that we are the cause, and that until we are completely convinced, we can't afford to act. The Stanford University climatologist Stephen Schneider asks how much certainty is necessary to act. He believes the evidence of human-induced climate change is at least 70 percent certain, a figure that skeptics pounce on as far too uncertain for action. Schneider responds by asking rhetorically, if we were told a sandwich had a 70 percent chance of containing a deadly poison, would we eat it? Of course not. So if we are performing an experiment on the only home we have, planet Earth, what level of certainty do we require, especially if the warnings of scientists are accurate and the consequences of not doing anything will be catastrophic? Even if those scientists are wrong, taking action will lead to enormous benefits in health, greater energy supplies, cleaner environment, and vast economic savings.

The projected effects of rising greenhouse gas levels are based on the amount of fossil fuels burned, methane liberated from landfills, chlorofluorocarbons (CFCs) released, and so on. But it is known that there are massive deposits of methane, a much more potent greenhouse gas than carbon dioxide, frozen beneath the permafrost in the Arctic and on the ocean floor. Inuit people in the circumpolar countries have been warning for years that permafrost is melting, something even the rabidly anti-climate-change senator from Alaska, Ted Stevens, has finally acknowledged is happening in his state as dozens of villages report their buildings are sinking. As permafrost melts, it will liberate massive amounts of methane into the atmosphere, accelerating the warming process far beyond the predictions of current computer models in what is called a positive feedback loop: rising levels of greenhouse gases induce warming, which melts permafrost, which in turn releases more greenhouse gas, which accelerates the warming even more.

In addition, the well-documented melting of polar ice sheets may have catastrophic effects on the movement of heat through ocean currents. There are enormous movements of water masses through the Atlantic and Pacific oceans. In the North Atlantic, water from the equator absorbs heat, which is moved by currents northward along the coast of Europe, raising the winter temperature above the levels expected for that latitude. As that water mass releases its heat and cools on its passage along the coast of Europe, it curves around and sinks at its northernmost point, slowly making its way south deep in the ocean. It is like a continuous stream of water through the ocean.

As ice sheets and glaciers melt more rapidly, fresh water floods the ocean and interferes with the current. This flooding can happen rapidly and has occurred in the past, shutting down the ocean currents and thereby bringing about a colder period or ice age in Europe. It seems counterintuitive that global warming might shut down the "heat engine" of this current and cause a catastrophic cooling of Europe, but in November 2005, scientists reported in *Nature* that currents appear to have slowed by 30 percent.

EVEN AS THE SKEPTICS persist in their claim that the IPCC scientists are missing or ignoring bits of evidence that "disprove" climate change, there are two types of evidence I find overwhelming. One comes from nature itself. If warming occurs, animals and plants that live within a certain temperature range will be forced to move to stay within that range. For organisms on mountainsides, that can be achieved by moving up. In a *Nature of Things* program entitled "Warnings from Nature," scientists documented that very kind of movement. In another case, a bird-watcher in the American Midwest has carefully recorded the comings and goings of birds through the seasons for fifty years. Her records clearly show that migratory birds are now arriving in her backyard up to two weeks earlier and leaving up to two weeks later. It's hard to believe that observational biases could be responsible for these results.

For me, the most powerful data are the annual atmospheric carbon dioxide levels extracted from the Antarctic ice sheets. In the topmost layers recording the most recent years, the carbon dioxide signature inflects sharply upward, rises steeply over the past decade and a half out of the background "noise," and now reaches a height beyond anything ever seen.

BY 1997, GLOBAL CONCERN about climate change had grown enough to warrant a gathering of delegates from most countries in the world at Kyoto, Japan. They were meeting to discuss a protocol for reducing emissions, with a goal of reaching a balance between emissions and the absorptive capacity of the biosphere. Collectively, humans were producing twice as much greenhouse gas, especially carbon dioxide from burning fossil fuels, as Earth could reabsorb, so overall emissions had to be reduced by 50 percent. But since countries like Canada, Australia, and the United States were disproportionately high emitters, our targets would eventually have to be reduced by 85 to 90 percent.

I found myself reluctantly attending this conference along with staff of the David Suzuki Foundation. I say reluctantly because, at these massive international affairs, much of the decision making goes on behind closed doors while groups such as ours merely buzz around like annoying gnats.

Kyoto is the cultural hub of Japan, and stepping out of the Shinkan-sen (bullet train), we were confronted with that strange contradiction of Japan, the traditional domes and pagoda shapes of its temples and the garish signs and monuments in plastic. After dropping off our luggage in our tiny hotel rooms, we walked through a light rain past the many shops and malls packed with Japanese shoppers. We were in a hurry, with little time to sightsee or shop or even seek out some good restaurants. When we reached the meeting halls, we were greeted by Green-peace's large blowup of Godzilla, the fire-breathing monster, created by garbage, a perfect metaphor for humanity's effects on the planet.

The halls were filled with the babble of people, official delegates from dozens of countries, environmentalists and other NGOs, lobby-ists for the fossil-fuels industry, and the media. Altogether, it was a mélange of perspectives and priorities. At the meetings, leading scien-tists talked about the latest evidence for climate change, environmental groups called for serious cuts in emissions, and government delegates wrestled with lobbyists working to sabotage the process by driving it off the rails. The Australian delegation complained bitterly that their

The Greenpeace display outside the conference hall in Kyoto

country was special, a big country with a sparse population that had few rivers for hydroelectric power and therefore was dependent on highly polluting coal-fired plants.

The insurance industry was the one large group in the business community that took climate change very seriously. Their actuarial data were dramatic—claims for climate-related damage like fires, floods, droughts, and storms were rising dramatically, as were the number of insurance companies going out of business.

The European Union (EU) was very concerned about climate change and wanted serious cuts in the range of 15 percent below 1990 emission levels. Aligned against them were the JUSCANZ countries (Japan, United States, Canada, Australia, and New Zealand), which formed a bloc working to water down the target. There were enormous debates about whether to allow Canada, and similar countries, to be given credit for the fact that its boreal forest absorbed carbon dioxide, therefore acting as a "carbon sink"; others wanted "emissions credits" to be traded so that polluting countries or industries could avoid reducing their emissions by paying for someone else's "share" of the atmosphere.

In such surroundings, the cynics could suggest the final decisions and targets were far too shallow to be effective and far too expensive for what would be achieved. But I believe the final outcome of the Kyoto deliberations was extremely important for what it signified. Kyoto signaled the recognition that the atmosphere is finite, that human activity has saturated it with emissions from fossil-fuel-burning vehicles and industries, and that we are adding more carbon dioxide and other greenhouse gases than the biosphere can handle. For the first time, governments and industries had to acknowledge that there can't be endless growth.

The atmosphere is not confined within national boundaries; it is a single entity shared by all people and organisms on Earth. The industrialized nations created the problem with their highly productive fossil-fuel-dependent economies. As an illustration of the disparity between the industrialized and nonindustrialized nations, Canada's 30 million people use as much energy as the entire African population of 900 million. In 1976, when I first visited China, which had thirty times Canada's population, it was using the same amount of oil and gas as Canada. I wrote at the time that if every Chinese wanted a motorbike, the results would be devastating. Now, a quarter of a century later, most Chinese aren't interested in bikes; they want cars, and with a booming economy and a growing middle class, more and more can afford them.

In 1997, the challenge was how to divvy up the atmosphere equitably. Countries like the United States, Australia, and Canada were heavy emitters, whereas countries like Russia were "under-emitters," since their antiquated and polluting industries were not globally competitive and were being forced to shut down; on a per capita basis, therefore, Russian people already had a lower emission output than the global emission target to be set at Kyoto. So, it was argued, such countries should be allowed to sell their "unused" share of the atmo-sphere to companies or countries that might not meet the target. This was a ludicrous idea, however, because even the lower emission rates were above the rates that would have to be reached to enable all green-house gases to be absorbed by plants. Allowing others to pay for the low emitters' "share" of the atmosphere was merely a loophole permit-ting those who had enough money to keep on polluting.

Alberta sent a delegation to lobby against the Kyoto negotiations. I remember Rahim Jaffer, the right-wing Reform party's member of Parliament from Edmonton, Alberta, loudly denying the evidence that climate change was happening, even though the overwhelming major-ity of delegates were not disputing the science. Europeans were appalled at the intransigence of the official JUSCANZ delegates, especially from the United States, which is the largest emitter on the planet; they were determined to set lower emissions targets. A stalemate loomed between those calling for significant reductions on the order of 15 percent below 1990 levels and those arguing that such goals were far too costly and ineffective. I didn't have access to the official Australian and Ameri-can delegates, but environmentalists from the two countries were out-spoken in their condemnation of the position of their governments. Many American environmentalists pinned their hopes on the arrival of U.S. vice president Al Gore.

Day after day the circus continued, as environmental groups per-formed a variety of stunts to try to gain attention from the media. Randy Hayes, the head of the Rainforest Action Network, led a conga line through the building to protest the position of his own country, the United States. I've always admired Randy for his originality and daring in the way he does things. I attended another conference in Japan at which he infuriated journalists by calling Japan an "environ-mental bandit."

At Kyoto, the David Suzuki Foundation called a press conference in which we used stacks of pop cans to illustrate the disparity in energy use

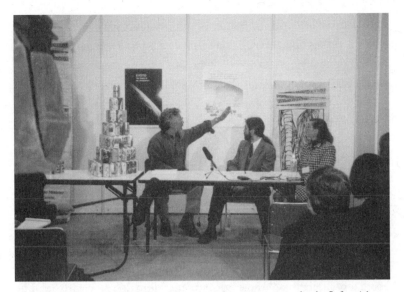

Press conference using pop cans to represent greenhouse gas emission levels. *Left to right:* me, Steven Guibeault (Greenpeace Canada), and Louise Comeau (Sierra Club Canada).

by industrialized and developing countries. Energy use by an average person in African countries like Zimbabwe was represented by 1 can, India and China by 5 and 15 cans, respectively, and Japan and European countries by 55 to 65 cans. Canada came near the top with 96, and the U.S. was tops with a whopping 120 cans. It made for a great photo.

The JUSCANZ allies were at loggerheads with the European Union, which wanted an aggressive approach to reducing emissions. Again, cynics argued that EU nations could make deeper cuts more easily. For example, Germany was aided by the fact that when East and West Germany were united, the antiquated, polluting plants of East Germany were shut down, thereby reducing the unified country's overall output and making it easier to meet targets. Since then, however, Germany has become the world leader in wind power, erecting windmills at home and exporting the technology abroad. Germany stands as a shining example of the opportunities created by taking the challenge seriously. Great Britain was also phasing out its outmoded coal-burning plants and therefore would find it easier to meet any target. Since then, however, Prime Minister Tony Blair has committed the United Kingdom to a 60 percent reduction in greenhouse gas emissions by 2040 and promises that cuts can be ramped up even further if the science demands it. Now that is a serious commitment.

BECAUSE OF JUSCANZ OPPOSITION, it began to look as if the proceedings would fail. But then Vice President Gore arrived. Environmentalists adored him because, as he described in his book *Earth in the Balance*, he understood the issues.

In 1988, while preparing for the radio series *It's a Matter of Survival*, I had interviewed Gore when he was visiting Canada, and he sent shivers up my spine as he answered my questions; I had never heard a politician state the environmental situation so clearly, and he articulated the solutions that were needed to overcome the problems. At the end of the interview, I turned off the tape recorder and begged him to immigrate to Canada so that I could work to get him elected prime minister.

Then I asked more seriously, "How can journalists like me help politicians like you?" His answer surprised me and put me on the path I have followed to this day. He said, "Don't look to politicians like me. If you want change, you have to convince the public there is a problem, show them there are alternatives, and get them to care enough to demand that something be done. Then, every politician will trip over himself trying to get on the bandwagon." Watching Gore perform as a presidential candidate in 2000, I felt the prescience of his advice to me. He didn't talk about the environment during his campaign because the American people weren't ready for it.

I had read Gore's book when it came out. It was a powerful document that I found very moving because he considered the environmental challenges from the standpoint of his Christian faith, parenthood, and politics. He didn't separate them into different areas but folded them together to come up with an integrated outlook and response. He pointed to the problems as he had encountered them as a journalist and politician, considered the implications as a parent and religious person, and outlined a program to respond to the threats, one that was both politically and economically sound. Upon his arrival in Kyoto, the environmental NGOs flocked around him as he brokered a deal with the EU countries. I later met an American environmentalist who had criticized Gore and the administration of U.S. president Bill Clinton for being too slow and too cautious, and he had been punished by being excluded from any further access to meetings with Gore. That's politics.

Much to the disgust of the private U.S. lobbyists, Gore settled for a target of a 6 percent reduction in greenhouse gas emissions by 2010. This was in 1997. Even if he had succeeded Clinton as president for two terms, he wouldn't be in office when the United States would be held to account for achieving the target, so it could be suggested he had nothing to lose by advancing the deal. Environmentalists hailed Gore as the savior of the Kyoto Protocol, which was signed by the attending delegates and would become law pending ratification by enough nations.

At the time, I was deeply disappointed because I knew Gore understood the implications of global warming and knew that deeper cuts were needed. In his book, he had called for massive investments in more efficient use of fossil fuels and in developing alternative energy sources, so a 6 percent cut seemed too trivial. But thinking now about the enormous lobbying pressure, I see his brokerage of an actual cut as a major step. The deal allowed Australia a huge concession—it would be the only industrialized country permitted to set an emissions target *above* 1990 levels (8 percent). All the others were expected to come in below that level.

I have never understood the Australian plea for special dispensation. Canada has the longest marine coastline of any country in the world, but the entire boundary of Australia is ocean, and the first consequence of warming of the oceans is expansion—sea levels will rise

David Suzuki Foundation gang at Kyoto. *Left to right:* Sarika, Tara, Severn, Me, Catherine Fitzpatrick, Ted Ferguson, and David Hocking.

as warmer water expands, and the impact on Canada and Australia will be immense. Canada, as a northern country, could complain that its energy needs are greater than those of other countries because of the cold climate, but Prime Minister Jean Chrétien ratified the Kyoto target in the knowledge that 70 percent of the public wanted it.

Whenever I land in Australia, I am always struck by the fact that the country has vast amounts of something Canadians would love to have more of—sunlight. Yet driving through the cities of the nation, one has to look very hard to see a solar panel anywhere. In many poor tropical countries, water barrels on top of houses or stands are simply heated by the sun. How can Australia justify opposition to Kyoto when all of its hot water could be provided by free, nonpolluting sunlight? With its vast desert expanses, Australia should be harvesting sunlight with immense solar collectors, developing innovative ways to exploit this resource, and finding markets for solar technology. It is disgraceful that John Howard, the prime minister, has sided with the United

States, and theirs are the only two industrialized nations refusing to abide by what is now an international treaty.

Will Kyoto make a difference? Many opponents of Kyoto, including U.S. president George Bush, have argued that its fatal flaw is the exclusion of the developing nations, especially India and China, as signatories. It's an argument that doesn't hold water.

If India and China follow our path of profligate energy use and pollution, no matter what the rest of the world does, the ramifications will be overwhelming. But we cannot compel them to take a different path if we do not show that we recognize the problem and are acting to reduce the hazards. If we don't set the example, we will have no moral credibility with other countries that look to us as role models. And finally, Canada (and especially the province of Alberta), Australia, and the United States are among the richest jurisdictions on Earth. If we argue that acting to minimize the hazards of climate change is too expensive, when will we be able to afford to act? And if we don't change our ways, why should India, China, Brazil, or Indonesia behave any differently?

THE FINAL AGREEMENT AT Kyoto was completed late at night on the last day of the meeting. As delegates blearily congratulated each other, few could have anticipated the challenges that lay ahead. The Kyoto Protocol would not come into effect until individual countries comprising a total of at least 60 percent of the world's population had ratified it. The ratification process would take years, and Canada, for one, had called for "voluntary compliance" to meet the target, even though experience already indicated this would never work. The private sector always opposes government regulation and, when pressured, promises to work things out voluntarily—but it never works. In the years since Kyoto, Canada's emissions have increased steadily to a point where, if we now wish to meet the goal, emissions will have to be cut by 32 percent. Hurricane Katrina revealed the folly and cost of ignoring the advice of experts, and Canadians should demand that our so-called leaders weigh scientific and technological advice far more heavily than the yelling of economists and industrialists.

Even though Gore took credit for the Kyoto agreement finally being adopted, he knew it would not pass through the United States Congress. When he ran for the U.S. presidency in 2000, he hardly talked about the environment at all. Upon election as president, George W. Bush quickly indicated he would not support the ratification of Kyoto. Since the largest energy user (and polluter) refused to consider reducing emissions, it was difficult to get the rest of the world to ratify the protocol.

As the United States' largest trading partner and foreign source of energy, Canada was under enormous pressure not to ratify. After Prime Minister Jean Chrétien went ahead and ratified the Kyoto Protocol in December 2002, I was thrilled to receive a letter in January 2003 thanking the foundation for making it possible for him to do so. His letter concluded: "Your personal efforts and those of your foundation have been an important part of the consultation process and have also contributed to informing Canadians about the issues."

Canada's signing was a very significant step but did not deliver the numbers needed to make the protocol internationally binding. The last country that could make that difference was Russia. I don't know what kind of pressure the United States exerted to keep President Vladimir Putin from signing, but I am sure it was considerable. Russia was in a position to blackmail both the Americans, who wanted Kyoto to fail, and the rest of the world, which needed the signature. Although I have no idea what finally tipped the balance, I would be amazed if it was because Putin wanted to do the right thing for the planet. Instead, I suspect he received assurances from the EU that there would be economic benefits to be had by signing. Nevertheless, in an atmosphere of despair and pessimism among environmentalists, Russia ratified Kyoto on November 18, 2004, thereby making the protocol international law ninety days later, on February 16, 2005—seven years after it was completed and a mere five to seven years before its end.

Iraq and Katrina should be wake-up calls to an administration that sometimes behaves like an international renegade, but the Bush–Cheney administration remains focused on its own course and agenda. I have absolutely no doubt that reality—more and more severe weather events, droughts, fires, climbing oil prices—is going to awaken the United States from its slumber on this issue.

I vividly remember the shock of realization that the Soviet Union was advanced in science and engineering in the fall of 1957 when Sputnik was launched. Americans did not cry "we can't do anything about it" or "it's too expensive" as they took on the challenge of the space race. Instead, money, energy, and resources were poured into the effort that not only succeeded in winning spectacularly with the manned lunar landing, but spun off a revolution in telecommunications, astronomy, and space research. And today, Nobel Prizes continue to be awarded to Americans disproportionately because of that commitment to science and engineering.

If we can get this great entrepreneurial nation to devote even a fraction of what is spent on military budgets and homeland security to use energy more efficiently and find energy alternatives, there will be a revitalization of the economy with green initiatives.

chapter SIXTEEN

REFLECTIONS ON SCIENCE AND TECHNOLOGY

TODAY THE MOST powerful force affecting our lives is not politics, business, celebrity, or sports, despite the coverage they receive in the media. By far the greatest factor shaping the world is science as applied by industry, medicine, and the military. We can't go anywhere on the planet without using the products or encountering the debris of science and technology. When I tell children there were no televisions or computers when I was their age, they find it hard to believe and often ask me, "What did you do?" because they can't imagine what one did in such an ancient and bereft civilization.

Each innovation changes the way we do things and renders the old ways obsolete. Looming are even more fantastic technologies, from intelligent machines to cloning, nanotechnology, stem cell regeneration, space travel, and much more. There will also be enormous problems in addition to the ones that already beset us, like global warming, toxic pollution, species extinction, overpopulation, alienation, and drug abuse. Without a basic knowledge of scientific terms and concepts and an understanding of how science differs from other ways of knowing, I don't believe we can find real solutions to such issues. Scientists and educators alike have failed to ensure that scientific literacy is as much a part of what is considered a core value as mathematics, reading, and writing. The consequences of scientific illiteracy among the general public are not trivial.

In the fall of 1987, I was part of a group that examined the degree to which our elected representatives comprehend science. Looking at the thirty-eight Cabinet ministers of the Canadian federal government, we found that of the thirty-two who could be assigned a profession outside politics, twelve were from business, ten from law, three from farming, and two from engineering. Thus, almost 70 percent of those thirty-two were from business or law, perhaps explaining why governments are so preoccupied with economic and jurisdictional issues. Why such a disproportionate representation from those two areas? I think it's because more of the practitioners in these fields can afford or are funded well enough to run for office and risk the enormous costs if they lose.

In a related study in 1987, fifty members of Parliament were administered a very simple test of their comprehension of scientific terms and concepts. Those with backgrounds in business and law scored absolutely rock-bottom. Yet these people will have to make informed decisions about climate change, alternative sources of energy, farmed versus wild salmon, intelligent machines, space research, space missile defence shields, biotechnology, stem cells, cloning, and other issues that require at least a basic grounding in science. No amount of simplification by technical staff will overcome the barrier of scientific illiteracy.

So decisions will end up being made for political reasons. How scientifically literate do we believe U.S. president George W. Bush is apropos of space-based missile defenses, teaching of intelligent design in science courses, foreign aid for HIV/AIDS, or responses to avian flu? Do we believe Australian prime minister John Howard understands the science behind global warming as he opposes the Kyoto Protocol?

Given the degree of scientific illiteracy among politicians, it's not surprising that we can't reach informed, rational decisions on these issues. I have spent a lot of time trying to bring new ministers up to speed when they are appointed, but they get moved around, and we have to start from scratch when a new person is put in the job. Only when scientific literacy is a central part of our education and culture will we have the possibility of a government that can make fully informed political decisions.

IN THE EARLY HISTORY of the human species, the invention of a spear, bow and arrow, needle, pottery vessel, metal implement, and domestication of plants and animals ushered in monumental changes that often reverberated for centuries and transformed individual lives and social arrangements, rendering the old ways extinct. Today multiple technological changes occur at an ever-accelerating rate, thereby ensuring that the world I knew as a boy is no more.

In my childhood, I wasn't permitted to go to movies at all or public swimming pools in the summer because my parents worried that I might catch polio, a viral disease the Sabin and Salk vaccines later pushed into obscurity. Each year around the world, hundreds of thousands of people suffered agonizing deaths or horrible scars from the now-eradicated disease of smallpox. The world I grew up in lacked jet planes, oral contraceptives, heart transplants, transoceanic phone calls, CDs, VCRs, plastics, photocopying machines, genetic engineering, and so much more.

Not only does each innovation alter the way we do things, many may change the very definition of what it is to be human. We love technology because we design it to do specific things for us, but we seldom reflect on the consequences or have any inkling of what the long-term repercussions might be. Thus, we discovered biomagnification of pesticides, the effects of chlorofluorocarbons (CFCs) on the ozone layer, and radioactive fallout from nuclear weapons only *after* the technologies had been created and used. Consider the impact of the automobile: it

Starting out as a fruit fly geneticist at UBC, when doing good basic science was all that was required to receive a grant. (Don't be fooled by the lab coat, which I seldom wore.)

liberated us from being local creatures, killed tens of millions of us, facilitated urban sprawl, caused massive loss of land under roads, created global pollution, and accelerated the depletion of resources. Television has had a corrosive effect on communities and social mores and has led to commercials and consumerism and the general dumbing down of issues and thought processes. Technology has huge costs.

When I began my career as a scientist, we took pride in exploring basic ideas of the structure of matter, the origin of the cosmos, or the structure and function of genes without having to justify the expansion of human knowledge. Medical genetics was considered intellectually inferior to the kind of work we carried out with fruit flies.

In 1972, a special Canadian Senate committee under Maurice Lamontagne had examined the role science plays in society and concluded there was a need to tie research more directly to society's needs. "Mission-oriented" work was to be encouraged, presaging the enormous pressure that would be put on scientists to make their work economically useful. Scientists are led, by necessity, by the priorities underlying the granting procedure. If good basic science is all that is required to receive a grant, then scientists will be much more honest about what they are doing. But when there is pressure to find a cure for cancer, for example, then scientists engage in a game that ultimately undermines science by creating a false impression of what science is.

Why do we support science? Former Canadian prime minister Pierre Trudeau seemed to feel science is a frill we support when times are good. I couldn't disagree more. We support science because it is a part of what it means to be civilized, pushing back the curtains of ignorance by revealing bits and pieces of nature's secrets. But more and more, we are under a demand that science deliver practical uses. This is a dangerous requirement, because it imposes an urgency that can lead to shortcuts, unwarranted claims, and deception.

Canadian scientists make up a very small proportion of the total number of scientists around the world. Our total grant money is minuscule compared with the U.S. total, and globally, it is even less. If we assume the quality of science is about the same everywhere, then on average perhaps 2 percent of important discoveries will be made in Canada. Thus, the probability that some fundamental "breakthrough" (how I hate that misused and overused word) will be made here is very small, and one might suppose that Trudeau was right—we should simply parasitize the world's literature and focus on rapid capitalization of new ideas.

But that is not how science works or how it leads to applications. The really exciting creative moments are in conversation with leading scientists at conferences and on visits, or in closed meetings where a handful of the elite in a field gather to bat around ideas that are still in the embryonic phase and not available in publications. Such meetings are exciting, creative, and exclusive, open only to the top people. That's why we support the members of our small but top-notch Canadian scientific community—they are the price of a front-row seat at the action. Without them, we aren't plugged in to the cutting-edge work going on around the world.

Canada's granting process was an outmoded system that worked when there wasn't a lot of pressure and the community was small. I sat on one of the granting panels that chose which applicants would be funded and was surprised at how much political considerations entered into the final awards. We scientists on the grant panel spent a lot of time assessing and rating the applications on their scientific merits as best we could and then allocating the funds. But our decisions were only recommendations, which we submitted to the National Research Council. When the final decisions were announced, it was obvious that additions and deletions had been made to our recommendations according to geographic distribution and whether an institution seemed to have a disproportionate amount or was shut out of any support. It was a ridiculous way to give out money. Our policy seemed to be: pee over a broad expanse of ground and hope plants will sprout up everywhere.

But if our bladder is small, we should at least direct the fertilizer to where the seeds are, not sprinkle it around.

When I was still active in research, Canadian granting agencies didn't seem to have the courage to identify the outstanding scientists and provide them with as much money as possible while turning down the rest. Today, much larger sums of research money are allocated and the rejection rate is much higher, but when I had a lab most applicants got grants at very low levels of support. We should focus on new, young scientists, because at the start of their careers, they are ambitious and have the energy to work hard. They are the ones who should be given substantial funding with few formal demands other than following wherever their interests lead for three or four years. At that point, they will have a body of work that can be evaluated for originality, quality, and quantity. From then on, those who have done promising work can be supported very well. We don't create excellence by funding institutions or infrastructure—it is individuals to whom we should pay attention and provide support.

Science has never been considered an important part of Canadian culture or celebrated in the way we celebrate the arts. Wisely, the Science Council of Canada was established as a Crown corporation, supposedly with an arm's length relationship with government. I say "supposedly" because when Stuart Smith, who was leader of the Liberal party of Ontario, became head of the Science Council, he had a difficult time reappointing me to the board for a second term because of a B.C. senator who opposed it. Nevertheless, in a time when the most powerful effect on our lives and our society is science, we need a body to look at the implications and provide counsel to guide us into the future. In 1993, Prime Minister Brian Mulroney abolished the Science Council (along with the Economics Council), thereby ensuring that we would move into the future with greater uncertainty and make decisions for political reasons, ignoring science-based assessments of the issues.

THE FORMER HOST OF CBC Radio's *Morningside,* Peter Gzowski, richly deserved the adulation expressed upon his untimely death in 2002. Gzowski was quintessentially Canadian. I cannot imagine him or someone like him with his stuttering, humble, low-key way making it as a star in London or New York. But in Canada, he touched a deep chord.

He interviewed me a number of times on *Morningside,* and I had also appeared several times on his painful venture into television, *90 Minutes Live.* There was much resentment within the *Nature of Things* unit about the money lavished on Gzowski's television program, but I loved the idea of a nightly showcase for Canadian talent. It's unfortunate that what worked so well on radio was a disaster on television. Gzowski felt I was a strong contributor, and he wanted me to appear as a regular on the show. I was flattered, but I didn't want to simply be a reporter on the "Golly, gee whiz, what will they think of next?" or "Isn't that scary?" aspect of science, so I declined.

One of the high points of my appearances on *90 Minutes Live* was the night I appeared with Kurt Vonnegut Jr., and Timothy Leary. Vonnegut and I got on famously, and we were both appalled at Leary, who was in his phase of pushing SMIILE, which stood for Space Migration, Intelligence Increase, Life Extension, the kind of techno-optimism that makes my teeth ache. It was great television, and the sparks were flying between the three of us when Peter broke in for a commercial. When the break was over, we were cut off, and he went on with the next act, which was a man with a bullwhip knocking cigarettes out of his son's mouth.

Much later I spoke with Alex Frame, the executive producer of *90 Minutes Live,* and he admitted it had been a mistake to stay so wedded to the prearranged schedule rather than let the energy of Leary, Vonnegut, and Suzuki carry on. The next day, Tara and I went out for breakfast with Vonnegut, who was charming and insisted on taking us to a bookstore to get one of his books. The salesperson did a double take when he recognized Vonnegut and could do nothing but stare when Vonnegut asked where his own books were. Eventually Vonnegut found the book he wanted and signed it, and it is one of our treasured possessions.

I appeared sporadically on *Morningside*. Peter was laid-back, but I was always wary, expecting some nasty question to come at me. It never did. He was a very generous interviewer, asking a question and then letting me have my say rather than cutting me off to shape the interview the way he wanted, as so many hosts do today. But if he was genuinely interested in what I said, I couldn't understand why he didn't go on to espouse environmental causes. I have always been surprised that hosts of programs may report on frightening or urgent stories, yet when the show is over, they move on to the next issue. It was one of the problems Jim Murray, my boss and best friend at *The Nature of Things*, had with me. Because of a program we did, say, on the Cree in Quebec, the Kaiapo in the Amazon, or the Haida in Haida Gwaii, I couldn't help but stay engaged with them. So when the program had been broadcast, I'd still be working away with them, whereas Jim felt I should move on and concentrate on the next show, which was a perfectly reasonable position from the standpoint of the series.

Writing about himself in 2001, Gzowski admitted in *A Peter Gzowski Reader* that he

> had a pretty full life. On radio or television or with pencil in hand, I've got to meet the Queen, eight prime ministers (nine if you count Margaret Thatcher...), four governors-general, two chief justices, two Nobel Prize winners, the world yodeling, whistling and bagpipe champions (all Canadians) and every winner and most of the runners up of the Giller Prize for Literature.

Gzowski was clearly proud of having interviewed so many important people—and he should have been. The range of people he had met and interviewed in a career spanning almost twenty years, for three hours a

Jim Fulton and me presenting Prime Minister Paul Martin with our document
"Sustainability Within A Generation" in 2004

day, five days a week, must be mind-boggling. I always marveled at the sheer stamina and concentration needed for such a prodigious effort.

But it's the list Gzowski chose to write down that interests me. All those prime ministers and the Queen and Giller Prize candidates and winners, yet a measly two Nobel Prize winners. I was surprised he even bothered to mention them, and he failed to indicate whether they were scientists, writers, economists, or peace workers. Lester Pearson, prime minister of Canada from 1963 to 1968, was the recipient of a Nobel Peace Prize in 1957, but there have been four other Nobel Prize winners in science who continued to stay in Canada—Frederick Banting, Gerhard Herzberg, John Polanyi, Mike Smith—and I interviewed three of them (Banting had died in 1941). There are usually about ten to twelve winners of the prestigious awards in three science categories every year. I was the host of *Quirks and Quarks* for four years, and during that time I interviewed at least twenty Nobel Prize winners. A huge divide remains between scientists and the rest of society, and the paucity of scientist Nobelists on Gzowski's list reflects it. How can we as a society assess the potential impact of so many issues in which science and technology play major roles in both their creation and solution if we ignore them?

Nothing illustrates the consequences of scientific illiteracy better than the situation in the United States. President George W. Bush received an education at Yale University, one of the top institutions in the world, and rose to head the wealthiest and most powerful nation in history. Yet the country founded on a separation of church and state has seen the intrusion of a Christian fundamentalism into the very center of power. One shocking consequence is the debate about evolution, which has flared into a national movement, putting enormous pressure on teachers and educational institutions to relegate evolution to a theory that must compete with the biblical version of Creation. Once called "scientific creationism," this literal interpretation of the Bible has been modernized into Intelligent Design, with all the trappings and jargon of molecular biology. The fact that it continues to be considered a serious scientific alternative to evolution is a disgrace. Evolution is as real as the existence of an atom, DNA, or a black hole; we see it everywhere, not only in living systems, but in the geology of Earth and the dynamic universe. The mechanisms and processes of evolution are far from understood, but the fact of its occurrence is not. Scientists have failed to inculcate an understanding of what lies within the scientific realm and where religion intrudes without justification.

But President Bush's kind of faith in science and technology also enabled him to push an agenda of space travel to Mars within a decade or two. I have visited the Houston Space Center many times to film and have shot the mock-ups for the Mars trip. They are unbelievably crude, and I don't believe for a minute that getting to Mars and back will be possible within my children's lifetime, if ever; nor is the cost of trying worth it. It is a political gimmick, a proposal Bush will not have to be accountable for, merely a bauble offered to the electorate if it demonstrates leadership and vision.

Of a more serious nature is the proposal to build a space-based missile defense system reminiscent of Ronald Reagan's Strategic Defense Initiative, or Star Wars. Now deprived of an Evil Empire, the Soviet Union, to justify such a costly boondoggle, Bush is left pointing to an Axis of Evil that may include North Korea, Cuba, and who knows who else among this terrifying group—Libya's three million people? Grenada?

The dangers posed by nuclear-tipped missiles are their speed, accuracy, and destructive power. Armed with multiple, independently targeted warheads, such weapons might be loaded with reflective materials to confuse radar. A defence system would have to pick up a missile immediately after it is launched to maximize the time window in which to respond. Computers would have to identify the missile correctly and not mistake commercial planes, flocks of ducks, or UFOs for the missile. The trajectory, probable target, and payload would have to be analyzed very rapidly to respond in time to knock down the attacking vehicle before it reached the United States (chances are this scenario would be played out over Canada).

Now here's the rub. Someone—a human being—is going to have to recognize the implications of what the entire system has detected and spat out: namely, that one or dozens of missiles are headed to the United States. If I were going to launch such an attack, I would do it at an inconvenient hour, like 3:00 AM on New Year's Day or after the Super Bowl. Some poor military person sitting in a silo somewhere in the Midwest, quietly playing a computer game or more likely napping, would have to notice what's going on and calmly assess the information and immediately pass it up the line. Assuming his or her superior was available, awake, and alert, he or she would have to assess the material and pass it on until eventually someone would have to go and wake the president so that he could push the red button or put in a key or whatever it takes to release the defensive weapons.

Can we assume all of the assessment and decision making would take place in seconds as it was passed up the chain of command and that finally someone somehow would enter, knock, blow a whistle, or do something else to wake the president? Can we assume the president would be fully awake instantly, able to assess the information lucidly and with care, ponder the consequences of not acting or responding, and not be distracted by thoughts of the country, his loved ones, or the stock market? Would he become sick or, as we saw him do in Michael Moore's documentary *Fahrenheit 9/11* after Bush received the news that two jetliners had crashed into the Twin Towers in New York in 2001—sit there for several minutes with a totally blank look? I know I would.

With a response-time window of minutes, even with the most efficient system the pressures would be too great for any human being to respond rationally. So if one believes in the technology, it has to be programmed to assess what is happening as each second ticks by, measure the effective time for response, and then decide when that critical moment is reached and order a response without interference by fallible humans.

The technology required to detect and respond to any possible threat—space satellites with sophisticated detectors and systems to relay information to ground stations, underground command centers, missiles in silos, and so on—is enormously complex. I do not believe for a minute that such a vast array of components will function perfectly from the time it is in place (my smoke detector didn't work the one time it was needed), but the only time we will know will be the first occasion it is put to the test. To function properly, the entire system will depend on the speed and accuracy of the supercomputers that are at the heart of the defense program. The computer program required to analyze all of the data will be more complex than any software ever designed, because every possible contingency has to be anticipated and programmed for without countermanding or interfering with different sets of instructions.

We know that any new program has numerous "bugs," and the only way to eliminate them is through thousands of people beginning to use it and finding them. Can a program be designed to respond to an attack without being tested by the real thing? It will have to be perfect the first time, something scientists not working for the military or receiving grants from the military tell us is virtually impossible. Only a scientifically literate president can even begin to truly assess the technical aspects of the proposed system.

SINCE I WROTE *Metamorphosis,* I have abandoned the doing of genetics, which had consumed me for a quarter of a century. In the 1970s, when geneticists began to learn to isolate and manipulate DNA in very sophisticated ways, it was immediately obvious there were enormous social, economic, and ecological implications. For decades writers, philosophers, and geneticists had been speculating about genetic engineering and discussing the potential ramifications of such powers. I never dreamed that within my lifetime, not only would the entire dictionary of sixty-four three-letter DNA words be deciphered, but we would also be able to purify, read, and synthesize specific sequences of DNA and insert them into virtually any organism at will. The day of human-designed organisms was at hand.

I knew there would be tremendous repercussions. Having belatedly recognized the dangers that our inventiveness posed from the battles over the insecticide DDT and then CFCs, I felt genetic engineering would encounter the same problems—our manipulative powers were great, but our knowledge of how the world works is so limited that we would not be able to anticipate all of the consequences in the real world. In my view, we had to be very cautious.

But there was tremendous pressure in my lab to begin working with the new technologies of DNA manipulation, because the techniques were so powerful that they had become molecular equivalents of a microscope, an indispensable tool for virtually every kind of genetic study. However, if my lab began to exploit these new technologies, I would have a strong vested interest in defending their continued use and ultimately application. Wouldn't this make me just like a scientist working for the tobacco industry, someone with a perspective and motivation that bias the way he or she carries out tests, interprets results, and draws conclusions? I had achieved far more in science than I ever dreamed. I hadn't set out to win honors or prizes or make a fortune; I only ever wanted the acknowledgment of my scientific cleverness by my peers.

As a result of the grotesque misapplication of a genetic rationale during the early part of the twentieth century in the eugenics movement, and in the Japanese Canadian evacuation, and then in the Holocaust, I knew a debate about genetic engineering had to be engaged and I wanted to participate in it with credibility. So I began to write a series of disclaimers, stating my intent not to become involved in such research, even though it was perhaps one of the most exciting moments in the history of genetics. That made it all the more imperative that some people with a background in genetics be able to enter the discussion without a stake in the technology.

Nevertheless, I continue to take vicarious delight in the enormous technical dexterity of today's molecular geneticist and revel in seeing answers to biological questions I never thought would be resolved in my lifetime. I watched my daughter carrying out experiments in undergraduate labs that were unthinkable when I graduated with a PhD. It is no wonder geneticists are exhilarated—indeed, intoxicated with excitement. But the rush to exploit this new area as biotechnology has me deeply disturbed.

I am equally distressed at the rush of my peers and colleagues in genetics to tout the potential benefits of this powerful technology with virtually no consideration of the hazards. Like scientists employed by the tobacco, fossil fuel, pharmaceutical, and forest industries, geneticists who set up companies, serve on boards, receive grants, or carry out experiments using the new techniques have a commitment to the technology that biases their pronouncements. As issues of cloning, stem cells, and release of genetically engineered organisms in the wild continue to crop up, there is a dearth of scientists trained in genetics who don't have a stake in the technology. Those few of us who are out there are often dismissed as has-beens who don't know what's going on. In their exuberance about the astonishing advances being made, scientists have expunged the history of their field and speak only of the enormous potential benefits of their work while dismissing the equally plausible hazards.

I have long agonized over the misapplication of genetics in the past, from the ludicrous claims of eugenics to prohibitions on interracial marriage, restrictions on immigration of ethnic groups, claims of racial inferiority, the supposed racial affinity of Japanese Canadians, and the Holocaust. Because of that, I wrote a series of columns that led to my eventual withdrawal from research to maintain my credibility in the discussions about the implications. In *Science Forum* in 1977, I wrote:

> For young scientists who are under enormous pressure to publish to secure a faculty position, tenure or promotion, and for established scientists with "Nobelitis", the siren's call of recombinant DNA is irresistible ... In my own laboratory, there is now considerable pressure to clone *Drosophila* DNA sequences in *E. coli* ... My students and postdocs take experiments and techniques for granted that were undreamed of five or ten years ago. We feel

that we're on the verge of really understanding the arrangement, structure and regulation of genes in chromosomes. In this climate of enthusiasm and excitement, scientists are finding the debate over regulation and longterm implications of recombinant DNA a frustrating roadblock to getting on with the research.

I concluded that I wanted to participate in the debate about the implications of genetic work and that if I did, I could not also be involved in research using the revolutionary techniques. I continued:

> Can the important questions be addressed objectively when one has such high stakes in continuing the work? I doubt it. Therefore I feel compelled to take the position that . . . no such experiments [on recombinant DNA] will be done in my lab; reports of such experiments will not acknowledge support by money from my grants; and I will not knowingly be listed as an author of a paper involving recombinant DNA.

As a geneticist, I believe there will be monumental discoveries and applications to come. But I also know that it is far too early and that the driving force behind the explosion in biotechnology is money. I graduated as a fully licensed geneticist in 1961 and was arrogant, ambitious, and filled with a desire to make my name. We knew about DNA, and the genetic code was just breaking; it was a delirious moment in science and we were hot. But today when I tell students about the hottest molecular ideas in 1961, they laugh in disbelief because forty years later, those ideas seem ridiculously far from the mark.

Those same students seem shocked when I suggest that when they are professors twenty years from now, today's hottest ideas will seem just as far off the mark. The nature of any cutting-edge science is that most of our current ideas are wrong. That's not a denigration of science; it is the way science progresses. In a new area, we make a number of observations that we try to "make sense of" by setting up a hypothesis. The value of the hypothesis is not only that it provides a way of thinking about the observations but also that it allows one to make a critical test by experiments. When the experiments are complete and the data in, chances are we will throw out the hypothesis or radically modify it, then do another test. That's how science progresses in any revolutionary area, which is what biotechnology is. It becomes downright dangerous, then, if we rush to apply every incremental insight or technique within a theoretical framework that is probably wrong.

Geneticists involved in biotechnology make breathtakingly simple mistakes and assumptions. With the power to isolate, sequence, synthesize, and manipulate pieces of DNA, it is easy to conceive of all kinds of novel creations—bacteria that will spread through our bodies to scavenge mercury or other pollutants and then extrude them from a pimple, plants that photosynthesize under much lower light intensities or at twice the rate, plant crops that can live on highly salinated soil or fertilize themselves from air, and so on. Even though these are just pie-in-the-sky speculation, companies are often set up on such ideas. But if such notions are considered real possibilities, transfer of sterility genes to wild plants, genetically engineered fish that destroy ecosystems, and new deadly diseases are every bit as plausible. We just don't know.

Biotechnologists generally deal with a characteristic they want to transfer from one organism to another—for example, a product that behaves as an antifreeze in flounders that enables the fish to live at temperatures below freezing. The DNA specifying the antifreeze substance is isolated and then transferred, say to a strawberry plant, on the assumption that in that totally new environment, the DNA will function just as it did in the fish. But natural selection acts on the sum total of the expression of all of the genes in the cascade of reactions that occurs from fertilization to development of the whole organism. The entire genome is an entity selected to function in the proper sequence. When a flounder gene is inserted into a strawberry plant, the fish DNA finds itself in a completely alien context, and the scientist has no idea whether or how that gene will express itself in the new surroundings. It is like pulling rock star Bono out of his group U2, sticking him into the New York Philharmonic Orchestra, and asking him to make music in that setting. Noise might emerge, but we can't predict what it will sound like.

It is far too early to begin to create products for food or medicines or to grow them in open fields at this stage in biotechnology's evolution if we wish to avoid unexpected and unpredictable consequences. But because the driving force to get novel organisms out is money, when I say such things I am confronted with angry biotechnologists demanding to know when we will ever know that a genetically engineered product is ready to be consumed or grown in the open.

My response is that when a field of experimentation is immature, virtually every bit of research yields a surprise and ultimately a publication; last time I looked, there was a profusion not only of articles but of biotechnology journals. The science is in its infancy. When it has reached a point where an exact sequence of DNA can be synthesized or isolated and inserted at a specific sequence in a recipient's DNA and the resultant phenotype predicted beforehand with absolute accuracy and replicability, then the science is mature enough to proceed to the next stages of wider testing. We're a long way from that. The science is exciting, but the applications are frightening in view of our ignorance.

I deliberately stopped research but did not immediately lose all of the knowledge that made me a geneticist. I am proud of my career and contribution in the field, yet the minute I ceased doing research and began to speak out about the unseemly haste with which scientists were rushing to exploit their work, people in biotechnology lashed out as if somehow I no longer understood what is being done.

It is young people, relatively unencumbered by distractions like administration and teaching, who are able to expend the energy to do research. As scientists get older, they acquire layers of responsibility that take them away from the bench. There is always the pull to keep publishing to validate their standing as scientists. It is unfortunate that older scientists aren't afforded recognition and respect for their past achievements and acknowledged as elder statespeople who can afford to look at the broader picture.

THE POWER OF SCIENCE is in description, teasing out bits of nature's secrets. Each insight or discovery reveals further layers of complexity and interconnections. Our models are of necessity absurdly simple, often grotesque caricatures of the real world. But they are our best tool when we try to "manage" our surroundings. In most areas, such as fisheries, forestry, and climate, our goal should be simply to guide human activity. Instead of trying to bludgeon nature into submission by the brute-force applications of our insights (if planted, seedlings will grow into trees; insecticides kill insects), we would do better to acknowledge the 3.8 billion years over which life has evolved its secrets. Rather than overwhelming nature, we could try to emulate what we see, and that "biomimicry" should be our guiding principle.

But even reductionism—focusing on parts of nature—can provide stunning insights into the elegance and interconnectedness of nature, and reveal the flaws in the way we try to manage her.

A good illustration of both the strengths and weaknesses of science and its application is the temperate rain forest of North America. Pinched between the Pacific Ocean and the coastal mountain range, this rare ecosystem extends from Alaska to northern California. Around the world, temperate rain forests are a tiny part of the terrestrial portion of the planet, yet they support the highest biomass of any ecosystem on Earth. That's because there are large trees like Sitka spruce, Douglas fir, red and yellow cedar, hemlock, and balsam. But the heavy rains wash nutrients from the soil, making it nitrogen poor. How, then, can it support the immense trees that characterize the forest? For several years, the David Suzuki Foundation funded studies to answer this question by ecologist Tom Reimchen of the University of Victoria.

Terrestrial nitrogen is almost exclusively ^{14}N, the normal isotope of nitrogen; in the oceans, there is a significant amount of ^{15}N, a heavier isotope that can be distinguished from ^{14}N. Throughout the North American temperate rain forest, salmon swim in thousands of rivers and streams. The five species of salmon need the forest, because when the forest around a salmon-bearing watershed is clear-cut, salmon populations plummet. That's because the fish are temperature sensitive; a small rise in temperature is lethal, so salmon need the shade of the canopy that keeps water temperatures down. In addition, the tree roots cling to the soil to prevent it from washing into the spawning gravels, and the forest community provides food for the baby salmon as they make their way to the ocean. But now we are finding that there is a reciprocal relationship—the forest also needs the salmon.

Along the coast, the salmon go to sea by the billions. Over time, they grow as they incorporate ^{15}N into all their tissues. By the time they return to their natal streams, they are like packages of nitrogen fertilizer marked by ^{15}N. Upon their return to spawn, killer whales and seals intercept them in the estuaries, and eagles, bears, and wolves, along with dozens of other species, feed on salmon eggs and on live and dead salmon in the rivers. Birds and mammals load up on ^{15}N and, as they move through the forest, defecate nitrogen-rich feces throughout the ecosystem.

Bears are one of the major vectors of nitrogen. During the salmon runs, they congregate at the rivers to fish, but once a bear has seized a fish, it leaves the river to feed alone. A bear will move up to 150 yards away from the river before settling down to consume the best parts—brain, belly, eggs—then return to the river for another. Reimchen has shown through painstaking observation that in a season, a single bear may take from six hundred to seven hundred salmon. After a bear abandons a partially eaten salmon, ravens, salamanders, beetles, and other creatures consume the remnants. Flies lay eggs on the carcass, and within days, the flesh of the fish becomes a writhing mass of maggots, which polish off the meat and drop to the forest floor to pupate over winter. In the spring, trillions of adult flies loaded with ^{15}N emerge from the leaf litter just as birds from South America come through on their way to the nesting grounds in the Arctic.

Reimchen calculates that the salmon provide the largest pulse of nitrogen fertilizer the forest gets all year, and he has demonstrated that there is a direct correlation between the width of an annual growth ring in a tree and the amount of ^{15}N contained within it. Government records of salmon runs over the past fifty years show that large rings occur in years of big salmon runs. When salmon die and sink to the bottom of the river, they are soon coated with a thick, furry layer of fungi and bacteria consuming the flesh of the fish. In turn, the ^{15}N-laden microorganisms are consumed by copepods, insects, and other invertebrates, which fill the water and feed the salmon fry when they emerge from the gravel.

In dying, the adult fish prepare a feast on which their young may dine on their way to the ocean. Thus, the ocean, forest, northern hemisphere and southern hemisphere form a single integrated part of nature held together by the salmon. For thousands of years, human beings were able to live on this productivity and achieve the highest population density of any non-agrarian society, as well as rich, diverse cultures.

When Europeans occupied these lands, they viewed the vast populations of salmon as an opportunity to exploit for economic ends. Today in Canada the responsibility for the salmon is assigned to the Department of Fisheries and Oceans for the commercial fishers, to the Department of Indian and Northern Affairs for the First

Nations food fishery, and to provincial ministers of tourism for the sport fishers. There are enormous conflicts between the ministries, even though they are responsible for the same "resource," because their respective constituencies have very different needs. The whales, eagles, bears, and wolves come under the jurisdiction of the minister of the environment, and trees are overseen by the minister of forests. The mountains and rocks are the responsibility of the minister of mining, and the rivers may be administered by the minister of energy (for hydroelectric power) or the minister of agriculture (for irrigation). In subdividing the ecosystem in this way, according to human needs and perspectives, we lose sight of the interconnectedness of the ocean, forest, and hemispheres, thereby ensuring we will never be able to manage the "resources" sustainably.

A CULTURE OF CELEBRITY

I T IS ASTONISHING and frightening to see the extent to which the phenomenon of celebrity has come to dominate our consciousness. Not only tabloids and magazines like *People* and *Us Weekly* but also the mainstream media seem obsessed with celebrities—and not just for days or weeks but for months and years. When the media lavish as much attention (or even more) on celebrities as they do on weightier issues, how can people distinguish what is important from what is not? The result of our preoccupation with celebrity is that the opinion of someone who might be a lightweight or a fool carries as much heft as the words of a scientist, doctor, or other expert.

Consider how information is packaged in a newspaper: entire sections are devoted to celebrity (entertainment), sports, business, and politics, yet few newspapers assign reporters to write specifically about science or the environment. Our focus on economics often results in big headlines for a developer, promoter, or hustler, while the environmental or social implications of industry are ignored. But when more than half of all living Nobel Prize–winning scientists sign a document of warning—as they did in November 1992, when the Union of Concerned Scientists declared that human activities were on a collision course with the natural world and, unchecked, could result in catastrophe in as little as ten years—they are virtually ignored.

Their predictions have been corroborated by reports about threats to significant portions of mammalian and bird species, the melting ice sheets and permafrost of circumpolar nations, and coral bleaching due to warming oceans. In 2001, I accepted a position on the board of the Millennium Ecosystem Assessment, a United Nations–appointed committee created to assess the state of global ecosystems and the services they perform (exchanging carbon dioxide for oxygen in the air, pollinating flowering plants, fixing nitrogen in the soil, filtering water, and so on). The reports from this $24-million project, which involved some 1,300 scientists from more than seventy countries, painted a devastating picture of the natural world on which we are all ultimately dependent.

The final report was released in March 2005 and in Canada was covered in an article on page 3 of the *Globe and Mail* newspaper. The next day, Pope John Paul II was taken to hospital, and his illness, death, and succession pushed our report out of the news. So a major study warning that Earth's ecosystems are being degraded at an unsustainable rate was a one-day, inside-page wonder.

We live in a time when the military, industry, and medicine are all applying scientific insights, with profound social, economic, and political consequences. As a result, ignoring scientific matters is very dangerous. It's not that I believe science will ultimately provide solutions to major problems we face; I think solutions to environmental issues are much more likely to result from political, social, and economic decisions than from scientific ones. But scientists can deliver the best descriptions of the state of climate, species, pollution, deforestation, and so on, and these should inform our political and economic actions. If we don't base our long-term actions on the best scientific

With Jane Fonda and Tom Lovejoy at a conference in Malibu, California

knowledge, then I believe we are in great danger of succumbing to the exigencies of politics and economics.

SOME "CELEBRITIES" DO DESERVE attention. Noam Chomsky is an academic I admire enormously. As a linguist, he is widely respected by academics for his idea that language and syntax are built into the human brain by heredity. His celebrity status, however, rests on his role as an outspoken critic of American foreign policy.

He has near cult status in Canada, where each of his books rockets to the top of best-seller lists, and he has gained a wide audience through the National Film Board documentary *Manufacturing Consent*. His forays into Canada are met with a rapturous response from his fans, a striking contrast to the reaction in his own country, where he is reviled as a traitor by large segments of American society. When Tara was teaching at Harvard, she saw an announcement that Chomsky was speaking on campus, so she went to the hall early to get a seat. To her surprise, there was no one else there, and by the time Chomsky spoke, there may have been thirty students in the room. He has a large following in Europe, Australia, and Latin America, where his left-leaning analyses strike a chord with activists.

I first met Noam Chomsky in the early '90s, when he was in Toronto to speak at Ryerson Institute of Technology. At that time, the CBC offices I worked in were at the corner of Bay and College, only a few blocks from Ryerson, so I dropped in to see whether I might meet him. It was a few hours before his talk, and he was in an auditorium checking the audiovisual system with a few students. To my delight, he greeted me warmly, informing me that Canadians regularly sent him my newspaper columns, and he complimented me on what I was writing. He is a superstar, and it was flattering to be acknowledged so generously.

For years after I began to speak out about environmental issues, as I said earlier, I felt as Chomsky does—that it was not up to me to tell people what to do or where the solutions were; I was simply a messenger trying to catalyze public concern. But I have read many books and articles, met many people, acquired information and knowledge, and reflected a lot about issues, all of which has shaped the way I see the problems. It has become clear to me over the years that it would be very difficult and time-consuming for people who are starting to get involved to wade through the same volume of material in a short period. And if the issues are urgent, then those of us who are pressing those issues have a responsibility at the very least to help people avoid unnecessary material or sources and get up to speed faster, still on their own but with some shortcuts to assist them. Chomsky refused to give any tips or recommendations when asked.

American consumer advocate and reformer Ralph Nader once spoke in Vancouver in the same week that Chomsky lectured at the city's Queen Elizabeth Theatre. It was almost too much to have two such prominent figures on hand at the same time. Nader's performance two nights later was a huge contrast to Chomsky's presentation. Nader had been invited by nurses who were involved in a dispute with the government. Instead of the grand surroundings of the Queen Elizabeth Theatre, his event was in a movie house in a rougher part of downtown Vancouver. It too was packed, and Nader gave a stirring speech in which he praised Canadians for our leadership in social issues (with Duff Conacher he had written a best-selling book about Canadian firsts) and compared Canadian social values with those of the United States. He received a standing ovation. Unlike Chomsky, when he was asked what could be done, Nader immediately listed off people, organizations, and strategies that could be contacted and worked with.

Nader has spent his career motivating people to take action, setting up public-interest research groups in universities across Canada. But it's a lonely life. From his earliest venture as a consumer advocate against the automobile industry, the lawyer has been subjected to intense scrutiny for any signs of vulnerability. I had met Nader while I was in Washington to film for *The Nature of Things*; I decided to drop in and meet him as a hero of mine. He greeted me warmly and was clearly informed about issues in Canada. His office was cluttered, books and articles heaped in piles. As we strolled through the room, he loaded me up with books, pamphlets, and articles. He really believes in empowering people with information.

Before he arrived in Vancouver for his speech, his office had called and said he would like to have dinner with me. When I asked what kind of food he liked, I was told he had no great preference but that since he is of Lebanese origin, Middle Eastern would be good. So Lebanese it was. Tara and Severn went along with me, and Ralph was accompanied by an associate and a nephew who lived in Vancouver. It was a lively and stimulating evening with lots of animated discussion.

Famed First Nations actor Graham Greene in a gag shot

Ralph is a very serious and intense person. This became obvious when a belly dancer appeared and began clicking her castanets, throwing her scarf around the necks of diners, and pulling them to their feet or their heads to her bosom. My jaw dropped as I watched. Ralph didn't even look her way and kept on talking. Finally she came over to our table, enticing a couple of people to get up to wiggle for a few seconds on the floor before stuffing some bills into her bra. Ralph never looked up but kept right on talking. The dancer eventually left without ever engaging him.

At the end of the meal, as we got up to leave, Ralph made no mention of the belly dancer but simply said: "That was a very nice meal. And no one overate."

WHEN I TAKE A trip—and especially before I used e-mail—faxes and mail pile up very quickly. So I have the mail separated into folders marked Urgent, Speaking Requests, First Class, Second Class, and Bumf. This system provides me with a way of responding first to the most pressing messages and working toward material to glance at and then file or discard.

In 1990, I arrived home from a couple of weeks away to find a stack of mail that Shirley Macaulay, my secretary, had left on my porch at home. Even though it was quite late at night and I was tired, I couldn't resist taking the top two folders, which were quite thick, to bed, and I began to sift through them. Shirley usually flagged with a little tab letters she thought were especially urgent, interesting, or important.

When I got to a handwritten letter of several pages with no tab, I figured it would be a struggle, because handwritten notes are so much harder to read and this was a long one. But the script was beautiful and easily read, so I started and was soon drawn into the content, which was the writer's response to a speech I had given a few months earlier. When I got to the thirteenth and last page, it was signed "Charles."

I thought, "Charles who?" I looked back at the letterhead on the front page, and it said Windsor Castle. It was from Prince Charles! I thought it must be an elaborate joke, but it wasn't. I've never discussed this letter in public before. It was the real thing, and this is how it came to be.

In January 1990, I gave a speech to the Food Marketing Institute in Honolulu, and apparently a transcript of my remarks was sent to Prince Charles. Not only did he read it, he sent me a detailed response in the handwritten letter. Unfortunately, when I asked his office for permission to reprint the letter, I was refused permission to quote even a sentence. But I can give the gist of what he said.

Prince Charles was especially struck by my use of the metaphor of the "boiled frog syndrome." According to psychologist Robert Ornstein, frogs that live in an aqueous environment have thermal receptors, sensory organs that detect large changes in temperature but not small, incremental shifts. According to Ornstein, if a frog is placed in a pot of hot water, it will immediately hop out. But if it is put in cold water and heat is slowly applied to the pot, the frog will eventually boil to death without ever registering the temperature change. The relevance of that frog as a metaphor to humans, who cannot sense thinning ozone, rising atmospheric temperature, background radiation, or toxic chemicals, is obvious.

Not only did His Royal Highness consider my analysis brilliant (his word, honest), he agreed with me about the gravity of the crisis, the destructive demand of conventional economics for endless growth, and the unwarranted optimism that technological innovation will get us out of any difficulty generated by our activities. He described his own experiences of the way people in developing countries are lured away from their traditional values by advertisements and our dazzling lifestyle.

Prince Charles told me that he and the BBC were discussing the possibility of his hosting a program on the environment. He was under enormous pressure to tone down his remarks, however, even though he felt there was a need for the kind of strong statements I had made in my speech. He ended by telling me that he would send copies of my speech to businesspeople and other influential folk, and he asked me to let him know if I was ever in his neck of the woods.

Now, like many people, I had read stories in the popular press portraying an eccentric king-in-waiting who was reputed to talk to plants and have weird ideas about architecture, but this was an unusually thoughtful letter. And since he had responded so generously to my ideas, of course I knew he must be brilliant. My parents-in-law are English, so I figured I would win a lot of brownie points with them when I showed them the letter. And I was right—they were most excited.

Because the letter had ended with an invitation to drop in, Tara and I decided we would take a trip to England built around a visit to Prince Charles. He had given a number to call, so the next day I called it, and I reached his personal secretary. I suggested a number of days when I could visit, and he promised he would check the prince's calendar and get back to me, which he did within a couple of days. We were scheduled for a half hour at Highgrove, the prince's summer place, which was near Tara's birthplace in Wotton-under-Edge in Gloucestershire.

Soon we had booked a plane and made our summer plans around our English visit, only to read a few weeks later that the prince had fallen off a horse while playing polo and broken his arm. I figured our visit would be off, so I called his secretary, telling him I had heard the prince was cancelling appointments. "Yes, he is," the secretary confirmed, "but not the appointments he wants to keep, and yours is still on his calendar."

Tara and I flew to England and after dropping our children off with relatives in Wotton-under-Edge went to Highgrove, where we were ushered into a large room whose walls were covered with pictures. I recognized the famous portrait of George III, the mad king thought to have suffered from porphyria, a hereditary disease; under his reign, the United States had broken away. Sitting on some of the tables were numerous family photos of the prince's siblings, children, and friends, but not one of Diana. We waited for several minutes—long enough to have a good look around without being snoopy. The apparent lack of security was quite stunning, although I'm sure today things are different. When we arrived at Highgrove, I had simply called out my name at the front gate, and we were let right in, then left alone in the room.

Finally Prince Charles walked in with his arm in a sling and greeted us warmly, making a self-deprecating remark about his clumsiness while playing. He is so familiar and famous, yet so personable and relaxed. He's only a human being, but he has been bred for this kind of rarefied life and exudes that in the way he carries himself. We had been briefed about what not to do—for example, refer to the Queen as "your mother" or call him Charles. I was impressed by how trim he was—not a hint of fat around his waist, yet think of all those fancy dinners he attends.

We spoke of many things. He mentioned that the critics had blasted him for expressing his views on modern architecture, since he had no credentials. He was keenly interested in environmental issues but wanted to avoid being attacked again in the same way he was by architects, so he asked if it was all right for him to consult me if he ever needed to have some backup expertise. I readily agreed but have never heard from him again, so I hope he does have others with expertise to advise him. He told me how to address the envelope of a letter so it would get to him in person, but I have never taken advantage of that information.

Toward the end of our meeting, which lengthened into an hour, he suddenly asked Tara and me what we thought about Muslims. The question came out of left field, and both of us sputtered that we hadn't really thought about them. "I think they are a very important group that we have to reach out to," he answered, adding that imme-

Queen Elizabeth visiting the CBC in Toronto

diately after we left, he was meeting some Muslim leaders. History has revealed how prescient he was.

I did meet him twice more. Once, when Bob Rae was the New Democrat premier of Ontario, I was invited to a noon luncheon with the prince and a group of leaders from the ethnic community. The prince was very informal and suggested we make it a working lunch and chat while we ate. He opened the discussion by asking what we each felt were priorities for Canada. A banker originally from the Caribbean got up and talked about racism; the first day he had gone to work at the bank, a guard had mistaken him for the janitor. A Chinese Canadian recounted her experiences of discrimination during her time in Canada, and a European Jew voiced her concerns about religious problems.

As the luncheon went on, I realized I must have been invited as representing another visible minority. I finally raised my hand and said that as a Japanese Canadian, I knew about the reality of discrimination, but I felt there were other priorities for all people that were worth mentioning. "I've been involved with environmental issues for a while, but today I feel as if we're all in a giant car," I said, making up my metaphor on the spot, "heading at a brick wall at a hundred miles an hour, and everyone in the car is arguing about where they want to sit. But it doesn't matter who is sitting in the driver's seat, someone has to shout, 'Turn the wheel and put on the brakes!' "

It got a laugh from a few people, including the prince, as we realized that we had focused on our immediate and personal issues but that there are also matters that envelop all of us. I have since used the metaphor many times, elaborating on it by adding that "those of us who are calling out to turn the wheel and put on the brakes are locked in the trunk so no one can hear."

I met Prince Charles once more in Ottawa when a lot of important Canadian people were called to have a buffet lunch with the Prince and Princess of Wales. I don't like these events, because I always feel awkward and find it difficult to engage in chitchat while gawking and being gawked at. I admire the way Prince Charles circulates apparently effortlessly, because I cannot imagine doing it day after day, year after year. When he was brought to my part of the room, he gave the impression in the way he greeted me that he recognized me. We had chatted for a minute or so when Diana sidled up (I was surprised at how tall she was) and said in a rather loud whisper, "How much longer?" She was clearly bored and couldn't wait to get out of there. I didn't hear his answer as I quickly ducked out of the way.

While I'm on the subject of royalty, I have to say that although I'm not a monarchist, I think it's great to have a governor general representing the Crown (and lieutenant-governors in the provinces) to kiss babies, give out awards, cut ribbons, and otherwise perform an important role with the public. It gives our prime minister and premiers a welcome reprieve from these activities so that they can concentrate on the business of governing. The United States suffers because presidents have to perform both functions.

When the former CBC journalist Adrienne Clarkson was considering accepting the position of governor general, I ran into her partner, the Canadian writer-philosopher John Ralston Saul, and told him I thought he would be prevented from taking part in the important discussions he writes about. He assured me he had no intention of being muzzled, but I was skeptical. But just as he had said, once Adrienne was installed, he continued to speak out and write as he always had. My admiration for both of them increased as they added glamor to their roles and brought together Canadians to think about key matters. I was disgusted by petty criticism over the tax money spent as they went about their job, which I think they did well.

More than twenty years ago, Tara attended a function in Ottawa that featured Prince Philip, father of Prince Charles. She was chatting in a big meeting hall with Noreen Rudd, an expert in human genetics, when Prince Philip hove into view and asked what they did. When Noreen answered that she was a human geneticist interested in the effects of environmental factors on fetal development, the prince riposted, "My mother bumped into a record player when she was pregnant with me but it didn't do any harm, do any harm, do any harm."

THE DALAI LAMA IS another man who deserves his celebrity status. In 2002 I received a letter from a leading Tibetan Buddhist from Dharamsala in northern India, the Dalai Lama's home in exile, asking me to talk about the environment to a select group of Tibetan monks living in India, in a program organized annually by their leader. I was flattered to receive the invitation, but I turned it down because it was for January, when I knew air pollution would be at its worst; I didn't want to risk further harming my lungs, which had been seriously weakened when I was in India filming the story on dams.

However, when my daughters learned I had declined the invitation, they were incredulous. "How can you turn down an invitation from the Dalai Lama?" they demanded. "It wasn't the Dalai Lama. It was someone high up among his monks," I protested. Nevertheless, they begged me to reconsider because they wanted to meet the Dalai Lama. I knew he had an enormous following, including high-profile celebrities like the actors Richard Gere and Goldie Hawn, but I did not consider the Hollywood glitz and faddishness reasons to want to meet him. However, I loved the idea that the family might travel together and share time in India, so I wrote back and asked whether I could be reconsidered.

Fortunately, I was reinstated in the program and, in fact, a half-hour private session was arranged with His Holiness in New Delhi, the Indian capital. The girls were thrilled. We flew to Delhi several days before we were scheduled to meet him. On the way to our hotel from the airport, the cab stopped at a traffic light and we were besieged by children begging. One small girl came up to my window pointing to her empty sleeve—she had only one arm and held her one palm up. I pulled out my wallet and gave her a few rupees as she scampered away and the car moved on. At the next light, more children surrounded us, and one came over to my window, pointing out his empty sleeve. That's when I realized these children could find easy targets like me by hiding one arm inside their shirts. I was tickled by their ingenuity.

A meeting with the Dalai Lama was arranged in a grand hotel at 9:30 in the morning. We knew what a privilege it was. People often tried for years to get up close to him, and here we were being granted a half hour with only us. We arrived early, in a state of excitement, and were ushered into an area where we were told to wait. People were everywhere—guards, confidants, supplicants—but they were kept away from our waiting area. Many minutes passed, and we realized our scheduled time had come and gone. I began to wonder whether we would be told, "Sorry, but he has run out of time for you."

Finally, forty-five minutes late, we were told to go down the hall to meet him. As we walked along the dimly lit corridor, the Dalai Lama himself suddenly popped out of a doorway, looked down the hall, and giggled, "I know you! I watch you on the Discovery Channel!" His is a world-recognized face, and he was acting as if I were the famous one.

We sat with him, and he talked warmly with almost a childlike openness and innocence. I had read a book about his early life and knew the ordeal of exile from his people. Yet here he was, so full of humor and mischief. We told him about our environmental interests and concerns, and he agreed with the thrust of our comments. We talked about how it seemed that money had become more important to people than other things. He reached over, took Tara's hand, and said, "Dogs and cats can do this," as he pretended to lick and nuzzle her hand. "But money can't do that." He was such a playful man, and his words were so direct and moving that at one point Severn began to weep. His Holiness didn't bat an eye or turn away embarrassed. He took Sev's hands into his, looked her straight in the eye, and kept on talking to her.

When he turned to environmental issues, we asked what he thought could be done. "Education," he said, "has to be the answer." I was a bit mischievous myself as I parried, "But we have an American president who graduated from Yale, one of the best universities in the U.S." "That's not the kind of education I'm talking about," he replied, and I felt silly for having been a smart-ass.

I knew he was getting all kinds of signals from his handlers that he was running late, but he never gave any indication he was under pressure or in a hurry, and he spent three-quarters of an hour with us. Finally, he stood to indicate our time was up. We had been instructed to give him white scarves, which we did, and he in turn placed them around each of our necks. He called over one of his people and urged him to take pictures with our cameras as he seized our arms and grinned away. "Take another one," he kept saying so that we would be sure to get one good picture. He was incredibly generous with his time and left us with an indelible souvenir of our meeting.

The family meeting the Dalai Lama in New Delhi

The Dalai Lama apparently has long had an interest in science and believes his monks should not focus just on matters spiritual. For a number of years, he has invited scientists to speak to a group of monks selected from across India. Thus, in January 2003, I was one of four scientists volunteering our time to teach those monks. One lecturer was a nuclear physicist from Georgia Tech in Atlanta, another a chemist from Long Island, and a third an evolutionary biologist from Harvard, while I was there to speak about genetics as well as the environment.

In January in the foothills of the Himalayas, it is quite crisp at night. We were put up in a hotel with stone walls and tile floors, which were unbelievably cold. There was no hot water in our room. At best we might get enough lukewarm water to just cover the bottom of the tub, so bathing was a pretty quick activity. In the morning, we would walk for a mile or so across fields to a village for orphaned Tibetan children, where the monks were staying. Actually, many were not truly orphans but had been sent out of Tibet by parents who remained in the Chinese-held nation.

Each day I wore long johns, a thick sweater, a fleece jacket, and a down coat to teach in the unheated classroom. With all my layers of clothing, I looked like the Michelin Man, while the monks sat cross-legged with bare arms and shoulders. I gave two lectures a day, each lecture two hours long with a half-hour break between them. Any university professor in Canada would be delighted with students like those monks—they were attentive, asked insightful questions, and had a wonderful sense of humor. The translators were fabulous. We had two young men who took turns translating and would transform a simple statement into a drama, full of gestures, body movements, and exclamations. I might make a two-sentence statement, after which the translator would go on for what seemed minutes, amplifying the statement and perhaps even adding his own two cents' worth. If I made a joke, about half of the students would immediately laugh, as they clearly understood English; then there would be a delayed laugh from the ones who understood only the translation.

I began my part of the course with material from my book *The Sacred Balance,* showing that we are not separate from the air, water, soil, and sun. I talked about how air was once referred to as *spirit,* which is the basis for the words *inspire* and *expire*; how we are all embedded in this matrix of air that links all life together and throughout time. It was so clear this resonated powerfully with the monks' spiritual teachings.

Severn and Sarika were invited to give a talk to the children who lived in the village. Like the monks, the children were tremendously attentive and responsive to the discussion about the environment and what youngsters can do. So despite being a reluctant participant, I ended up feeling grateful for having met His Holiness and for the opportunity to teach those monks and the children.

I SUPPOSE IF PUBLIC attention is a criterion, I am a celebrity in Canada. I never sought or desired celebrity, but television provides a kind of intimacy that movies do not. Someone can watch a show while going to the bathroom, lounging in front of a fireplace, or stretching out in bed. So when people run into me, they often greet me as a familiar friend. I can't help being startled each time someone addresses me, though almost always it is to say something very kind. I must admit, I am not able to respond generously because greetings are still a surprise and intrusion, and my teenage reticence to engage in conversation returns.

Back in the '70s, there was a lot of resentment of my viewpoint, especially from businessmen, and they openly expressed their disagreement. Even today, there are those who dislike my stands. I opposed the current U.S. administration's invasion of Iraq and applauded Prime Minister Jean Chrétien's decision that Canada would await the UN search for weapons of mass destruction. A few weeks after President Bush ordered troops into Iraq, I flew to Edmonton, Alberta. After we landed and I stood up to deplane, a man behind me recognized me, leaned over with a smile, and said, "I guess you are rooting for your friend Saddam" (Hussein, toppled president of Iraq and at the time being hunted by the Americans). I was speechless, but before I could even stutter a clever retort like "f--k you," the woman standing next to him berated him loudly and he slunk away. Good to have friends nearby.

Another time, I was working out at the YMCA in Winnipeg. I was exercising on a cross-trainer, one of the few machines I can tolerate with my knees gimpy from years of jogging, when the young man next to me said, "You're Suzuki, aren't you?"

"Yeah," I replied, "but here I'm just an old man trying to stay healthy." I thought he might chuckle, but instead he retorted, "You know, you've got a lot of nerve spouting the crap you do. You should be pulled off the air. CBC is a waste of taxpayers' money." Well, this

With the Canadian singer Bruce Cockburn

time I didn't lose my wit and told him where he could shove his ideas, expecting him to lash out at me. Instead, he meekly dismounted his machine and left. It's funny, but even though 95 percent of all people who call out to me are friendly and generous, it's the ones who disagree so obnoxiously who stick in my memory.

When the CBC began to tout its search for "the greatest Canadian" for a television series of that name in 2004, I was interviewed on radio and asked what I thought about the idea. I scoffed at the notion that it meant anything. Greatest what? Greatest crook, moneymaker, athlete, looker, writer? Besides, how can we select one person out of millions who are Canadians and conclude that one individual is the greatest. My mother, for example, never made the newspapers or a television report, but she finished high school, worked hard all her life, brought forth four children, and raised them to be responsible, contributing citizens of the country, and to me, she was the greatest. I feel the same about my father.

One of the towering figures in the American environmental movement, David Brower

I now realize that the exercise of trying to define the greatest Canadian was not a wasted or even frivolous effort. I was astonished to watch and listen to conversations, often quite heated, about Canada and Canadians. It was great to hear the talk and feel the passion— it got us thinking about this country, its values, and what makes us special. I was surprised and CBC management was delighted when the project took off. According to Slawko Klimkiw, the man then in charge of television programming, 60 percent of the votes in the first round were submitted by women. I don't know how he got that statistic, because not one woman appeared among the top ten nominees. I felt there should have been four categories—men, living and dead, and women, living and dead. But as an exercise to get people involved and thinking, it worked.

As not only a scientist but also an environmental activist, I had no idea that I would be anywhere on the list, so when the names were first announced, I was surprised to be placed among the top ten. As I said later in an interview, I would have been honored to be in the top one thousand. What a remarkable list—not a single businessperson or, sadly, woman, but *three* scientists (Sir Frederick Banting, Alexander Graham Bell, and me).

The United States dominates Canada in so many ways. I kept thinking about people on the Canadian list in comparison with any Americans might select. Ultimately Canadians chose as number 1 Tommy Douglas, a socialist preacher and politician who championed national medicare and many other social causes—would such a person have even appeared among the top one hundred Americans? I felt our list alone indicated how Canada is different from the U.S.

It is funny to look at the list of "greatest Americans" as voted by Britons in an Internet poll before a BBC program titled *What the World Thinks of America*. Of 37,102 votes cast, the top ten were: 1. Homer Simpson (47.2 percent), 2. Abraham Lincoln (9.7), 3. Martin Luther King (8.5), 4. Mr. T (7.8), 5. Thomas Jefferson (5.7), 6. George Washington (5.1), 7. Bob Dylan (4.7), 8. Benjamin Franklin (4.1), 9. Franklin D. Roosevelt (3.7), and 10. Bill Clinton (3.5).

Among 2.4 million votes cast by Americans for the "greatest American" poll, the results were: 1. Ronald Reagan, 2. Abraham Lincoln, 3. Martin Luther King, 4. George Washington, 5. Benjamin Franklin, 6. George W. Bush, 7. Bill Clinton, 8. Elvis Presley, 9. Oprah Winfrey, and 10. Franklin D. Roosevelt. Interesting. Six presidents, including two (Reagan and Bush) I am sure historians will judge harshly, two blacks (King, Winfrey), one scientist (Franklin), and one woman (Winfrey).

The original search for the "greatest" was launched by the BBC, and over a million votes were cast for the top ten Britons, who were: 1. Winston Churchill (28.1 percent), 2. Isambard Kingdom Brunel (24.6), 3. Diana, Princess of Wales (13.9), 4. Charles Darwin (6.9), 5. William Shakespeare (6.8), 6. Isaac Newton (5.2), 7. Queen Elizabeth 1 (4.4),

8. John Lennon (4.2), 9. Horatio Nelson (3), and 10. Oliver Cromwell (2.8). Two women, but really, is Diana one of the ten greatest Britons? And I had to look up engineer Brunel.

The CBC was extremely discreet in its handling of the list of nominees for its *The Greatest Canadian* program. For one thing, though working for the corporation, I never had even the tiniest hint that I was on the list. CBC staff must have been contacting people I'd worked with in the past to locate film footage, as well as friends and family for personal photos, yet no one leaked the information to me. When the list was announced, I was floored. How I wished my parents were still alive, because they would have savored it the most. After going through the rejection implicit in the expulsion of Japanese Canadians from British Columbia and the hardships they endured in this country of their birth, Mom and Dad would have been thrilled to see their child held in such high esteem.

ON THE NIGHT OF the final results of the contest, we got a call from our Gitga'at friend Art Sterritt in remote Hartley Bay. "Congratulations on coming in fifth," he said. "Since everyone ahead of you is dead, that makes you the greatest *living* Canadian!"

"But Art," Tara protested, "the program comes on three hours from now, so how do you know?"

"Oh, we have a satellite dish," he replied. "We watched it from Newfoundland!" Hartley Bay is a tiny village in northern B.C. that can only be reached by plane or boat and is thousands of miles from Newfoundland, but thanks to technology, it is more plugged in than we are in the big city.

Only a few weeks later, *Maclean's* magazine in Toronto published the results of a poll in which women across Canada were asked with whom they would most like to be stranded on a desert island. They were asked to select from a small list that included me; CBC Television

Vanity Fair portrait of eco-heroes. *Left to right:* L. Hunter Lovins, Tim Wirth, Leon Shenandoah, Bonnie Reiss, Jack Heinz, Oren Lyons, Ed Begley Jr., me, Dr. Thomas Lovejoy, Cesar Chavez, Tom Cruise, and Olivia Newton-John at an environmental conference held in Malibu, California.

newsreader Peter Mansbridge; Canadian prime minister Paul Martin; *Canadian Idol* TV series host Ben Mulroney; and Calgary Flames ice-hockey superstar Jarome Iginla. I was flabbergasted when a writer with the magazine called to tell me I had been selected first, by 46 percent of the women (55 percent in Alberta), while the runner-up was young Mulroney at 16 percent!

"Where were all those women when I was young and single?" I sputtered. Later, when I did a little strutting and suggested to Tara that I must be hot, she replied matter-of-factly, "David, women aren't stupid. They know you can fish. You were a meal ticket." Ah, reality.

chapter EIGHTEEN

THOUGHTS AS
I GROW OLD

O N MY BRIEF VISITS to Cuba, I have been impressed by the contrast between Fidel Castro and Che Guevara in the public eye. Posters and T-shirts with pictures of Che and slogans from his writings before the Cuban Revolution leader was killed in Bolivia in 1967 are ubiquitous, but I have never seen a sign, statue, or picture of President Castro in the streets. The absence of his image is in keeping with his reputed attitude that nothing is permanent—even the sun will die in a few billion years—so why should people care about their legacy after they're gone?

I have never sought honors or fame, though one honor I received brought pleasure for what it enabled me to do. In 1986, I received the Royal Bank Award, which was presented in an elaborate ceremony in Vancouver before a tuxedo-wearing crowd that included my in-laws and my father and his companion, Fumiko. The award was a tax-free $100,000, and the pleasure it gave was the purchase of our beloved Tangwyn, a small piece of paradise on Quadra Island. When we finally purchased *Kingfisher*, a small cabin cruiser, in 2003, Tara proclaimed, "David, we've got everything we need in life. We don't need any more

The family at Tangwyn

stuff." If I ever receive another award of money, it will go straight to the David Suzuki Foundation's endowment fund. .

Tara and I also believe we have given our children the best any parents could—unstinting love, a variety of experiences at home and in other parts of the world, and a good education. What more support do they need from us to face the future? Now our parental responsibilities are complete; though one may do so, there is no further obligation to pass on money, valuable goods, or property to them.

When Tara and I first met, one of the places we spent time together was her parents' waterfront cottage on Sechelt Inlet on British Columbia's Sunshine Coast. We loved it there. Across the inlet was a muddy beach where we would dig for clams, feel cockles beneath our feet, and set our crab traps. I would cast out from the family float and catch ling cod, and we would take the rowboat offshore and fish for rock cod. We even got lucky and caught the occasional salmon.

But the relentless pressure of people like me meant that over time the ling have disappeared, easy victims of their ferocious appetites and aggressive territoriality. The rock cod on which we depended for breakfast became scarcer and smaller, while more and more cottages sprouted up around us with the inevitable increase in boom boxes, outdoor parties, and water skiers. Across the inlet, an entire hillside was shaved bare of its trees, and then poles and roads appeared, warning of the huge development that followed and the homes that now light up the night. After fifteen years, it was time to find our own place to retreat to from the city.

We began the search with the help of Tara's retired parents, who could check out some of the places that interested us. We spent months scouring properties for sale on the islands between the British Columbia mainland and Vancouver Island in the search for an ideal site that would give us a sense of isolation yet was affordable and reasonably accessible to Vancouver. We had focused on three pieces of land that were available on Quadra and Cortes islands near Campbell River on Vancouver Island. When we walked onto the land Tara later named Tangwyn (Welsh for "place of peace and restoration"), we knew instantly it was what we sought. Its ten acres contained some magnificent old-growth Douglas fir trees, a small creek, and perhaps a third of a mile of waterfront that included beaches, rocky promontories, and at low tide a huge tidal pool. A land bridge connected Tangwyn and unoccupied Heriot Island adjacent to us. Tangwyn became our talisman, the place where we wanted our children to feel a strong bond to nature. And it became the place where the girls and our grandchildren would learn how to fish, then clean, cook, and eat their catch.

I love to fish, because fish are a major part of my diet and of who I am. I know sportspeople and conservationists advocate catch-and-release fishing, but I don't. There is no question that when we "play" a fish, the animal is struggling for its life. Usually a fish is worked to exhaustion before being released, so upon liberation, it is an easy tar-

Enjoying my favorite pastime around the corner from Tangwyn and the cottage

get for predators like birds and seals. Fishing for trout in a lake in the Okanagan region of south-central B.C., I noticed loons hovering near the canoe and soon realized they had learned to take a fish right off the hook or to grab it when it was released. Marine seals have learned the same thing.

The fish don't volunteer to be a part of our "sport," and the notion of torturing them for pleasure and then releasing them as if we are being considerate and protective simply perpetuates the notion that nature and other species are playthings for our enjoyment. I know vegans condemn the catching and eating of fish as antithetical to a reverence for life, but I accept that as an animal, I depend on the consumption of other life to survive (plants are life forms too), and I try to do it with respect and gratitude.

IF WE AVOID TRAFFIC jams and make all the ferry connections just right, it takes just over five hours (six if we're unlucky) to get from

Vancouver to Tangwyn. As we ride the last ferry from Campbell River to Quathiaski Cove on Quadra, our excitement grows and we delight in the sight of the island hills covered in forest, the dense schools of herring, the fishing boats pursuing salmon, and the ever-present eagles ready to swoop down and take a careless fish. We feel the joy of arriving back where nature is still abundant and intact.

But when we talk to our neighbors who have lived in the area for fifty years or more, they describe a world that no longer exists around there: bays filled with abalone, red snapper, gigantic ling cod and rock cod as long as an arm, herring so abundant they could be raked off the kelp to fill a punt in minutes, and schools of salmon so thick they could be heard coming as their bodies slapped the water miles away. Today all of that is gone. Six years after we had bought Tangwyn, we were fishing for rock cod when Tara hooked a large ling. I watched in disappointment yet admiration as she removed the hook and carefully returned the fish to the water. "This is the first big ling we've seen in six years," she said. "We can't kill it."

Even in the brief time Tangwyn has been part of our lives, we have seen the herring vanish because of the insane fishery permitting the capture of spawning herring for the females' ovaries, which bring a high return in Japan. I call it insane because herring are one of the key prey species for salmon, seals, whales, and other carnivorous fishes, and First Nations have long harvested their eggs without killing the fish. Because the spawning herring form large schools, they become such easy prey that the Department of Fisheries and Oceans actually has had ten-minute openings—seiners are allowed ten minutes to set their nets with the potential to make a year's worth of pay for the crew members. What kind of a delusion is it to think a ten-minute season is a fishery that is sustainable? Years ago, one opening for the herring roe fishery wiped out the large populations around Tangwyn, and they still haven't come back.

Abalone were once abundant throughout the islands in Georgia Strait, but when scuba divers were allowed to "harvest" them, they quickly disappeared and have not come back. In the fifteen years we have gone to Tangwyn, we have found two live abalone—essentially they are extinct, and it is highly doubtful they will ever come back within my children's lifetime.

Geoducks (pronounced "gooey-ducks"), the huge clams whose siphons are highly prized in Asia, are being blasted out of the ocean bottom by divers wielding pressure hoses. The clams are like nuggets of gold but are exploited with almost no idea of their biology or life cycle; they may reach decades if not a century or more in age. I watched in helpless fury as divers spent two days off the shores of Tangwyn pumping geoducks out of the ocean floor. We were delighted to find a small patch of perhaps fifty geoducks at low tide that had been missed by the commercial divers, only to see them trashed by oyster farmers dragging heavy loads of spat-laden shells across them.

Rock cod, which we once took for granted as a dependable meal, have been depleted by commercial fishers, who ship them live to the Asian market. When the DFO announced a quota for sport fishers of one rock cod a day, it was clear the fish should be declared totally off-limits to all fishing until they can replenish themselves.

We tend to think of the oceans as a homogeneous environment from which we can catch creatures that are somehow magically replaced without end. We know that as a rule, the bigger, older animals are far more prolific than younger fish, yet we allow fishers to keep the largest and return the small ones as if somehow this is good management. I believe we should allow fewer fish to be caught, encourage release of large ones, and mandate that fishers stop letting the small ones go until a trophy fish is captured. Once sport fishers have caught their limit of salmon, they often target other fish, like ling and halibut, loading up with hundreds of pounds of fish. They may proudly display halibut more than six and a half feet long and weighing over 165 pounds and release the chickens (under 30 pounds), which is exactly the opposite of what should be done.

Since our purchase of Tangwyn, logging on Quadra has gone on steadily. As we drive from the ferry terminal at Quathiaski Cove and turn onto the road to Heriot Bay, the large swath of forest to our left was clear-cut long before we got there, and the section to our right was cleared a few years ago. The cynical strip of trees left standing beside the road cannot hide the devastation of clear-cutting. Every day, truckloads of trees leave the island; yet one of the ironies of globalization is that at the lumberyard on Quadra, the only lumber sold comes from California.

Another problem is that most of us today live in large cities: we've become urban animals, occupying a human-created environment that is almost devoid of biodiversity. We have a few domesticated plants and animals that we like to have around us, and we tolerate the pests we can't eliminate, but basically we live in a biologically impoverished region wherever we dwell. That means the baseline against which we judge the wildness of nature is so shallow that to us, the Tangwyn of today seems rich and abundant.

And that, it seems to me, is a major challenge we face as humanity explodes in numbers and consumptive demand—our collective memory is so short that we soon forget how things were. We take for granted a small cluster of trees in an empty lot, and then suddenly one day the trees are gone. Soon after, an apartment complex goes up. Within months, we barely remember the trees and open land that were once there. And so it goes all across the planet as we lose links to and reminders of a richer world that has disappeared in the name of economic development.

When I was growing up in Vancouver, Dad would row a boat around Stanley Park in downtown Vancouver, and catch sea-run cutthroat trout. We would jig for halibut off Spanish Banks on the city's waterfront, catch sturgeon in the Fraser River, and ride horses up the Vedder River to catch steelhead and Dolly Varden trout.

My grandchildren have no hope of experiencing the richness I knew as a child. And there is no longer any living memory of passenger pigeons, of prairie lands covered by millions upon millions of bison, which were preyed upon by grizzly bears all the way across to Ontario and down to Texas. And so we continue to celebrate our imprint across the land, taming the wild and reminding ourselves of what once was with the names of suburbs and streets—Oakview Lane, Forest Hills, Arbutus Drive.

When we purchased Tangwyn, the agent took great pains to inform us it could be subdivided into three pieces. "You could sell two and pay for all of it," he said, as if that were an incentive and option. It wasn't. We are privileged to claim to own what was once First Nations land and would like to see it become a part of a larger entity, the forest. Subdividing it into smaller parcels that would be sold off to be developed further will not do that. Somehow we have to find a way to maintain the integrity of wild areas.

It's not all hopeless if we can transcend the current conceit that what is the latest is the best, that history and the past are mere academic pursuits. We can learn much from lessons of the past; indeed, we can find ways to husband scarce resources and even replenish and expand them by applying ancient methods.

In 1995, a geologist, John Harper, was flying in a plane along the British Columbia coast at low tide when he noticed semicircular structures radiating out from shore at the tide line. He recognized that they were not natural and must have been made by people. He investigated these structures, which have now been found up and down the coast of B.C., and today it is recognized that the original people on the coast created them by placing stones at low tide. Over time, the incoming tide would wash shells, sand, and debris over the rocks and into the semicircle, perfect beds for clams. In fact, these were "clam gardens," deliberately created so that clams could be harvested on a regular basis.

When Severn began her graduate degree with the noted University of Victoria ethnobotanist Nancy Turner, she learned about clam gardens and met Adam Dick, a Kwakwaka'wakw elder who was traditionally educated and knew about many of the traditions lost by most tribes. Severn was sure the rock structures along the connection between Tangwyn and Heriot Island were not natural and took Adam to look at it. "Oh, yes, that's a *loki way*," he said, matter-of-factly. It was indeed a human-made clam garden, and that also explained the midden we had found on the property near the beach.

For centuries, explorers finding new lands occupied by aboriginal peoples have dismissed those peoples as primitive savages lacking the technological evidence of civilization. We are only now realizing that, in fact, thousands of years of observation and thought had created a profound knowledge base that allowed people not only to exploit nature's abundance but also to enhance certain parts of its productivity, from clams to forests.

SEX HAS BEEN A driving force in my life. In today's liberated society, the ideas about sex I grew up with seem quaint at best, naive at worst. Chastity and premarital virginity of prospective brides were still hoped for and highly prized. Where the men were to gain their experience, I have no idea, because certainly paying for sex was not socially acceptable. Puberty hit me like a concrete wall, testosterone hammering through my body and wreaking havoc on my brain when I was about twelve. Only as age has brought relief from the high titer of sex hormones have I been freed of thinking of sex once a minute. Now it's about once every five minutes.

I am delighted to see the role sex plays in the lives of Tara and my daughters; it is part of their lives but doesn't necessarily mean a permanent commitment. It just seems so much healthier to be able to have

have sex instead of the prolonged and agonizing petting sessions that passed for sex in my youth. When I was a boy, it was widely believed that for many women, if not most, sex was not a pleasure but something to be borne. Frigidity was widely regarded and accepted as most women's lot, a notion I am sure women today would vehemently reject. My generation placed far too much value on the act of sex itself.

As well as being liberated to explore their bodies and sexuality to the fullest, women are breaking down gender barriers as I never dreamed would be possible in my lifetime. My daughter Tamiko decided to play team hockey when she was in her late thirties, and though I never saw her play, she is such an athlete that I'm sure she did very well. I say "did" because she was forced by knee problems to give it up after a few seasons. When I was a young man, we would never have imagined teams of middle-aged women playing ice hockey. I have delighted in cheering on Severn and Sarika as they played a kind of basketball that wasn't practiced in my youth; when I was in high school, girls in "bloomers" were allowed to dribble the ball twice before passing, a completely different game from the rough-and-tumble sport today. My niece, Jill Aoki, was a soccer star, as is my granddaughter, Midori.

As women have been widening their athletic opportunities, academically they have exploded ahead. I well remember my high school graduation in 1954, when perhaps 10 percent of my class went on to university and boys captured most of the prizes and awards. Almost fifty years later, when I attended Severn's and then Sarika's graduation, girls earned most of the awards and held incredible records of community and extracurricular service.

Women now make up more than 60 percent of university undergraduates, more than half of students in graduate studies, medicine, and law schools, and a rapidly increasing number are enrolling in engineering, agriculture, and forestry, areas traditionally male domains. The social ramifications of this huge gender shift will reverberate through society for decades, I am sure.

Troy and me in the hull of the *Klondike,* a sternwheeler boat in Whitehorse, Yukon, that Troy was helping to restore

I wonder, however, about the boys who are not winning the awards they once did and who are not going on to university, but not because I think they should be represented fifty-fifty. Personal experience tells me that women mature socially and intellectually much sooner than boys. I know I was brain-damaged by testosterone and figure I'm just starting to catch up to women, except that senility threatens to intrude any minute. My son, as much because I was his father as anything else, did not complete university and graduated instead from Emily Carr Institute of Art + Design in Vancouver. He has become an excellent carpenter and, more recently, an accomplished boatbuilder, and I am very proud of what he has become. Yet I worry as I watch him inform others, almost apologetically, that he never completed university.

Has university become the standard by which we measure a person's worth? If so, it is a mistake. I have as much regard for Troy's talent as a carpenter and boatbuilder as I have for any academic with a bachelor's degree or even a PhD. And every time my car breaks down or my sewer gets plugged, I am very grateful to and admiring of the tradespeople who come to my rescue.

The declining proportion of men in academia may, as the Fraser Institute suggests, reflect discriminatory standards, although I doubt it. I believe we have the opportunity to get our priorities and values right. Yes, we need academically trained people, as we need violinists, artists, and so many other talents. In a multicultural society such as Canada's, diversity has become our great strength, and we have to find ways to honor that diversity, especially as gender barriers are removed in most occupations.

One serious challenge of this gender shift is the conflict between a woman's professional ambitions and the biological imperatives of her body. The decline in fertility after the age of thirty is quite dramatic and often leads to heroic medical interventions, such as in vitro fertilization for older women. Could we develop ways for women to have it both ways, to pursue a career while also having children?

My wonderful secretary, Shirley Macaulay, worked for me for more than twenty years until she was forced to retire by the university. I despaired of finding someone who could replace her as both efficient secretary and friend. When Shirley and I finally interviewed Evelyn de la Giroday, we both agreed she would be an ideal replacement, younger, experienced, and willing to be firm if necessary. I was very disappointed to learn that Ev was pregnant and that she wanted to spend quite a while with her baby before returning to work. "What about bringing the baby to the office, where you could nurse her and still work?" I asked.

Ev was a bit dubious, but we agreed to try it out. After Ruthie was born, we set up a playpen in my office at the University of British Columbia while Ev worked in the room adjacent. It worked very well. The baby slept a lot, and besides, I was out of the office most of the time anyway. Evelyn could feed or change the baby in the privacy of my office and still carry out her duties. What surprised me was the protest raised by faculty and students. Ruthie very seldom cried loudly enough to be heard outside my office, but people became aware there was a baby around, and rather than being intrigued by the experiment, academics were indignant at what they felt was an inappropriate presence in their hallowed halls. Fortunately the arrangement worked for long enough for Ev to be happy to find a sitter to take care of Ruth at home, and Ev worked for me for years after.

BEING A PARENT IS the most important thing I have done in life, and I have always been completely committed to my children, though not in the same way my father was. Through my childhood memories, it seems to me my father devoted a huge amount of his time to me. Whether at work or play, he included me on his trips, which were important parts of my formative years, and he spent hours listening to my childish prattle and questions, trying to respond and answer as fully as he could. I have failed to emulate that with my children.

After my first marriage had ended, I endeavored to be with the children every day I was in Vancouver and was aided by Joane's generosity in allowing me unrestricted access to them. But often my mind was distracted, not totally focused on them but off somewhere else. I was too selfish to give myself over to being Dad 100 percent, and I regret that, not only for the children's sake but also for my own. I was just unable to give myself totally to the moment and fully enjoy them.

Joane was my first love, and though we have met less and less often over the years, she has always had my greatest respect and gratitude for the years we did spend together and for never using the children as a weapon to punish me for my shortcomings. They had been conceived in love. When our marriage ended, we didn't negotiate conditions for the amount of money I would pay her in alimony because, as she told

Laura, Tamiko, and Troy

the stunned lawyer, "I trust Dave." I have always tried to live up to that faith. I supported Joane so that she could be a full-time mother, a job she did wonderfully.

When I told Joane seven years after our separation that my remarriage was going to be a financial strain, without a word of protest she told me she could resume her career now that Laura, our youngest, was in school. Well trained as a lab technician at Ryerson Institute of Technology in Toronto and experienced with the electron microscope at the University of Chicago, Joane was soon running the lab for Pat and Edith McGeer, the famous neurobiology team at UBC.

Tamiko went away to McGill University in Montreal and studied biology. She hoped to improve her French while she was there but was disappointed at how easy it was to continue speaking English. At McGill, Tamiko fell in love with Eduardo Campos, a Chilean Canadian who was enrolled in engineering and was a computer whiz. They married after graduation and decided to have a footloose life, working for periods and saving enough to travel to different parts of the world. They had decided they would forgo a family for a more gypsylike life.

But Eduardo's Latin American parents felt it was a mistake, and I did too. When Tamiko approached thirty, she began to reassess the decision, and in 1990 she gave birth to Tamo, my first grandson, and three years later to Midori, my first and (so far) only granddaughter. Tamiko has become one of those supermoms, holding down a job as a chromosome analyst in a hospital while caring for two supercharged children who have grown to be star athletes. Eduardo has used his fluency in Spanish and English to take jobs working in South America and spends a lot of time away from home. In many ways, Tami is repeating the role Tara has played in our home, multitasking because of the absence of her partner much of the time.

Tamo and Midori were born when Sarika was still a child, so suddenly I had a young daughter and grandchildren when I was spending a lot of time away. It has been unfair to my grandchildren that I have not had the time with them I wished for. I loved attending basketball games to cheer Sev and Sarika when they played in high school but have seldom been in town when Tamo and Midori have had hockey, soccer, snowboarding, and football competitions.

Grandchildren are such a delight because the relationship is so different from the relationship with one's children. Every human relationship—between lovers, parents, or children—has moments of frustration, anger, and resentment. It's inevitable, because we are human beings with fallibilities and needs that may conflict with those of others. But in a loving relationship, we work these conflicts out, and the benefits and joys more than offset those awkward or trying moments.

With grandchildren, however, there isn't the chafing that can result from living together day in and day out, so every get-together is a celebration and fun. We can do all those things with grandchildren that we carefully avoided as parents, like buying candy or extravagant toys, then drop them back with their parents to pick up the pieces. It is sheer joy and no responsibility. And because they don't live with us, grand-children don't see all the flaws in us that their parents know so well—so they can just worship us for what they think we are. It's great.

When it became clear that we had the financial support to make the television series based on my book *The Sacred Balance*, Amanda McConnell had the brilliant idea of including Tamo, both to repre-sent me as a child and as a reminder that the next generation had to be included in our perspective. Although I had taken Tamo when he was younger to experience seaweed camp in Gitga'at territory, I was nervous about spending so much time with him alone. "What do I do to keep him entertained?" I wondered. As an enticement on our first shoot, I met him in Florida and took him to Universal Studios, where we shared some incredible rides and had a delightful three days together. He was a wonderful companion and performer throughout the filming.

Laura chose to attend Queen's University in Kingston, Ontario, where she majored in psychology. I was delighted when she fell in love with and later married Peter Cook, a fellow cartoonist on the school paper and also a psychology major. Peter made Laura laugh and drew her out as a personality. Jonathan, their son, is a beautiful child who was found to have suffered oxygen deprivation at birth and has cere-bral palsy, a debilitating problem of varying severity, depending on the area of the brain that is damaged. Jonathan has severe prob-lems, will probably never walk, and though blind, he apparently has developed an alternate neural pathway that enables him to recognize symbols and patterns and actually to read.

What has been so impressive and humbling to me has been the par-enting of this heroic young couple, Laura and Peter. They are mag-nificent parents, pouring love and energy into developing Jonathan's capabilities to the maximum. As my grandson has constrained their

Son-in-law Peter Cook with Laura and my grandson Jonathan

world and activities, success and joy have come from struggle and incremental achievements. I have often pondered how strong I would be were I faced with a severely disabled child, whether I would be up to the job. By their actions, Laura and Peter demonstrate the good and the potential that I hope are in all of us when adversity intervenes.

Troy spent many years trying to figure out his relationship with me, but he stayed very close to my father, moving in with him for several years. As we have become close again (thank goodness for e-mail), I wonder where he's going in a life still evolving. Like many younger men today, he has chosen not to follow the high-pressure, competitive path that was the model of a "successful" male when I was younger. And as a result, in so many ways, he has led a more varied, interesting life than I have.

Severn and Sarika are out of the nest but still strongly attached to the family. It is wonderful to have them spend weeks at Tangwyn with boyfriends in tow. Horizons for the girls seem limitless compared with what was expected for Tara's generation of women.

After graduating from Yale University in 2001, Severn traveled for two years and gave inspirational speeches to adult and youth groups across North America. She then decided to go back to graduate school to study ethnobotany and is now working with Nancy Turner at the University of Victoria; through Sev, Tara and I are vicariously learning about the exciting discoveries of aboriginal gardening along the west coast.

Although as children of a faculty member my children could have attended UBC without paying tuition, I had informed all of them I would pay for their postsecondary school education, but they would have to take it outside B.C. because I believe being away from home is half of what this experience is about.

I had urged Sarika to take one of the acceptances she received from Mount Holyoke College and Smith College in Massachusetts, the two women's colleges near my alma mater, Amherst. But in the end she decided against an all-female school and went to the University of California at Berkeley to study marine biology. Now, through her, I enjoy learning about fish that have so long been important in my life. Tara and I have offered to be her research assistants any time.

All of my children have become vibrant, interesting human beings, all of them committed environmentalists and contributors to society. If my children and their children know anything, I hope it is that they have my unconditional love and can always depend on that.

WHAT IS THE MEANING of life? Although I'm an elder, I haven't come close to answering that question. The 1960s were all about enjoying the moment. I remember students having a confrontation with faculty at UBC and one of the leaders who was challenging professors, marks, and classes saying life is about "fun" and university was irrelevant because it wasn't fun. For me, life has been and continues to be about *work*. I find it impossible to live in the present and to simply relish the joy of the moment. Life for me seems to be all about responsibility and the need to fulfill obligations. It hasn't been fair to Tara, or my children or grandchildren, but a sense of duty and being busy has taken me away from them, even when I am physically with them.

I have been a pushover for certain kinds of requests for help—from underdogs, like a woman in Woodstock who had struggled for years to galvanize concern about local environmental issues, so I helped her by going and giving a speech that raised money and support for her. I hate it when I hear stories of bullies, like the owner of a marine aquarium in the Niagara region who took a small group of people to court for handing out leaflets urging people to consider the plight of the captive killer whales. I gave a speech to a sold-out crowd and helped the defendants raise tens of thousands of dollars for legal fees to fight their case. I keep trying to help when appeals come from isolated First Nations communities fighting high suicide rates among youth, problems of contaminated water, or arrogant authorities like provincial hydroelectricity corporations.

But all of these do-good efforts take me away from the family and home, because most of the time I end up visiting and speaking on weekends. It has been utterly selfish for me to put these activities ahead of time spent with family and certainly a conceit to think I can be the one to make a difference.

My devotion to work has also resulted in an almost obsessive need to be punctual. The one thing that creates tension between Tara and me is our totally different approaches to time. She is motivated by a desire to get as much out of every minute as she can, and that means not wasting time by leaving and arriving early, so she pushes things to the very last minute. In contrast, I like to leave lots of leeway for unexpected holdups and am much happier arriving early and waiting. I practically go bonkers when Tara is late. She claims I once allowed so much time for traffic and the unexpected when we left for a movie in West Vancouver that we arrived two hours early. But that is ridiculous

Family gathering in June 2005. *Left to right, front row:* Sarika, me, Jonathan (grandson), Marcia, Richard Aoki (Marcia's husband), and his grandson, Malevai. *Back row:* Severn, Tara, Peter Cook (son-in-law), Laura, Delroy Barrett, Jill Aoki (niece), and Makoto.

and must be untrue. It is true, however, that I am "anal," as my daughters constantly remind me.

My friends and even my family believe it will be impossible for me to retire, but I don't agree. Retirement to me does not mean not doing anything interesting and meaningful and just waiting for death. There have been many things I've wanted to do, but I have never been able to devote the time and attention that are needed to do them fully and well. For example, I would love to try my hand at painting, and when I told this to my sister Aiko, who was an artist, she sent me all of the necessary equipment, including a how-to-get-started book, but I've never even removed the wrapping. Many years ago, when I expressed regret that I had never learned to read music or play an instrument, Joane bought a beautiful recorder for me, but I never touched that either.

To follow these pursuits seriously, I couldn't just put in an hour a day or every other day; I want to be able to focus on them without

Continuing the fishing tradition: Sarika and Severn with a ling cod

distractions of time or other commitments. Maybe it's just a rationalization for doing nothing, but to me, retirement means having the time to do a few of the things I want to do—paint, learn Spanish, do some carving, study geology—before I pass on and the atoms in my body are returned to the natural world from which they came.

HUMAN BEINGS BEAR THAT terrible burden that self-awareness has inflicted on us—the knowledge that we, like all other creatures on earth, will die. That's what religions attempt to provide solace for, the unbearable thought of our disappearance forever. Belief in a life after death is one way to bear this truth, although it pains me to see people who seem to care little about this life because they believe they will live forever after they leave it. It even seems that blowing oneself up is preferable to a life fully lived if the promise is seventy virgins in paradise (over eternity, those virgins won't satisfy very long). I have been an atheist all my adult life, although as a teenager, I desperately wanted to believe in a god.

I don't like to even think of death because it makes me very uncomfortable, not because of fear about the process of dying, although any form of dying other than from instant death in an accident or from old age strikes me as a crummy way to go. No, what I don't like is the idea that this guy looking back at me in the mirror, this person locked into my skull full of memories that make him who he is, this fellow who has known pain, joy, thoughts, having existed for such a brief flash in all of eternity, is going to vanish forever at his death. Forever is such a long time, and seventy, eighty, ninety, even a hundred years is such a tiny interval in all of time.

As an atheist, I have no illusions about my life and death; they are insignificant in cosmic terms. That's why I have turned down requests to name schools after me, to let my name stand as a candidate for the presidency of a university, and to run for chancellor of another

Mom and Dad on their 50th wedding anniversary (March 21, 1984),
only two months before Mom's death

university. I don't have time to try to pad my curriculum vitae or take a
position that is merely honorific.

I attended a potlatch, a ceremonial gathering, for Haida Chief
Watson Price's hundredth birthday. As I pondered the significance of
his birthday, I found it overwhelming to think of the world he was born
into, a world without planes, refrigerators, television, computers, or
even cars. He grew up in the tradition of his people, which had its roots
thousands of years ago. And in remembering the stories and lessons of
his grandparents, he represented a living memory going back to the
early 1800s. For most of us, we will be remembered far more briefly.
In the end, as we reflect on the meaning of our lives and our legacy to
the future, what more could we ask for than to be remembered with
affection and respect by a few people who will survive a decade or two
further, by our children and grandchildren? I hope when it's my time
to die, I do so with the dignity of my father.

Parents-in-law Harry and Freddy Cullis on her 86th birthday

After my mother died, Dad met a woman named Fumiko Gondo, who had come from Japan to live with her daughter, Naoko, who worked in Vancouver. Fumiko was a Korean who grew up in Japan, and she did not speak English. She and Dad began to take walks together, and Dad enjoyed the opportunity to brush up on his Japanese. Eventually they started spending all their time together, and Dad even gave away Naoko when she married in Japan.

Fumiko was a lovely woman, and she and Dad were a great pair. In the early 1990s when Dad developed a cancerous tumor in his abdominal cavity, Fumiko was devastated. Although he had no pain, he lost his appetite and began to lose weight and strength, and it became clear he was dying. Dad had always said he had no great fear of death. "I've had a great life and I have no regrets," he would say.

Fumiko boiled large quantities of rice over and over to produce a thick gel of rice concentrate, which Japanese consider extremely

Christmas 2003. *Left to right, front row:* Severn, Huckleberry, Tara, Eduardo Campos (Tamiko's husband), and Tamo (my grandson). *Back row:* Tamiko, Midori (my granddaughter), and Sarika.

nutritive with medicinal properties. As I encouraged him, Dad would doggedly try to get a few spoonfuls down but often gagged with the effort. Finally, a neighbor who was a doctor told me that at this stage of his cancer Dad would not die of starvation, so we shouldn't worry about feeding him if he couldn't eat. It was a huge relief.

I moved in with Dad to be with him in his final weeks of life. He was still alert and interested in what was happening in the family. Each night, Tara and the girls would come over, and they sometimes brought slides of one of our trips, often ones we had taken with Dad and Mom. He would greet Tara with, "Well, what adventure have you got for me tonight?"

In the last week, my sisters arrived, and we reminisced about our lives. What struck me was that at no point did we complain about how hard life had been or all the things we had missed out on. Instead, we laughed and cried over stories about family, friends, and neighbors and the things we had done together that had enriched our lives. There was no boasting about possessions or wealth or accomplishments, only human relationships and shared experiences, which are what life is all about.

Dad's great achievement each day was to get out of bed and walk to the bathroom, where he would try to have a bowel movement. He had grown so painfully thin that the skin around his buttocks hung in sheets, and he was so weak that getting to the bathroom and back became quite a feat. Sometimes, in the effort to get his legs off the bed and onto the floor, he would leak a bit, causing him huge embarrassment. We bought rubber mats to go under the sheets, and I finally suggested diapers would solve everything. He was adamant that he would not wear them. Finally, when he had had a particularly messy accident, I called Tara and asked her to get some diapers for Dad. He overheard me and again objected weakly that he wouldn't wear them. Within hours, he slipped into a coma, and his breathing became more erratic and finally stopped. I still think the thought of being made to wear diapers was the final indignity, and he simply checked out, a peaceful death at eighty-five.

As he was dying, I wrote Dad's obituary and he fine-tuned it. "Don't say 'passed away,' " he said. "Say 'he died'." Here's what the obituary said:

Obituary, May 8, 1994

Carr Kaoru Suzuki died peacefully on May 8th. He was eighty-five. His ashes will be spread on the winds of Quadra Island. He found great strength in the Japanese tradition of nature-worship. Shortly before he died, he said: "I will return to nature where I came from. I will be part of the fish, the trees, the birds—that's my reincarnation. I have had a rich and full life and have no regrets. I will live on in your memories of me and through my grandchildren."

Dad had become interested in Shinto near the end of his life, and his Shinto beliefs fit well with the First Nations sense of connection with nature. Certainly if the laws of physics apply to our bodies, we are made up of the earth through the air, water, and food we ingest, and when we die, the atoms that comprise our bodies don't vanish but are eventually recycled back through the biosphere. So we return to nature, which gave us life in the first place, and as Dad's obituary said, we will still be everywhere. I like that idea, although it doesn't satisfy—as religion does—that egotistic desire to continue on in some conscious state.

Years after Dad died, an interviewer, knowing how important Dad had been to me, asked whether his death was one of the most painful moments of my life. I had to answer no. How could it be? I miss him and Mom tremendously and think of them every day, but Dad had a rich, full life, had been lucid until hours before his death, and had no pain or fear of death.

THE SENTIMENTS INCLUDED IN Dad's obituary are what I hope will be included in mine. I have had a rich and full life. I've selfishly acted on my priorities and impulses, often when I should have spent some of that time on those I love. I have hurt others, including my own family, but not deliberately out of meanness, and I hope that my life can be summed up as a positive addition to the human family.

Perhaps one or two programs I've done on television or radio will be played again after I'm dead, perhaps a book or two I've written will be read. That would be nice. But the one true legacy of any value is my children and, through them, my grandchildren. My grandchildren may remember something they learned from me or shared with me and, if I'm lucky, they may even pass that snippet on to their grandchildren. So at most, I might be remembered for four generations. My mother was the most decent, self-effacing person I've ever known; it hurts me to realize that when my sisters and I die, she will disappear from

My favorite photo of Dad, in repose at Windy Bay, Haida Gwaii

memory quickly in the fragments of memory among my children. Why, then, would I wish for any more than she did? My father made a point of leaving trees as gifts, a gesture that ensures that so long as those plants flourish, he will be there in some way.

This is a sad time to depart from this life. I have witnessed the disappearance and destruction of so much of the natural world that I loved. Extinction of a species is natural in the evolutionary scheme of life on Earth—99.9999 percent of all species that have ever existed are extinct. But we are an infant species, arriving very recently, perhaps 150,000 years ago in the plains of Africa, and yet now the once unthinkable, the coming extinction of our own species, is actually conceivable. Our trajectory to dominance of the planet has been spectacular, but we have not fully comprehended the price of that success. It has been my lot to be a Cassandra or Chicken Little, warning about imminent disaster, but it gives me no satisfaction at all to think my concerns may be validated by my grandchildren's generation.

My grandchildren are my stake in the near future, and it is my most fervent hope that they might say one day, "Grandpa was part of a great movement that helped turn things around for us." I also hope that they might remember my most valuable lesson and be able to say, "Grandpa taught us how to catch and clean a fish. Let's go catch one for dinner."

The notorious fig leaf shot for the show "Phallacies"
for *The Nature of Things with David Suzuki*

INDEX

ALSO FROM DAVID SUZUKI
AND GREYSTONE BOOKS

ADULT BOOKS

Wisdom of the Elders: Native and Scientific Ways of Knowing about Nature, with Peter Knudtson
(ISBN: 1-55365-193-6)

Tree: A Life Story, with Wayne Grady, Art by Robert Bateman (ISBN: 1-55365-016-6)

From Naked Ape to Superspecies: Humanity and the Global Eco-Crisis, with Holly Dressel (ISBN: 1-55365-031-X)

The David Suzuki Reader: A Lifetime of Ideas from a Leading Activist and Thinker (ISBN: 1-55365-022-0)

Good News for a Change: How Everyday People are Helping the Planet, with Holly Dressel (ISBN: 1-55054-926-X)

The Sacred Balance: A Visual Celebration of Our Place in Nature, with Amanda McConnell and Maria DeCambra (ISBN: 1-55365-065-4)

The Sacred Balance: Rediscovering Our Place in Nature, with Amanda McConnell (ISBN: 1-55054-963-4)

CHILDREN'S BOOKS

Salmon Forest, with Sarah Ellis, Illustrated by Sheena Lott
(ISBN: 1-55365-163-4)

Eco-Fun, with Kathy Vanderlinden (ISBN: 1-55054-823-9)

You Are the Earth: Know the Planet So You Can Make It Better, with Kathy Vanderlinden (ISBN: 1-55054-839-5)

Available wherever books are sold.
Visit www.greystonebooks.com for more information.

PHOTO CREDITS